W0254195

ELECTRONIC INFORMATION DELIVERY

Electronic Information Delivery

Ensuring Quality and Value

Edited by Reva Basch

Gower

© Reva Basch 1995

All rights reserved. No part of this publication may be reproduced, stored in retrieval system, or transmitted in any form or by any means, electronic, mechanical, photocopying, recording, or otherwise without the permission of the publisher.

Published by
Gower Publishing Limited
Gower House
Croft Road
Aldershot
Hampshire GU11 3HR
England

Gower
Old Post Road
Brookfield
Vermont 05036
USA

Reprinted 1996

British Library Cataloguing in Publication Data
Electronic Information Delivery: Ensuring
Quality and Value
1. Basch, Reva
025.4
ISBN 0–566–07567–9

Library of Congress Cataloging-in-Publication Data
Electronic information delivery: ensuring quality and value / edited
by Reva Basch.
p. cm
Includes bibliographical references.
ISBN 0–566–07567–9
I. Database management. 2. Databases—Quality control.
I. Basch, Reva.
QA78.9.D3E548 1995
025.04—dc20 94–12967
CIP

Typeset in Great Britain by Bournemouth Colour Graphics, Parkstone, Dorset and printed in Great Britain by Antony Rowe Ltd, Chippenham, Wiltshire

Contents

List of figures

Introduction

AN OVERVIEW OF QUALITY AND VALUE IN INFORMATION SERVICES

Reva Basch, President of Aubergine Information Services, an online research and consulting firm in Berkeley, California

The current concern about quality and value in information products can be traced to the beginning of the decade, when the Southern California Online Users Group devoted its 1990 annual retreat to a discussion of the subject. The SCOUG Rating Scale appeared to have inspired some serious thinking about quality issues, as evidenced by several of the papers in this collection. Whether it actually marked the genesis of the quality movement in electronic information products, or was simply a sign of the times, is not certain and ultimately not important. The fact is that all three of the major online conferences in 1990 – the National Online Meeting, Online/CD-ROM '90 and the International Online Information Meeting – included official declarations that quality would be the watchword of the 1990s. One of the liveliest sessions at International Online in London that year was the audience participation that followed a formal panel discussion on database quality. The 1991 round of conferences also included quality tracks, as have subsequent information industry meetings throughout the world. Obviously, the interest in quality is ongoing.

In this volume, Mintz, Hudnut and Beutler talk about standardization, consistency and accuracy in the context of database production, while Quint, Tenopir, Juntunen *et al.* incorporate discussions of those and other SCOUG quality measures into their user-oriented discussions. However, it is worth reiterating the basic SCOUG criteria in their original form.

It was intended that these should become the framework for a quantitative method of judging database performance in ten broad categories:

- Consistency
- Coverage and Scope
- Timeliness
- Accuracy/Error Rate
- Accessibility/Ease of Use
- Integration
- Output
- Documentation
- Customer Support and Training
- Value-to-Cost Ratio.

Consistency

In a way, consistency is at the heart of the entire quality issue – the idea that any well-designed database system would follow the same general rules from file to file, that the same editorial policies and indexing practices would be in effect, and that, within any given database, all records would be structured comparably with regard to field assignments, field labels and other data elements. *Consistency* is an overall principle, a meta-category, although it feeds into several of the other criteria as well.

Coverage and scope

Evaluating the coverage and scope of a particular database involves asking some comparative questions: At the source level, how well does the file cover its subject, relative to others in the same field? Do searchers who specialize in this area consider it the authoritative database? What do they view as its special strengths and its weaknesses? Does it cover the major journals in the field? Are those journals indexed cover-to-cover? If not, what portions are omitted, and does the database producer document those omissions? Is there any consistency in what material is routinely included and excluded? At the database level, coverage over *time* is also critical. Are there any significant lapses and, if so, are these documented? Are temporary gaps in coverage due to technical problems adequately flagged at login?

Timeliness

Databases vary tremendously not only with regard to their frequency of update, but also in terms of the currency of the *contents* of each update. Weekly updates do not imply equivalent timeliness of the material contained in the update. Some database producers give priority to one type of publication, or one title, over another, which means that some sources are much more up to date than others in the same database.

Accuracy/error rate

This is the criterion most frequently associated with database quality: typographical errors, misspellings, information assigned to the wrong fields, incorrect sales figures, inaccurate citations, oddly formatted records and other kinds of dirty data. As Jacsó points out, many of these problems are relatively easy to identify. Fortunately, they are usually relatively easy to fix as well. NewsNet has garnered points among users for instituting the FIXIT command based upon searcher input. When faulty data points to some sort of systemic problem, information providers seem more willing than they did in the past to re-examine their production process or their quality control cycle and institute some changes. Beutler discusses an organizational approach to quality control from a CD-ROM manufacturer's viewpoint, and Lawrence and Lenti from that of an online database producer.

A more subtle problem, addressed by Armstrong, involves the validity of the source material itself. What sources are being packaged and repackaged as information products, and how credible are these sources in their various electronic versions? This is a complex question. We don't expect every book or magazine article we read to be absolutely accurate; how much more accountability, if any, is it fair to expect from database publishers? Norman, Armstrong and others point out that, with the rise in end-user searching, the quality control that was once inherent in both book selection and intermediated database searching no longer pertains; the user cannot assume that a knowledgeable information professional has acted as a sort of *de facto* quality filter somewhere along the way. The bottom line, reiterated by several contributors to this volume, is *caveat searcher* – let the searcher beware.

Accessibility/ease of use

More than anything else, the unifying premise behind SCOUG's work on quality is that anything that stands in the way of access to information, or that limits the depth and flexibility of the search process, is *ipso facto* a quality issue. Accessibility includes logistical considerations with regard to connecting to the online service. The need for dedicated search hardware or software is a barrier, as is the requirement for written contracts as opposed to online signups. Gateway access is a plus, as is around-the-clock availability and support for higher baud rates.

System features affect access as well. As Juntunen *et al.* point out, lack of full proximity searching, pluralization, displayable thesauri, consistent and in-depth indexing, built-in equivalencies for variant spellings, and other limitations that characterize some of the smaller and less sophisticated database systems in particular, are barriers to use, and therefore constitute quality issues as well.

Integration

Integration refers to the inter-relationship of comparable databases on the same online service, and to the standardization of basic database conventions, like field tags and form of entry, from system to system. Hudnut explores these issues in depth, putting them in the context of important functionalities like the ability to do multi-file searching and remove duplicates, to invoke cross-database search aids, like journal lists and company name finders, and to link bibliographic records with their full-text equivalents, either in the same or different databases.

Output

The form in which information is delivered has quality implications, since it represents the result of one's efforts, the end product. Some of the quality-related issues here reflect on system capabilities, such as the ability to order offline prints or downloads, to sort search results or rank them by relevance, to define custom formats or print portions of a document selectively, to download an answer set into a spreadsheet or a database management program, and to retrieve tables and graphical material that were part of the original document.

Documentation

Database documentation varies tremendously in quality. Aside from basic issues like availability and cost, users must judge depth and content, timeliness and useability. Controlled vocabulary indexing and the use of codes and similar access points should be supported by both print and online thesauri and other documentation. Online help should be context-sensitive rather than generic. Error messages should not only alert users to an error condition but should suggest ways of recovering from it. Logon banners should be used to inform users about new features, reloads, changes or temporary problems with certain files.

Customer support and training

Organizations with a commitment to Total Quality Management (described from two complementary perspectives by Lawrence and Lenti, and by Oberts) place a strong emphasis on customer service. A well-trained, knowledgeable and responsive support staff is crucial. Other quality checkpoints in this area relate to access – hours of staffing, toll-free telephone numbers, availability from outside the country in which the online service or database producer is located, and electronic mail capabilities.

Training in 'beyond the basics' is important. Specialized seminars in various subject areas, workshops sponsored jointly by two or three databases producers whose files complement each other in particular applications, and cross-disciplinary training – sessions like 'Patents for business searchers' and 'Chemistry for the non-chemist' – are all indications that an information provider is taking its commitment to quality seriously. Training should include hands-on practice time and/or free time for practice on the system afterwards, and should ideally be supplemented with low-cost training files, cheap after-hours options for practicing searching skills, and/or 'free file of the month'-type programs.

SCOUG, at its quality retreat, emphasized the importance of establishing partnerships – whether in the form of user advisory panels, national and local user groups, or formal update sessions – among database producers and online services on the one hand, and the users who constitute their most sophisticated and vocal customer base, on the other. Armstrong, Norman, Gilchrist, Juntunen *et al.* describe various initiatives that demonstrate the information industry's commitment to building ongoing, two-way communications with its customers.

Value-to-cost ratio

Value to cost is the last of the broad SCOUG categories, and the one in which the group attempted to assimilate all the other quality checklist items and to factor them in with the very significant element of *pricing*.

Value might be regarded as a function of *quality* and *price*. A high quality product is of little value to a user who cannot afford to pay for it. A reasonably-priced product with some quality shortcomings may actually represent a better value for some users. When it comes to assessing value, everything is relative.

Overall system characteristics come into play here, factors like speed and performance, pricing structures and display options, that affect one's ability to do efficient and cost-effective searching. Waiting while display screens fill, line-by-line, is a negative factor; the ability to scroll documents continuously and to interrupt both search processing and output where necessary, are positive ones. So is the existence of free or inexpensive display formats, including Key Word in Context, for browsing documents and evaluating interim results. Consistency with regard to display and print charges is a plus as well.

At the general system level, one must factor into the value-to-cost equation such variables as surcharges for higher baud rates; any up-front subscription costs, monthly service charges or minimum usage fees; premiums or special fees for global or multi-file searches that are not cancelled out by connect time savings; and the availability of accurate cost estimates at any point during the search session. Broader, administrative issues include the opportunity to search more economically by taking advantage of any volume discount programs, flat-fee contract options, or frequent searcher bonuses that might be offered.

The legacy of SCOUG

When SCOUG actually attempted to subdivide these categories into their component parts, and to quantify and prioritize each element, it became apparent that they were dealing with an incredibly complex structure. Not only would they have to account for at least three distinct types of databases – bibliographic, directory and full-text – they would have to adjust the criteria in each case according to the expertise of the searcher – whether they were a novice or an experienced professional, or an experienced professional searching an unfamiliar system. Not only that, they realized that each online service has its own quirks, special features and preferred ways of handling the data. In effect, each database would have to be evaluated as a unique entity on each online host that carried it.

These were sobering realizations, to put it mildly. Although SCOUG members had resolved to publish an official position paper, to begin the evaluation phase with a small group of directory databases (since the problems in those files seemed easiest to identify and isolate), and to recruit additional evaluators at the upcoming Online/CD-ROM '90 meeting, none of these efforts were realized, at least not in a direct sense. However, SCOUG's preliminary work, which consisted in large measure of delineating the overall scope of the database quality situation and identifying the issues involved, either paralleled or formed the basis for much of the work currently in progress in Finland and in Europe and the UK, and discussed by Armstrong, Norman, Gilchrist and Juntunen *et al.* In fact, SCOUG will be cooperating with the Centre for Information Quality Management, as described by Armstrong, in its systematic efforts to flag and report quality problems.

SCOUG's efforts also captured the attention of the US online industry. NFAIS, the National Federation of Abstracting and Information Services, set up a task force on quality to work with users on some of the specific issues the group had raised. The Information Industry Association established an informal liaison with SCOUG and set up a formal user–vendor working group that was showcased in a 1992 IIA conference program.

Equally important, several database producers and online services took direct and immediate action to fix some of the specific problems that had been identified at the SCOUG retreat. Examples include:

- Dialog's duplicate detection feature, followed by Data-Star's *improved* duplicate detection feature;
- Dialog's introduction of 'metabases' like the Journal Name Finder and Company Name Finder;
- BRS's introduction of a linking capability between bibliographic and full-text records;
- Inspec's major reload, which indicated that at least *one* database producer *had* found a practical means of retroactively correcting older records;
- IAC's Company Intelligence file, which documented the means by which basic company data was collected – telephone, written questionnaire, etc. – and the date that the individual record – not just the database as a whole – was

last revised;

- NewsNet's FIXIT command, which allows users to identify faulty records and tag them for repairs. NewsNet later won an Online Product of the Year award for this enhancement;
- Data-Star's establishment of a special online bulletin board for searchers and database producers to talk to each other. Producers can post messages about enhancements, training sessions and new products, while users can ask questions, report problems and make suggestions about quality-related issues.

Of course, concern with quality has not been limited to the *online* industry. At the beginning of 1992, Marydee Ojala tracked the rise of quality as an issue in the management literature as a whole.[1] As Gilchrist points out, the roots of the quality movement lie in the manufacturing sector and have only recently migrated to the service sector, of which the electronic information business has traditionally been considered a part. Arnold even casts this assumption in a different light, with his 'information manufacturing' paradigm. Ojala noted that several of the criteria for the Malcolm Baldrige Quality Award, which has been given in US industry since 1988, are particularly relevant to the information business:

1. Quality is defined by the customer;
2. Senior management must create clear quality values and build those values into the way the company operates;
3. Companies need to communicate quality requirements to their suppliers and work to elevate supplier quality performance.

With regard to the first point, the customer as the ultimate determinant of quality is a theme propounded, either implicitly or explicitly, by most of the contributors to this volume.

With regard to the second point, the role of top management in commiting to and setting the tone for a quality operation is stressed not only by the contributors who describe the implementation of formal TQM operations within their companies, but also by those who emphasize the importance of standardization and accuracy in database production and distribution, and by the consumers of information products who insist that attention to quality and responsiveness to customer problems must be pervasive throughout the organization.

The third point, the need to involve suppliers as well as users in the quality process, is an interesting one. It is problematic insofar as it invokes the liability chain that both Halvorson and Norman consider in depth. In the electronic information business, the lines between supplier and distributor, or wholesaler and retailer, are often indistinct. Database publishers might be vendors as well; producers are sometimes also suppliers. Mounting a file on an online host or as a CD-ROM product is a collaborative effort in the most fundamental sense. Negotiating a license in the information business is not like placing an order in the garment industry.

Yet, when it comes time to accept responsibility for quality matters, the line between producer and distributor seems, suddenly, to be razor-sharp. We hear comments like these:

> From online hosts: Dirty data is the responsibility of the database producer. From database producers: It's the online host that prevents us from making corrections in a timely manner.
>
> From database producers: Inadequate field length? We would lengthen them, but the online service won't let us. Lack of standardization? We had to make *our* perfect data structure work in *their* shabby environment.
>
> From users: We don't care who's responsible, we just want it fixed. From hosts and database producers: Fixes are expensive; you must prioritize, and you must expect to pay more. In the meantime, *caveat searcher*.

Overview of contents

This volume examines not only the implications of the customer-oriented quality markers outlined by SCOUG and other user organizations, but also far more fundamental issues like the application of quality engineering principles to information products; assigning responsibility and determining accountability for the way such products are built, distributed and used; and building a permanent, workable partnership among the producers, resellers, intermediaries and ultimate customers of these products. Despite the variety of different perspectives represented, there is consensus among the contributors on several grounds: the basic criteria for judging the quality of an information product or service; the belief that information products should, indeed, be subject to the same rules of performance as other kinds of goods and services; and the conviction that information quality management is an ongoing and altogether essential function.

Arnold begins by establishing a historical context for the development of the electronic information industry and suggesting that the same principles that apply to quality control and quality assurance in other types of industries can be applied to this kind of 'manufacturing' as well. Hudnut's paper contributes to the historical perspective, describing the extent to which traditional database providers and online services have been limited by mainframe hardware and software constraints as well as their own short-sightedness, and suggesting some ways of surmounting the lack of standards and integration that still plagues the information industry today.

Mintz picks up Hudnut's theme, depicting many of the same issues from the perspective of a primary information supplier, a print publisher who is well-acquainted with the exacting requirements of maintaining quality and some degree of standardization during conversion to a variety of different electronic formats. Beutler also deals with the challenges of maintaining the integrity of source data, from the viewpoint of a CD-ROM publisher charged with accomplishing such conversions. The final paper in the information provider sequence, Lawrence and Lenti's description of TQM in a database production environment, places the concerns about timeliness, accuracy, consistency and completeness expressed by the previous authors in the context of a formal and fully-implemented organizational quality effort.

In the following section, Oberts and Quint consider these same issues from the standpoint of the professional searcher charged with providing quality results to end-users. Oberts focuses on the information services unit within a large corporation, and applies the same principles of Total Quality Management to assuring quality on the 'human' side of the scale. She stresses staff training, competence, responsiveness and resourcefulness, as well as the importance of clear and ongoing communication with the requestors who constitute not only her customer base but also the final consumers of the information products mediated and distributed by her staff. Quint focuses on the interface between online searchers and online services. She refers to the former as the latter's ultimate quality control checkpoint, and depicts the myriad ways in which human intelligence and expertise must compensate for the imperfections and limitations of online databases and host systems.

The papers by Tenopir and Jacsó place the quality issues discussed in earlier chapters within the practical context of evaluation and testing. Tenopir relates general quality measures like database scope, indexing, accuracy and consistency to the specific elements of database design and structure that underlie them. She points out and assigns responsibility for some specific shortcomings, and sets the stage for the user-based evaluation effort that Jacsó describes in depth.

Halvorson picks up the important theme of liability and addresses it from the dual perspective of an intermediary online searcher and a US-based practicing attorney. Although he takes the position of an independent researcher, his comments and cautions apply to all professional users; they form a useful counterpart to Quint's description of what the working searcher must do to ensure quality output. Norman's two-part chapter lends a UK perspective to the question of liability, looking at the role of the institutional librarian or information provider as well as the independent researcher. She then proceeds to lay the groundwork for the final section of the book by describing various UK and European initiatives in the area of database and information service quality.

The last three papers – Juntunen, Miklos and Jalkanen reporting from Finland, Armstrong in the UK, and Gilchrist moving from the UK to a broader European and international perspective – portray ongoing quality efforts that parallel, enlarge on, and complement the database rating framework developed by SCOUG. The Finns describe how, by focusing on a small group of local databases, they were able to complete detailed evaluations and issue a summary report. Armstrong reports on events leading up to the establishment of the Centre for Information Quality Management, a clearinghouse for quality issues and communication along the information chain. Finally, Gilchrist summarizes the information quality movement to date, places it in the context of related international and inter-industry initiatives, and makes the case for its ongoing significance as the shape of the information industry continues to evolve.

The future of quality

The 1990s, the same period that saw the dawn of quality consciousness in the information industry, has been a time of dramatic change for that industry as well. Key players have emerged, formed strategic alliances, acquired other companies or been acquired themselves, achieved market dominance or disappeared entirely. Technology has fueled the development of innovative search software and massively powerful new retrieval engines, of graphical interfaces, new hardware platforms and storage media like CD-ROM. Full-text databases, natural language and other non-Boolean retrieval algorithms, automatic interest filters and wireless cellular communications are encouraging the growth of the much-heralded and long delayed end-user market. The Internet is radically redefining the nature and the experience of electronic information-gathering, while raising a whole new set of questions about copyright, liability and the reliability of information sources.

What all of this means for information quality management is that it, too, must remain a dynamic process, a work in progress. As the boundaries continue to blur among source publishers, database producers and information suppliers, and among intermediaries and end-users of information, we must constantly re-examine issues of accountability, liability and value. As Boolean logic, proximity operators and other command line mainstays are replaced or overlaid by relevance ranking, 'plain English' query language or personalized, pre-determined retrieval filters, we must continually adjust the criteria for acceptable system performance so that the emphasis is on results, not just on features. With the growth in full-text and other source databases, including image-based products, over the rigidly-indexed bibliographic files that predominated in the past, we must, again, look at issues of access, efficiency and value-for-cost, as opposed to simply file structure and vocabulary choice. The ultimate determinant of quality is accessibility to information – the desired information, in a form and at a price that users find acceptable. Here, the Southern California Online Users Group, the judges for the Baldrige Quality Award, the contributors to this collection and the various task forces, panels and public and private initiatives that they describe are in agreement: Quality, however we define it, is determined by the customer.

Notes

1. Ojala, Marydee (1992), 'Quality online and online quality. Column: The dollar sign', *Online*, **16** (1), January, 73–5.

Part I

DATABASE PRODUCTION

Chapter 1

INFORMATION MANUFACTURING: A HISTORICAL VIEW OF QUALITY ENGINEERING

Stephen E. Arnold, Information Consultant, Harrod's Creek, Kentucky

'The positive results of a technical enterprise are immediate. They are felt at once, as in the case of electricity or television. The negative effects, however, are long-term and are felt only with experience.' – Jacques Ellul[1]

'You build quality in, not try to control it.' – Public Broadcasting Service promotional clip for a program about quality.[2]

Electronic publishing – as the term is used by those who build commercial machine-readable files – has moved through several distinct phases in the industry's first 25 years and now attracts a wide and diverse collection of 'publishers'.[3]

As more electronic information becomes available, there will be more good information. If the bell curve traced by normal distribution is correct, however, there will be more bad information as well.

The focus of this essay is upon information manufacturing and one of its most important elements – quality. Before tackling some of the more troublesome issues associated with the caliber of information products and services, I will review trends in electronic database building, the essential components of information manufacturing, and some of the reasons quality has not been viewed as important in the past.

Trends in database building

The number, diversity, and scope of databases is increasing rapidly. There are text and numeric databases. There are hierarchical, flat, and relational databases. There are single-object and multi-object databases. There are public and private files. There are databases with terabytes of data and those with a few hundred records. Electronic information now embraces audio and video. Grassroots database building is exploding, and bulletin board systems are inching towards Internet connectivity and creating a new type of publishing medium.

To see the overall sweep of change, we must step back and view databases in a suitably broad context. This approach might blur some important distinctions for specific types of databases, but the advantage gained is an overview of the direction of movement in the 'information manufacturing' industry.

'Information manufacturing' refers to the process of creating machine-readable files, from the moment of conception in the producer's mind to the feedback provided by users of the final product. The concept of information manufacturing assumes that database building has progressed considerably from the artisan-and-craft approach of the early years of electronic publishing.

The first stage: Invention

The first stage of information manufacturing in the USA began in the 1960s. Scientists, entrepreneurs and the US government applied computer technology to scientific information storage and retrieval. By 1980, information manufacturing had moved from bold experimentation, where each solution was an innovation, to technique, the application of standard procedures.

The earliest database builders had to write programs to get the results they desired. The Magellans of electronic publishing wove these individual programs into a manual work flow. Each step in the database publishing process was defined according to the same procedures used for creating printed reference books.

The organization of information in machine-readable form was the principal value added by these pioneers. In some ways, the earliest commercially-available databases were similar to the wooden boats crafted in the United States in the 19th century. Unwieldy tools and uncooperative materials became, under the master craftsman's hands, richly detailed, carefully crafted products. Although there were superficial resemblances, each wooden vessel was unique.

In the early days of electronic publishing, certain processes were tailored to fit the capabilities of the mainframe computers which operated in batch mode. The electronic publishing process reflected the rigidity imposed by the systems. As different as electronic publishing and traditional print publishing are, they shared a set of tightly-defined processes.

The characteristics of the earliest stage of information manufacturing include:

- Little automation. Intensive 'human' involvement in design and development

Four Stages in Information Manufacturing		
Stage	**Name**	**Main Feature**
1965–1981	Invention	Development of original systems and procedures; emulation of print paradigms
1982–1992	Duplication	Innovation of particular features; emulation and enhancement of existing machine-readable files
1992–1997	Reconstruction	Databases with high value re-engineered for manufacturing in information factories using advanced systems and software; emphasis on replacing human effort with software and system processes.
1997–2001	Proliferation	Application of automated information manufacturing techniques to a broad, diverse range of products and services; embedded information in previously unintelligent products.

Figure 1.1 *Four stages in information manufacturing*

of database systems, procedures, and records.

- Print models. Reliance on established models or metaphors for record structure (for example, machine-readable databases were electronic versions of printed indices).
- Experts only. Followed by a slow but steady migration of the expertise needed to build (and use) a database from technical specialists to a broader audience.

The transition between the first stage and the second is interesting. By the start of the 1980s, enough tools and know-how were available to support more robust innovations. In the early 1980s, new databases and services started appearing with increasing rapidity. The number of machine-readable files doubled and then doubled again in a span of 18 to 24 months. Entrepreneurs offering specialized services like thesaurus development and off-shore data entry tested the feasibility of building profitable support businesses for the fledgling database publishing industry.

Information manufacturing processes grew more efficient as organizations gained database experience. As managers learned to harness reliable technology to a specific process to reduce costs or increase the number of records produced, work flow procedures were modified to allow computers and software to expedite specific functions like serials management or format verification.

The characteristics of databases designed and manufactured during this period include:

- Reliance on human intellect to select data for the file, but greater use of computers to verify elements of the database entry; for example, to confirm that a specific field contains data;
- Manual data entry, first at the database producer's facility and eventually at other locations, to help contain costs;

- Homogeneous records; that is, fixed or maximum field length, and other attempts at standardization of the record structure;
- Relatively little ability to increase production without adding staff.

Many of the most successful commercial files on which people rely date from this first stage of information manufacturing. Examples include: census data, commercial databases of company financials, and citation (index-only and index-and-abstract) databases. Many of the most frequently used databases on Dialog Information Services were created during the earliest stage of electronic publishing. There is a certain nostalgia associated with some of these old databases; many people long for the good old days of precise, controlled-term indexing and discrete records with a sharply-etched visual personality.

The second stage: Duplication

The second stage of database building extends from 1983 to the present. This 10-year period has yielded more databases and a steady refinement of the manufacturing processes anchored in the first stage.

One way to think of this stage of electronic publishing is in terms of its similarity to the small farms which once characterized the American Midwest. Individuals and organizations discovered that they could cultivate a modest acreage and begin to work it intensively. The nation's growing population created a natural market for the products of these modest enterprises.

Similarly, in the second stage of electronic publishing, many individuals and organizations discovered sources of information, input them, and processed them to add value. However, the output of the electronic publishers during the second stage were relatively modest. There were few, if any, economies of scale.

Overall, however, aggregated database manufacturing volume accelerated rapidly in this stage. First, technology migrated from the isolated altars of the computer room to the individual desktop. Secondly, the cost of hardware dropped, almost as rapidly as the computing horsepower rose. More powerful tools became cheap and plentiful, and electronic publishers put them to good use in tweaking the well-worn processes of first stage information manufacturing. Finally, knowledge diffused. Each week that passed pushed information out to a broader and deeper segment of the population.

During this stage, however, innovation was focused on moving information from print to electronic formats. Online services like West Publishing Company and Mead Data Central expanded their offerings by orders of magnitude: more databases, more technological power and more features.

For the most part, the databases created since 1983 built upon the machine-readable files already on the market. Of course, new types of databases were invented as well: in 1984, the first videodisc was introduced at an Information Industry Association meeting. This marvel combined sound, words and full-motion video. But products similar to those already available from other publishers continued to flow from competing information factories. This contrasts with the first stage of information manufacturing, when the data pioneers were wrestling with how-to's, not consciously creating me-too's.

Since the end of the 1980s, trade shows featuring commercial databases have become predictable, featuring lookalikes, repositioned databases, technical gadgets, and price changes. A hot market – business information, for example – attracted established publishers from other fields, like science and technology, as well as new entrants. 'Opportunity' in the database industry became synonymous with information saleable to business.

The characteristics of databases created in the duplication stage include:

- Incremental improvements of existing models; that is, the addition of enhancements wanted by customers or users.
- Increasing reliance on machine assistance for database creation; for example, optical character recognition or direct feeds of full-text materials, instead of manual data entry.
- Greater throughput. Integration of personal computers into the manufacturing process and moving labor-intensive tasks like data entry to Korea, Ireland, and other countries where the cost of labor was less.
- Emergence of integrated manufacturing operations which create primary data, process data from other information producers, and distribute the data to specific markets; for example, West Publishing Co. and VNU's Disclosure and Inforum units.

The greatest legacy of this stage was the foundation it created for the stage we are now entering: reconstruction.

The third stage: Reconstruction

Let me define *reconstruction*. Increasingly affordable computing, software, and graphics technologies are setting the stage for what promises to be a decade of manufacturing innovation. Files created in the next five to seven years will be rebuilds, not mere enhancements, of highly successful databases that now exist in digital form. The prime candidates for reconstruction are files that cannot be changed to meet the needs of their customers quickly enough to prevent competitors from trying to woo those customers with new and improved products. The successful reconstructions will entail a rethinking of the fundamental manufacturing policies and processes that underlie the original database. These are the policies and processes that make the manufacturing system difficult, even impossible, to change.

Just as advanced machinery increased the capacity of small farmers who adopted it, the newest technologies help electronic publishers deal with, and add value to, greater and greater flows of unprocessed information.

The benefits of adopting more advanced information manufacturing techniques are almost identical to those experienced in other business sectors that followed the same path:

- Machines allowed the enterprise to obtain more productivity per person.
- The machine-assisted information manufacturing process yielded greater consistency.
- The overall processes, in most instances, were accelerated.
- It allows more flexibility in distributing the product; in the case of information manufacturing, the goal is media-independent output, as opposed to just print or single-system online delivery.

Thus, reconstruction as a stage in information manufacturing coincides with the idea of re-engineering or retooling a work process in other manufacturing businesses. However, the term *reconstruction* carries three additional connotations in the context of electronic publishing:

First, new and advanced technologies let competitors duplicate – insofar as possible – known winners. Predicasts, Inc. has begun the job of evolving PROMT into a different construct by adding full-text records in what was originally an abstract and index database. Galen (formerly Humana, Inc. Louisville, Kentucky) has undertaken a similar effort by applying imaging technology to patient records across its dozens of hospitals. In some ways, the latter is more innovative. But the two examples reflect the same trend: use of technology to improve upon an existing information construct. This is not rocket science, but it will probably increase revenue and reduce costs.

Secondly, reconstruction opens wide the doors of opportunity for organizations whose principal business may not be electronic publishing as we understand the market today. Examples include: (1) A seed company may include data of significant commercial value to farmers. Access to the data requires buying the seed company's products. (2) A network software company bundles live data feeds with the operating environment. (3) Print publishers can produce electronic products at somewhat lower cost and with fewer administrative cartwheels than at any previous time. For instance, Knight-Ridder has nudged the San Jose (California) Mercury News into the world of electronic publishing with its electronic distribution of the newspaper via America Online, a consumer-oriented information service which is, in some ways, a competitor to Knight-Ridder's own Dialog Information Services.

Thirdly, reconstruction creates opportunities to redefine product categories, particularly in the area of multi-object database manufacturing and enhanced user services. Examples are: (1) Does the purchaser of a word processing package know what database of correctly-spelled words is used by the program's spell-checker? (2) Games on CD-ROMs can teach the player about anatomy, for instance. To what category does one assign a product that combines a game, scientific instruction, and images? (3) Lotus 1-2-3 for Windows includes animated tutorials to teach users how to complete certain tasks in the program.

Some of the characteristics of third-stage information manufacturing include:

- Greater dependence on machine generation of databases; for example, full-text and numeric databases built with minimal human input;
- Introduction of new types of information constructs which present data in a less restricted format, or which include certain 'data objects' wanted and needed by users;
- Proliferation of delivery options; for example, online, magnetic tape, direct broadcast, on-demand print and others.

Most importantly, there is now greater awareness of the importance of 'quality' in a machine-readable file. The customer can perceive inconsistencies and errors in a single database, of course. But if there is only one database on a subject, the question of quality is lower on the priority list. With many choices, quality moves up a few notches. The customer can do some comparison shopping, looking for a reasonable trade-off between expensive accuracy and lower cost, but still acceptable, information.

In short, greater familiarity with databases means more informed customers. Informed customers are better equipped to express their wants, needs, desires and demands. William M. Bulkeley coined the phrase 'reign of error' to express the importance of database quality.[4] Unfortunately, quality is not the burning issue for most users that some information professionals would like it to be. Most people believe that information delivered by computer is correct, but there is ample evidence to prove that, although electronic information makes research faster and easier, it does not necessarily make it cheaper or more accurate.

The driving force, as we leave the third stage of electronic publishing, is price. As one database marketer is fond of saying, 'You can have it faster, cheaper, or better. Pick any *one*.'

The fourth stage: Proliferation

Once the technologies are in place to allow existing information to be recast into more user-oriented forms, information manufacturing will be woven into the fabric of *things*. One almost-certain outcome will be the merging of the television, telephone and online information service. It is too early to know which consortium or partnership will win the 'informationizing' derby, but the horses in the race have good bloodlines. In the USA, they include AT&T, seven regional Bell operating companies, and a rich assortment of cable, motion picture and publishing companies.

What will happen in information manufacturing is roughly analogous to what happened to the cotton mills of the American Northeast with the advent of steam: manufacturing was suddenly cut free from water power. Owners could move their operations to sites where other factors were more favorable to the business; for example, closer to a source of raw material, or to a location where operating costs were lower.

Electronic information will have even greater manufacturing freedom. The availability of information will become universal. No longer will value be added simply by collecting and organizing data. Information manufacturing will make almost full use of automated tools for processing, formatting and shaping raw data into useful chunks.

Advanced technologies will become co-terminous with systems for distributing information. Thus, there will be a near-universal shift from manufacturing individual information objects (for example, a finely crafted index-and-abstract record) to redistributing media-independent output tailored to the needs of specific customers.

I am reasonably certain that electronic information will become a *consumer* product in the sense that household detergent is a consumer product; that is, virtually every home in the USA and other developed countries has soap in the cupboard. In the proliferation stage, machine-readable databases will become an environmental factor. A purchaser will acquire a product because electronic information is embedded in the product and gives the product attributes which meet customer needs. Examples are: (1) 'Information' in the washing machine will regulate water temperature, rinse cycle, even what detergent to add to the water. (2) An automobile will include digital mapping and traveler information as part of the vehicle's infotainment module. Database options will be available as well, e.g. enhanced bed-and-breakfast listings. Upgrades will consist of databases that offer the buyer more 'value' than the standard package.

Value, however, underscores the importance of customer perception about databases. The products of an information manufacturing process are intangible until the *data* are shaped – by a query, a technology, or a human intelligence – into something tangible. The result may be a printed report, a display on a monitor, a CD-ROM, an interactive game, or some other deliverable artifact. At that moment, quality stops being an abstraction and becomes tangible. Data quality is creeping from the shadows, closer to the blaze of center stage.

Modern information manufacturing essentials

Many industries are now undergoing or will undergo re-engineering of their processes. The increasing fragmentation of markets into smaller and smaller segments forces organizations to develop products and services for these different customer groups. Few business segments are immune to the effects of rising cost pressure. Customers, too, are becoming more and more demanding.

Shorter, faster product life cycles

One of the key drivers of modern manufacturing is fast-cycle operations. The Sony Corporation is one of the major proponents of this approach to electronic product manufacture. The time required to determine market need or respond to a competitor is reduced at *each* step of the manufacturing process. Sharp Corporation, one of Japan's second-tier electronics companies, views electronics as a fad product. The entire life cycle of the product, from initial concept to removing the product from the market, is measured in months.

The litany of many knowledge workers is, 'Marketing, marketing, marketing'. This mantra may reassure or at least shift responsibility from one shoulder to another, but marketing, like electronic information, is a slippery concept.

Peter Drucker offered these observations in his essay *The Emerging Theory of Manufacturing*:

> [A] plant must be redesigned from the end backwards and managed as an integrated flow ... few companies have enough knowledge about what goes on in their plants to run them as systems .... As soon as we define manufacturing as the process that converts things into economic satisfactions, it becomes clear that producing does not stop when the product leaves the factory.[5]

The customer's needs become the input for changing the manufacturing process to deliver products the customer will buy. Henry Ford, an authentic American genius, allegedly said in response to a question about the choice of paint for a Model T: 'Any color so long as it is black.' Customers today are unlikely to find their options so limited.

Gross distinctions based on basic functionality or subject discipline have begun to blur. In the near future, electronic information products will be evaluated on such attributes as:

- Price;
- Accuracy (correctness of spelling, factual precision);
- Presentation (appearance, usability);
- Trade-offs (completeness versus cost, ease-of-use versus accuracy).

We are entering a period when marketing will be increasingly dependent upon manufacturing to deliver what the customer wants. Organizations that can build machine-readable files that meet customer needs will then face the difficult job of differentiating their databases from others.

Despite the tendency to place great emphasis on marketing, managers of information factories must be skilled 'information engineers' and expert manufacturers if the organization's products are to gain wider customer and user acceptance.

In the United States, there are hundreds, if not thousands, of niche markets. Individuals in these markets use a variety of techniques and technologies to form virtual communities of interest. News and information about a new machine-readable file can rapidly reach individuals in a niche without much support from a marketing department.

Fast cycle manufacturing

The central issue here is what I call *fast-cycle manufacturing*. Fast cycle manufacturing means that an organization can *quickly* develop new products or prototypes of products without additional investments in infrastructure, excessive reliance upon costly external resources, unnecessary manual processes, or disruption of established work routines.

There are some very good reasons why, as we enter stage four, fast-cycle manufacturing is emerging as the essential ingredient for successful electronic information manufacturing.

First, as people become more experienced at using electronic information, their expectations change. The fastest PC available in 1985 is a museum piece to a power user today. The experienced user of information services can quickly form an assessment of almost any machine-readable file. A customer's specific requirements may change even more rapidly. The ability to respond quickly and effectively to a market's needs (a market which may consist of a single customer) is critical. The merry-go-round keeps turning, but only the information company that snags the brass ring continues to ride.

Secondly, mature electronic information products are often the most attractive target for competitors to attack niche by niche. Therefore, companies with mature products must turn to fast cycle manufacturing in order to respond quickly to competitive threats and to flow sufficient numbers of new products and services into their mature market in order to keep existing revenues from declining.

Finally, newer technologies allow greater automation of processes and, in some instances, radical re-engineering of work flows. Consider the impact of software which monitors a live news feed and prepares and prints a personalized daily newspaper. Such a product is now available for the IBM PC and compatible platform. This product – Journalist from PED Software in San Jose, California – costs about $130 and is only one example of the way in which certain information manufacturing functions can be reworked.

New product flow

A second essential in modern information manufacturing is product development. As the intervals between stages in the product life cycle and in the manufacturing process become shorter, it becomes more and more important to have a flow of new products in the pipeline. Therefore, the modern information manufacturing facility must be hard-wired to sources for new product ideas.

A third essential is that the manufacturing facility must be able to create the products that the market or the product developers specify. This means that the core manufacturing processes must be based upon systems that can be changed.

The contrast between this and the manufacturing approaches of the earlier stages of electronic publishing could not be greater. Flexibility is defined within specific, almost inflexible parameters. The more traditional information manufacturing

A Comparison of Information Manufacturing Concepts[1]		
	Traditional Manufacturing	***Fast-Cycle Manufacturing***
Organization	Serial	Parallel
Customer Input	Secondary to established process	Influences the processes in real time
Product development cycle	Separate day-to-day processes	Integrated into day-to-day processes
Turnaround time	Measured in weeks or months	Measured in hours or days
Flexibility	Little or none	Considerable
Structure of people relationships	Hierarchical	Peer-to-peer
Jobs	Compartmentalized	Fluid and open
Approach to quality	System defines	Customer defines
Computing environment	Static	Dynamic
Ability to make incremental improvements	Limited	Broader
Product attributes	Predictable (limited innovation)	Unpredictable (greater innovation)
Pricing	Rigid, aimed at protecting existing revenue	Flexible, aimed at increasing market share

1 These dichotomies are artificial. The purpose of characterizing these two approaches is to cast into relief the differences in the two systems. In reality, most modern electronic publishing systems share characteristics of each type of manufacturing, but one dominates or gets more emphasis.

Figure 1.2 *A comparison of information manufacturing concepts*

systems can produce machine-readable information, but they are often unable to accommodate changes to that data.

Now, new products can come from almost any source, from the blue or from inspired imitation. Electronic publishing companies have a suite of options from which to mix and match an approach appropriate for their needs. Among the new product development mechanisms I have encountered are:

- Customer-driven sources (for example, user groups, formal research, suggestions);
- Internal teams (for example, a new product department, ad hoc teams, informal 'skunk works');

- The competition (the source of 'me-too' products);
- Acquisitions (outright purchase of a company or its technology);
- Technical breakthroughs;
- Repackaging (for example, new formats, slight twists, incremental upgrades).

How is less important than *doing*. The organization that does not have a flow of new products runs three great risks. First, mature products may be eroded, so new products are needed to maintain historical revenue levels. Secondly, without new products, organizations will find growth difficult, if not impossible. Despite the fluid nature of electronic information, products and services must be tailored to each niche to achieve the best opportunity to return a suitable payback.

Marketing

The third essential is usually labeled marketing.

What is the link – this very moment – between information manufacturing, marketing, and equally foggy concepts like 'value' and 'quality'? *Marketing* is a word applied to a wide range of functions which position the product and facilitate sales.[6] Marketing functions today range from advertising and public relations to product planning to warehousing and sales.

This question is at the core of justifying the existence of machine-readable files. For example:

- In banking: 'We need to build a more effective database of our commercial customers. How much will this cost? How long will it take? What is the value of this investment to the bank?'
- In associations: 'We have a wealth of information about our members, including the technical material each provides to us. How can we create a database of these resources? What will be the payoff for the members? What is the cost of building the system? What is its value?'
- In publishing: 'Our customers tell us they want charts and graphs as well as full-text. How can we build a database that contains indices, full-text and page images? What is the cost of creating this type of manufacturing operation? What is the value of this type of database today and over the next five years?'

In summary, information marketing must deal with these tasks:

- Determining product needs (market research);
- Informing the user of the product availability (marketing communications);
- Supporting the user of the product (marketing support or customer service);
- Inputting user feedback to the organization (product development).

However, manufacturing is the central actor in this drama. If manufacturing does not make the change, marketing has a difficult task convincing the customer about the value or quality of this particular database.

What is most important?

The key to success appears to be a synthesis of two elements: (1) a consistent flow of new products, and (2) the ability to make these products. However, I want to reiterate the significance of a flow of well-manufactured new electronic information products. This is essential to the success of electronic publishers as information companies cross the boundary between Reconstruction and Proliferation. Why is this?

First, maturing information products can be easily challenged by competitors offering the customers something different. Often, the new offering consists of comparable information delivered in a more desirable medium at a lower price, or some other combination of technology-based attributes that the established product's producers cannot easily or comfortably match.

As the costs of technology drift lower and the knowledge requisite for fabricating electronic information becomes more widespread, smaller organizations, often one- or two-person start-ups, attack the mature information products obliquely. In the arena of pharmaceutical information, one thinks about the site licensing services of Current Drugs invading a select group of companies with new electronic information products. This relative newcomer has caught some established information companies flat-footed.

Secondly, smaller organizations can often move more rapidly. A mature information company is often a slow and unresponsive entity. The customers have been telling anyone who would listen what they need. However, companies with mature electronic information products must protect their revenue base. An innovative new product might cannibalize revenues from the flagship product. The sum of revenues from the mature product and the new product might not equal the previous year's annual turnover. There are, of course, many reasons why companies with mature products do not provide a flow of new products. Technology, the fuel that fires the competition, may be like a new pair of shoes, somewhat uncomfortable until broken in. The organization with a mature information product may be unwilling or unable to apply a newer technology to a product. Thus, an opportunity passes.

I do not want to dwell on the management reasons for not providing new products. Instead I want to return to a deeper concept of product development; that is, fast cycle manufacturing.

The ability to create new products is not enough. A successful company will be able to establish a process that permits:

- Rapid prototyping;
- Testing;
- Revising and modifying;
- Producing;
- Marketing.

The new product must be moved through the complete development cycle rapidly and in a cost-efficient, effective manner. It does an information manufacturing concern little good to have an idea, take six months to develop a prototype and three months more to get the product to market. Chances are the competition will have responded and moved forward again in the span of nine months to one year. A slow-reacting organization loses twice: the costs of product development are lost, never to be recovered, and the opportunity for new revenue has been snatched by the competition. Little wonder that information companies with outmoded, sluggish manufacturing facilities are under siege. They are sitting ducks for the competition. But, unlike ducks, they cannot move from harm's way.

The end as beginning: organization and quality

Database publishers have, therefore, taken an ambivalent view of the quality of their products. They have viewed the collection and organization of the source data as the most important functions. Stepping back from these functions and asking, 'Are the data correct?' has, until recently, been considered irrelevant.

As data become more and more readily available in electronic form, collection and organization *per se* are losing their market value. Thus, there is an inexorable shift from collection and organization to organization and quality control. Machine processes, when properly implemented, are more consistent than person-based processes. Human judgement is inconsistent, particularly when applied to certain types of information processes. In general, inconsistency is not desirable in machine-readable constructs. Therefore, the proliferation of electronic information is going to have a significant impact on manufacturing processes, the addition of value to electronic information, and the notion of quality.

Quality in the midst of rapid product development, fast-cycle manufacturing, and the proliferating information environment remains a concern of information producers and customers alike. The concern reflects a good news/bad news approach to the cluster of characteristics, opinions and facts that comprise information quality.

Good news and bad news

First, the good news. Advancements in technology give information manufacturers cost-effective ways to address certain operands in the quality equation. Machine checks on spelling, indexing, record structure and other formal, objective components of a machine-readable database are easy processes to implement *if the information manufacturer chooses to invest programming and system resources to implement them.*

As software begins to embed spelling checks and thesaurus look-up capabilities in the basic code, information manufacturers need merely 'flip a bit' in order to take advantage of what were, only a few years ago, complex and sophisticated features. Because such procedures are relatively easy to implement and cost nothing extra to activate, certain aspects of machine-readable files will undoubtedly improve: state, province, and country names will be consistent. Telephone numbers will have all the necessary digits – although individual numbers may still be wrong.

Now, the bad news. In the push toward fast-cycle processes, there will be a continuing temptation to focus on the sizzle, the zip and the bang of the new product. *Quality* does not have the cachet that true-color, multimedia, image-enabled databases have. The crackle and pop may drown out the voice that asks, 'But are the data accurate?'

In the proliferation of electronic information, there will be some victories for quality. There will be casualties as well. This is not to say that the majority of the new electronic information products will be seriously flawed or wrong. The message is *caveat emptor*, just as it has been since the first financial transaction.

Barriers to quality

At this point, you may be thinking, 'What a ridiculous situation. Information manufacturers should simply fix errors! They do, don't they?' My advice: Do some checking. Ask around. Scrutinize databases as a *consumer* of the data, not a neutral intermediary.

The reasons for ignoring user needs and wants vary by organization, of course. For our purposes, we will assume that the current information manufacturing 'system' cannot readily accommodate the change. Typical reasons for not responding to user input include:

- Programming cost is beyond the organization's resources;
- Priority of the change is too low to warrant investment;
- Change is technically impossible in the present manufacturing 'plant';
- Return on investment does not meet organization's target;
- Copyright or other legal issues block the change.

It makes little difference if the unresponsive provider of electronic information has the world's most superb marketing engine. The key is the ability of the information manufacturer to deliver what the customer wants. In practical terms, a machine-readable file can lose user and customer support if enhancements are not made. A competitor can enter the market and take customers.

If an information manufacturer does not respond to customer needs, is it likely the customer will seek an alternative? No-one seeks an alternative if no acceptable options exist, if no-one knows the data are flawed, or if one believes that *some* information is better than *no* information.

Marketing does not make a successful machine-readable file; manufacturing does. To state the obvious: the information in the database must be accurate, and the overall experience of accessing and using it must conform to the customer's expectations of fair value, ease of use and other subjective factors.

Proliferation and quality

One of the most visible signs of the acceleration of the move toward the proliferation phase is the clustering of information manufacturers into two groups:

1. Manufacturers using information factories that were constructed on policies, systems, hardware, and software developed during the 1982–1992 period or earlier. Some in this category are integrating newer technologies into their existing systems. Examples: (1) Dow Jones News/Retrieval's experiments with parallel processing computers; (2) The Whole Earth 'Lectronic Link's virtual communities and user-created databases.
2. Manufacturers using advanced technologies which will become the foundation for the 'reconstruction' stage that is beginning to gather momentum. Examples: (1) Voyager Corporation's multimedia CD-ROMs; (2) Indices built by agent software operating on Internet nodes.

Talking about what *will* happen is risky, of course. I want to point out that the principal difference between these two movements is mass production with some individualization, as opposed to information manufacturing specifically tailored to the individual's needs and requirements.

Skirmishes will be fought between information manufacturers who are making files that follow the assembly-line model of minor customization, and organizations that can create customized information constructs. The likely winners will not be any of the primary combatants themselves, but integrators who are able to resolve the differences and thus capture the customer's loyalty. Likely characteristics of such integrators will be:

- Ability to use data from other information manufacturers and reconfigure it to meet the needs of particular markets. Example: a producer of software tools that reside in a network operating system
- Lower costs for such features as indexing, machine translation and formatting. Example: software handles these functions; high-cost human labor is reserved for high value-added tasks.
- Flexibility in assembling the information objects needed to provide the desired machine-readable file.

As I write this, I know of no fully operational information factory or information integrator that is observing these principles.

Whose yardstick?

But what is *quality*?

This is a question with many answers. Toyota Motors defines quality as products which conform to the specification. Items which exceed allowed variances are, therefore, of poor quality.

Can electronic information be measured like an automobile fender? When does a database have quality? The answer depends on who asks the question, the expertise of the person evaluating the database and its records, and the use to which the electronic information will be put.

An information factory produces individual information a record at a time. (Other units of a database, in the jargon of numeric file manufacturers, are *data sets* and *time series*.) Some of the attributes of quality customers recognize are timeliness (e.g. real-time updates) and brand identity (e.g. Dow Jones). Other 'visible' factors include data consistency; that is, elements of the record are in a predictable 'place' and 'style' relative to other records in the file.

The databases as a whole have to be reliable; that is, they have to operate according to user expectations, or as past experience suggests they will. They have to be affordable, priced so the customer can afford to buy them, or at least see the value of having the data. There is a subjective aspect as well: the databases have to be usable; that is, they should not create confusion, disappointment or frustration.

At the May 1992 Workshop on Instruction in Library Use, representatives of North American academic libraries were invited to offer their opinions about the challenges posed by electronic information products. A surprising number of these librarians voiced concern about software features, local control of documentation, and functionality of CD-ROM and online public access catalog products.[7]

As I listened, I thought the group demonstrated consensus on one point: database producers seemed unable or unwilling to make product-related changes. CD-ROM publishers in particular found it easy to say, 'Changes are coming.' But any changes seemed to be partial at best.

Why are CD-ROM publishers resisting customer pleas for software enhancements? Consider online: Why are traditional timesharing services unwilling to expand electronic mail and user-created database services? Why are large text timesharing companies unable to accommodate user requests for data formatted for specific word processors? Why are database producers unable to provide charts and graphs in graphic and tabular formats? Why are information manufacturers blaming online vendors for limiting their ability to fix data errors? Why are online vendors saying that database quality is solely the responsibility of the manufacturer?

The reasons are rooted in information manufacturing processes and policies. The majority of electronic publishers, therefore, wisely try to steer a middle course. Certain features and functions are added if they can be provided at 'reasonable' cost, in a 'reasonable' period of time, and without necessitating an overhaul of the complete information manufacturing facility.

But as users and customers get smarter about machine-readable files, they want more. When an information manufacturer promises but cannot deliver, sales are lost. As a librarian from the American West might say, 'Big hat, no cattle.' Quality is rooted in manufacturing. When information manufacturing is recognized as the central issue, change will be possible, and the reconstruction phase of information manufacturing, on which we are now embarked, will gain momentum.

Marketing talks, manufacturing delivers, customers experience. The only road to database quality is through the information factory.

Notes

1. Ellul, Jacques (1990), *The Technological Bluff*, translated by Geoffrey W. Bromiley, Grand Rapids, Michigan: William B. Eerdmans Publishing Co., p. 73.
2. Aired on PBS stations, 30 May 1992.
3. The author wishes to acknowledge the comments and suggestions made by Martin Hensel, President, Martin Hensel Corporation (Newton, Massachusetts). Mr. Hensel's observations and insights are woven throughout this essay. I am deeply indebted to him for his unselfish contributions of time and knowledge.
4. *The Wall Street Journal*, 26 May 1992, page B6; in the occasional column 'Information Age.'
5. Drucker, Peter F. (1992), *Managing for the Future: The 1990s and Beyond*, New York: Truman Talley Books, p. 314.
6. Arnold, Stephen E. (1990), 'Marketing Electronic Information: Theory, Practice, and Challenges, 1980–1990,' in *Annual Review of Information Science and Technology*, (Ed. Martha E. Williams), Barking, Essex: Elsevier Science Publishers B.V. pp. 87–144.
7. A more detailed description of this conference appeared in *Library Monitor*, June 1992.

Chapter 2

STANDARDIZING ONLINE INFORMATION: AN IMPOSSIBILITY?

Sophie K. Hudnut, Dialog Information Services, Inc.

We live in a world filled with names: short names, nicknames, pseudonyms, abbreviations and acronyms. Pity the individual who wants to search online! Want to find an author whose first name is Jay? You might find him under Jay or James or J. or J. followed by his middle initial. Will you remember to look for Peg under Margaret or M. or P.? Is it KMart or K-Mart? How often do you scratch your head about ROI, or CEO and CFO, or DOE and DOA, trying to remember what the acronyms stand for, so you can look up the full phrase too? Better yet, what about the five-year-old article just loaded with unexplained acronyms which may have slipped from vogue already, with nary an explanation of what the letters stood for in the first place.

The rapid technological developments of the 20th century have introduced a wide variety of new terminology in our language. The increasing informality of the written and spoken word has led to a further proliferation of synonymous names and labels for people, organizations and products. The computer has made it much easier for us to access information than at any other time in history, but our rapidly changing language is making it much more difficult to find the desired information.

Standardizing online information presents something of a dilemma. Should the system accept anything the user enters and convert it to the proper equivalent? If so, who will be smart enough to program all the variations into the system? Is D. Smith actually Dean Smith or Doug Smith or D.L. Smith? Is there some happy medium where the system and the user do part of the work? My objective is to touch on a few of the problem areas in online searching impacted by the lack of standardization:

database design, data characteristics (such as names of people, organizations and products), bibliographic citations and the quality of retrieved results.

Historical perspective

Initially, online databases were derived from printed citation indexes. In printed works, it was desirable to devote most of the space to citation content, with a few pages devoted to subject and author indexes. To make the publication manageable in size, indexes and even the citations themselves were often heavily abbreviated. This approach was also suitable for early online databases, because data storage was limited and costly. Data fields were fixed in length, and if you guessed wrong on maximum field size, you had to abbreviate the entries to fit. There was a lot of pressure to keep data fields short.

Working on an early project to convert a library card catalog for online access, I remember having to abbreviate data on the fly, with little thought to its impact on retrieval. Indexers knew that what was put in an index was what would be used to find entries in it, but we had not yet realized that phrase indexes, where you could only access the first word, were going to be replaced by the ability to search on any word in a phrase. More significantly, it had not dawned on us that the computer was very precise and literal: you could only retrieve what you entered. Having grown up with the limited access provided by printed indexes and card files, few, if any, of us realized that we were making computerized information retrieval more difficult in the long run.

Database quality issues

Database characteristics, such as structure, subject coverage, record content and accuracy, play a significant role in defining quality and ease of use. The database producer gathers data from many sources with a goal of making the data consistent in form within the database. In developing a database, the producer must deal with issues such as what to cover, how to organize the data and how to keep adding new data over time. Should the database cover a limited subject area in depth or include a broad spectrum of subjects in a more selective manner? Retrospective coverage, the number of publications covered, the extent of coverage, international versus regional or local coverage, the kind of data to cover – all are important factors.

Record content is equally important. Abstracts, lead paragraphs, full text of the original source, subject indexing – the more information that can be provided, the better. As more databases go to full-text, online searchers also expect complete coverage of a journal, including those pieces, such as letters, fillers, etc., that have traditionally been omitted. Users see this as a quality issue, and expect to be told what is missing. If the information is not available, they will take their business elsewhere.

Subject indexing is an enhancement provided by the database producer, and it raises some interesting quality issues. The better the indexing, the easier the database is to use; but indexing is a costly operation if done manually, and automated indexing is still not sufficiently accurate. Database indexing can range from in-depth indexing that truly enhances retrieval, to little more than broad section headings or single words or even no indexing at all. For many years, it was argued that if full-text could be searched online, there would be little need for subject indexing. The user could search the natural language phrases of the article and find the needed information. Now we have discovered that full-text searching is difficult – it requires a much more precise query (Boolean ANDs are too broad) and some kind of filter to retrieve the desired information. If the author relies on colloquial terminology in the text, the searcher who is unfamiliar with the subject is not going to find the needed information. Subject index terms bridge this gap by providing synonyms and alternative terms for getting at a particular subject.

Database quality can also be affected by the design of the record and the data fields. If data is not properly organized into fields and entered in a consistent fashion, it may be difficult to isolate for searching. Data must be entered consistently into a field. If allowable field length is inadequate, data contained therein may be truncated, or so highly abbreviated in an attempt to squeeze it in, that it is virtually irretrievable. In fields such as author or date, the order in which the data is entered may determine how easily it can be made searchable by the search service.

Let us look at the problem of date fields. If the date is in the month–day–year format, for example March 25, 1993, it might be indexed as a complete phrase. Although the complete dates can be browsed in the date index, this form of entry is useless for searching by year since the year is at the end of the phrase, and it cannot be browsed in logical month order since the months are alphabetized. Any date entries added to the index in a different order, for example, 25 March 1993, would occur in a different part of the index. If the month–day–year date is word indexed, it makes the date index unbrowsable, except by year, since each piece of the date is in a separate location, and the complete date can only be retrieved by the use of proximity operators.

The date problem was solved by developing a standardized date format: YYMMDD, which allows dates to be grouped first by year, then by month and date. This solves the problem of indexing and retrieval but makes the date rather unfriendly to read as entered. But, if the date is indexed in a standard way, it can be converted to any format for display. So, either format, March 25, 1993 or 25 March 1993, can be displayed or even translated into other languages if desired, all because of the standardized form of entry. Furthermore, the search service can write an algorithm to translate whatever the user enters into the standardized form needed for retrieval.

Data accuracy and timeliness are critical aspects of database production. In bibliographic files, garbled source information makes it difficult to locate the original source. Statistical data must be extremely accurate – a transposed decimal point or incorrectly translated monetary unit can make a big difference, especially when organizations retrieving the data are likely to make business decisions based on the information. Typographical errors in the text may cause the user to miss a relevant publication. Data that is late can be useless to a searcher with a time-dependent deadline. Database producers have to provide updated information as quickly as possible while maintaining accuracy and continually improving the quality of their results.

The search service determines how a database will be used online, and the look and feel of the records. But it is dependent on the database producer for content and data input structure. A well-designed record, in which data elements have been divided properly into fields, can be converted more easily into a fully-searchable record than one in which several pieces of data are lumped together into one field. For instance, the source field often contains journal name, volume, pages and date. If this is the only place in the record where the date is found, the search service will usually attempt to build a date field algorithmically, but if there is much variation in the form of the date, for example as noted above, the date field may contain good as well as bad data. Ordering of data within a field is critical, too. An author name entered in direct order will be difficult to invert for 'last name' browsing because of the many variations that can occur in multi-word surnames or international names.

The search service builds in the search functionality for a database, including not only how the database is searched, but also the features that enhance the search process. These include searchable indexes, friendly display formats, consistency between similar databases, analysis techniques and a variety of other capabilities. To the extent possible, it is the search service that introduces standardization to facilitate searching across databases. The use of standardized field qualifiers for similar fields makes it easier for the searcher to move from one database to another or to search them together. Some field qualifiers, such as TI for title, are now being used by all search services to make it easier for searchers to move between services. Dialog has developed the Finder files to assist users in searching for non-standard data, such as journal names and company names, between databases.

The appearance of search system features that work across databases, such as duplicate detection and ranking of search results, has made us much more aware of quality and standardization issues. The lack of consistency between databases becomes very obvious when you look at records that describe the same work in very different ways. In Figure 2.1, records from five different databases describing the same patent are compared. Two of the records are from patent databases and three are from bibliographic databases. Field labels have been standardized to make the data differences more apparent. The table reflects the following events: four of the five databases announced the publication of a United States patent application, common for applications based on US government research. During the examination process the application was abandoned in favor of a later application not illustrated here. In reality, the four records describe a phantom publication. The point is that titles, assignees (who owns the invention), patent/application numbers and even dates do not match. No wonder identifying duplicates is virtually impossible to do automatically! Only the practiced eye of a knowledgeable and experienced searcher could identify these as the same document.

After more than twenty years of online databases, storage has become cheap and

Title: Combination primer/topcoat coating; Polyurethane binder with titanium dioxide and zinc salts
Assignee: US OF America Navy Secretary of
Patent No.: ABANDONED
Application No.: US 211026
Date filed: 880616

Title: Combination primer/topcoat coating
Assignee: Department of the Navy, Washington, DC (USA)
Patent No.: US A 7–211026
Publication Date: 16 Jun 1988

Title: Anticorrosive, flexible, chemically resistant, weather-resistant, opaque, single layer, light-weight polyurethane coatings
Assignee: United States Dept. of the Navy
Patent No.: U.S. Pat. Appl.; US 211026 A0
Publication Date: 881115
Application No.: US 211026
Date filed: 880616

Title: Flexible, adherent, weather-resistant, opaque coating compsns – comprising polyurethane binder, titanium dioxide pigments, and zinc-cpds., esp. useful as primer and top-coats for naval aircraft
Asignee No.: US Sec of Navy
Patent No: US 7211026A
Publication Date: 881129

Title: Combination Primer/Topcoat Coating (Patent Application)
Assignee: Department of the Navy, Washington, DC.
Patent No.: PAT–APPL–7–211 026 ← *Searched as Report No. not Patent*
Date filed: 16 Jun 88

Figure 2.1 *Representations of the same document in five different databases*

plentiful, but those early decisions about indexing and file structure continue to plague us. As online searching has grown in popularity, database producers have enhanced their databases by adding more fields and cleaning up problematic fields. Alas, such improvements are rarely retrospective, leaving the user unaware when a given field or search term does not apply to the whole database. The Medline database is unique in that subject heading changes are extended to retrospective records and are installed annually by all search services that offer the file.

As the search facilitator, the search service has an obligation to standardize, as much as possible, how similar databases are presented to the user. Whereas the database producer is concerned with quality, accuracy and consistency of the data provided, the search service is responsible for interpreting that data to the user in a consistent and accurate way, and providing a unified image of multiple databases to make them easy to search individually or together, irrespective of their origins. As we will see later, quality issues are further complicated by the primary publishers of data who differ among themselves on stylistic issues such as handling of names and bibliographic references.

In discussions of standardization, we must also consider the user. How much is the user expected to know about database selection, database content or the how-tos of the search process? Should the user recognize INSPEC as a database that covers electrical engineering? Should the user be expected to know to enter an author name last name first? Is it common knowledge that JAMA is a standard abbreviation for the *Journal of the American Medical Association?* Database producers and search services, as the facilitators in the search process, will have to wrestle with these issues for a long time to come.

Data quality issues

Much of the data that comes to search services, although similar in general nature, is not actually standardized. The standards applied by one database producer may differ from those used by another. To provide effective multi-file searching, the format of the data needs to be standardized. At the same time, providing good service to searchers with varying levels of expertise means accepting their requests in a variety of forms, and converting them internally to a standardized form for processing. Up to now, the online industry has not succeeded in either of these aspects of standardization.

A comprehensive search of a topic often involves the use of several related databases, so it is likely that some portion of the records will overlap. Different directory databases may include the same company but with somewhat differing data. Bibliographic and full-text databases may cover the same article but with unique enhancements, such as subject headings or informative abstracts. If the same journal is indexed in two bibliographic databases, duplicate records may or may not be retrieved. The absence of duplicates might indicate that the journal was indexed selectively, or that the article references were not entered consistently. Variations in style or content will cause records describing the same article or organization to look very different to the computer, making it considerably more difficult to recognize duplicates automatically.

Although individual databases are generally free of duplicate records, almost any multi-file search will retrieve some duplicates. Searchers complained for years about duplicate records, but it was not until Dialog started introducing features such as OneSearch in 1986 for multi-file searching, followed by duplicate detection in 1990, that we realized how 'dirty' data really could be. With the ID (Identify Duplicates) command, you could view the records in an answer set and 'see' the duplicate ones. Even worse, you could see the records that were actually duplicates but had not been recognized as such by the system software.

As duplicate detection was added to more search services, it became easy to see why these discrepancies existed. Even the search services did not always agree on what constituted a duplicate record; it depended on how each had defined their detection algorithms. Commonly, the standardization employed by one database producer did not coincide with that of another. For example, the two records in Figure 2.2 cite the same article, but with significant differences. The first record omits the author, and provides a strange-looking date but relatively easy to understand paging. The second record includes the author and has a traditional date,

HOME BAKING PURSUED . . . AGAIN	HOME BAKING PURSUED . . . AGAIN
<no author listed>	Hold, David F.
ViewText May 00, 1990 p. 8–10	ViewText v11 p8(2) May, 1990

Figure 2.2 *Comparison of records from different databases*

but abbreviated paging. With the first record, you know you can find it on pages 8 to 10, but on the second, you know only to start on page 8 and look for two more pages somewhere in that issue.

Many data fields suffer from a lack of standardization. Geographic names are quite a problem. Database developers in the USA seem to think that everyone in the world knows that AK is the two-letter code for Alaska – or is it Arkansas?! Even Americans don't always know. The point is that someone searching a particular state might be better off searching its full name; the same is true for cities and countries throughout the world.

The inconsistencies that occur between equivalent records in different databases stem from a variety of reasons. They may be due to an attempt to provide clarity (through enhanced titles, for instance), to differences in translation or in the record style adopted by the producer. Compensating for them in a computer algorithm can be very difficult, which makes the process of accurate duplicate removal difficult. To illustrate the extent of the problem, we'll look at specific fields that seem to present the greatest difficulties: title, author, organization, journal, citation information and numeric data. You will find that the numerous inconsistencies that can occur in these fields are a great part of what makes searching so challenging.

Titles

A title is the name of the article or work as selected by the author (or his editor). The title often reflects an author's idiosyncrasies and his/her assumptions about the community being addressed. Authors, particularly those involved in scientific research, often do not realize that their readers may not be knowledgeable in the subject area or the unique vocabulary of their specialty. Consequently, titles may contain unfamiliar acronyms or abbreviations, provide incomplete identification of geographic locations or even, as in the case of patents, have little bearing on the content that follows.

Some database producers will attempt to 'fix' the title by adding enhancements to make it clearer. A mountain region might be qualified by the name of the country in which it is found. The species name might be appended to the common name of a plant or animal. A phrase describing the type of work, for example 'letter', might be added to the title. Spelling variations due to local usage or translation idiosyncrasies (e.g. YOGURT vs. YOGHURT) can introduce unexpected differences, too. Figure 2.3 illustrates the kinds of variations that occur in titles.

• Changes in wording: Abbreviations
Caprolactam induces genetic alterations in early germ cell stages and in somatic tissue of *D. Melanogaster* Caprolactam induces genetic alterations in early germ cell stages and in somatic tissue of *Drosophila Melanogaster*
• Changes in wording: Acronyms
Characterization of a pyridine nucleotide-nonspecific glutamate dehydrogenase from Bacteriodes thetaiotamicron Characterization of a pyridine nucleotide-nonspecific glutamate dehydrogenase from *EC–1.4..41* Bacteriodes thetaiotamicron
• Variations in translation
Note: both titles are translations of 'Klammernaht oder Einzelknopfnaht? Eine kontrollierte klinische Studie zum Vergleich beider Hautverschlussmethoden' *Stapling of interrupted sutures? Controlled clinical comparison of 2 methods of skin closure* *Stapling suture or single button suture? A controlled clinical study of a comparison of both skin closure methods*
• Variations in molecular formulas
Corrosion of *silicon nitride* (*Si3N4*) and sialons in *vanadium oxide* (*V2O5*) melts Corrosion of *Si/sub 3/N/sub 4/* and sialons in *V/sub 2/O/sub 5/* melts Corrosion of *Si/3N//4* and sialons in *V//2O/5* melts

Figure 2.3 *Common variations found in duplicate titles*

Author and personal names

Author names can be amazingly inconsistent. The form of an author's name in a publication may depend on the author or on editorial policy. Although we have moved away from the old library custom of indexing pseudonyms under the author's real name, name searching is not any easier. When you look at online records, it is difficult to know whether to search for full first names, two initials or only one. Database producers can make this even more difficult by inserting or omitting punctuation, reducing first names to initials and even running initials together. Database producers often limit the number of author names that are included, with '*et al.*' a common substitute, particularly in older data.

Traditionally, author indexes are organized by surname and are phrase-indexed. This encourages index browsing and compensates somewhat for the inconsistent handling of first names. With names of Oriental, Middle Eastern or African origin, it is often difficult to judge which part of the name is the surname. Some databases do not invert such names unless the individual resides in a Western country, thus adding to the confusion on how such names are indexed and searched. Newspaper databases enter bylines with the surname following the first name. With the proliferation of compound names, it is difficult to write an algorithm to invert names accurately, hence author name indexes in newspapers are generally word-indexed and are not conducive to browsing.

For effective name searching in a mix of databases, the user may have to rely on several techniques. Author names entered in the traditional inverted form can be browsed by scanning the index. Bylines and names mentioned in text generally have to be reassembled using proximity operators. Non-Western names have to be explored from each part of the name on the chance that they were/were not inverted. You also have to stay on the alert for names that include titles, such as King, Doctor, Junior, Sister, etc., since they may be included with the name, may precede the surname, follow it, appear after the first name or initial, or be omitted completely. Figure 2.4 illustrates the kinds of variations that can occur in author names.

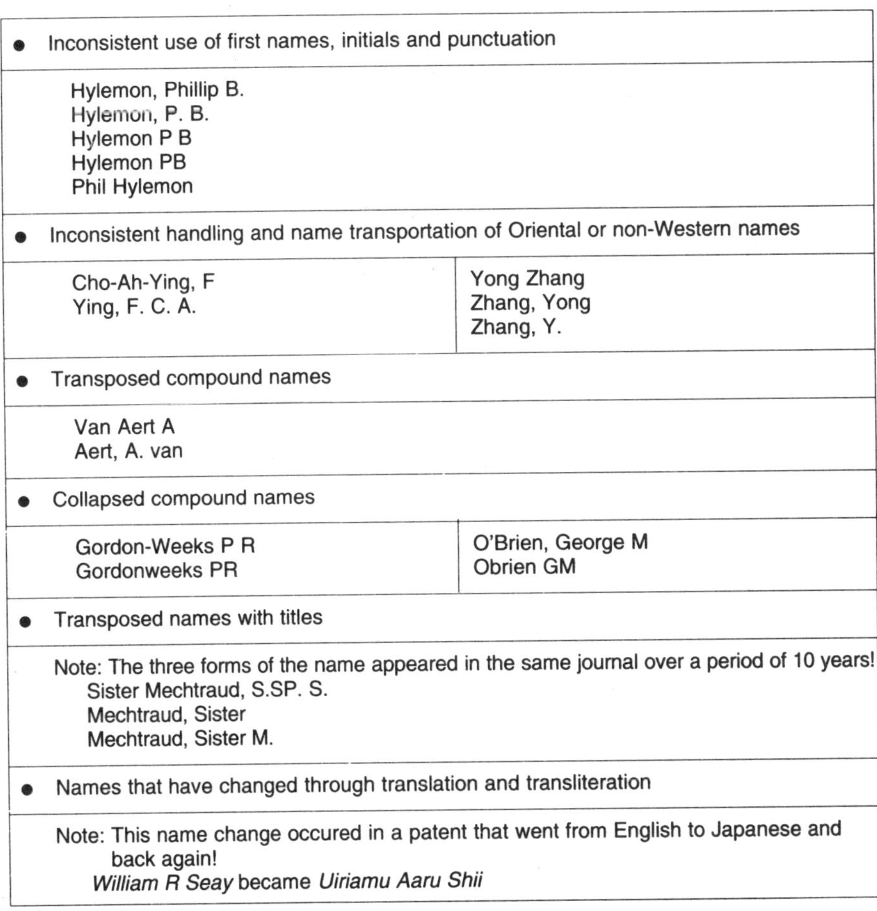

- Inconsistent use of first names, initials and punctuation

Hylemon, Phillip B.
Hylemon, P. B.
Hylemon P B
Hylemon PB
Phil Hylemon

- Inconsistent handling and name transportation of Oriental or non-Western names

Cho-Ah-Ying, F Ying, F. C. A.	Yong Zhang Zhang, Yong Zhang, Y.

- Transposed compound names

Van Aert A
Aert, A. van

- Collapsed compound names

Gordon-Weeks P R Gordonweeks PR	O'Brien, George M Obrien GM

- Transposed names with titles

Note: The three forms of the name appeared in the same journal over a period of 10 years!
Sister Mechtraud, S.SP. S.
Mechtraud, Sister
Mechtraud, Sister M.

- Names that have changed through translation and transliteration

Note: This name change occured in a patent that went from English to Japanese and back again!
William R Seay became *Uiriamu Aaru Shii*

Figure 2.4 *Common author name variations*

Journal names

Journal names identify the publication in which an article appeared. Historically, journal names have been abbreviated to save space. Unfortunately, this practice has continued in online databases, the very place where complete rather than abbreviated names would be most beneficial. Although many database producers follow abbreviation practices established by ISO or NISO standards, non-standard abbreviations do creep in. The same journal indexed by two producers may have different abbreviations. The names of professional society journals are frequently transposed. English language, cover-to-cover translations of international journals are difficult to match to their originals, since the information that would link them is rarely provided. Non-English or uncommon journal names can be especially difficult to identify when not spelled out in full, since it is unlikely that a searcher can recognize the abbreviation and equate it with the full name. Similarly, non-English speakers have trouble identifying heavily abbreviated English language journal names.

Further liberties are taken with the journal name and the form of entry; consequently, journal name indexes are littered with misspellings, unusual abbreviations and transposed word order. For example, *The Journal of the American Medical Association* has more than 150 variations. Then there is the occasional journal name that is identical for two publications published in different countries; only the addition of a city or country qualifier to the name differentiates them.

Journal names are usually phrase indexed, so their non-standard formats can make them difficult to search. Dialog's Journal Name Finder (JNF) database, introduced in 1991, is the first industry attempt to provide an easy way to locate journals in Dialog databases. Journal names are word-indexed in it, but the onus is still on the user to remember to include abbreviations when searching the JNF. Figure 2.5 illustrates the kinds of variations found in journal names.

Citations

To locate an article in a journal, you need to know the volume, issue, pages and date of the issue in which it appeared. Variations tend to be stylistic and differ from database to database. Dates may be exact or represented only as years. Pages may appear as a range or as a starting page followed by a count of the number of pages in the article. These small variations make it difficult to identify duplicate citations. Figure 2.6 illustrates the kinds of variations that can occur.

Organizational names in bibliographic and directory records

Organizational names appear in many different forms in online databases. Depending on the type of database, they may be labeled as corporate source, author affiliation, sponsoring agency, company name, owner, patent assignee, etc. The types of organizations vary as well; they may be corporations, foundations, research

• Highly abbreviated, difficult-to-identify names	
Am. J. Prev. Med. used for 'American Journal of Preventive Medicine' Z Deut Geo Ges used for 'Zeitschrift der Deutschen Geologischen Gesellschaft'	
• Use of non-standard abbreviations	
All of the following abbreviations are used for the word JOURNAL	
J	JOURN
JNL	JOURNA
JOURNAL	JOURNAL
JOUR	JRNL
• Transposed name elements, use of acronyms, abbreviations and variable punctuation	
Am. Med. Assoc. J. American Medical Association Journal Chicago, American Medical Assn J. AM. Med. Assoc. J. Amer.Med.Assoc. JAMA JAMA. American Medical Association Journal JAMA, Journal of the American Medical Association Journal of the American Medical Association	
• Duplicate journal names that are actually different publications	
Leukemia Research – actually two publications, one published in England and one in USA Leukemia – also known as 'Leukemia (Baltimore)' and 'Leukemia (Basingstoke)'	

Figure 2.5 *Common variations found in journal names*

• Use of issue number vs. month/day of publication	
Dec 10 1984, 146 (50) 1984, 146/50	
vol.2, no.23, Publication Date: 11 June 1990 Date: 1990 Volume: 2 Number: 23	
v. 90 (1) Feb 1983 90 (1) 1983	
• Paging variations	
p263–8 (263–268)	
• Inconsistent style and meaning	
136 (2) p78	(means volume 136, number 2, page 78)
v136 p78(2)	(means volume 136, page 78, column 2)

Figure 2.6 *Common variations in citation information*

institutes, universities or government agencies. The care with which an organization name is handled depends on the intent of the database. In most bibliographic databases, the organization name is treated as additional information which is not crucial to the retrieval of an article. The name is entered as provided by the author with little attempt to formalize it. Such fields often carry numerous inconsistent abbreviations in an obvious attempt to fit in long names.

Databases in which legal ownership is critical, such as patents, trademarks or copyright, sometimes attempt to standardize the name by providing additional codes. The name is usually left intact, but may be abbreviated in non-standard ways. Even though the organization names are part of a legal document, they are frequently provided in non-standard forms. A colleague who maintained an authority list for a patent database once told me that the only organization whose name consistently appeared in the same form was Corning Glass Works.

Directory databases sometimes do better with regard to standardized names. In its databases, Dun & Bradstreet provides organization names in the form in which they were registered in the state of incorporation. This, coupled with the DUNS number, goes a long way towards standardizing the parent name of a group of companies, but it doesn't always solve the problem. For example, if you search for *7/11 Stores* in directory files, you will find thousands of entries, many differentiated only by the store number or by inconsistent usage of punctuation in the name.

Dialog introduced its Company Name Finder (CNF) file in 1991. The database collects company names and owner names from directory and bibliographic databases with an identifiable company or owner name field. In 1992, the CNF contained about 45 million entries for organizations around the world; however, it did not include any corporate source entries – this would probably have doubled its size! This huge number of entries represents uncounted exact duplicates as well as near-duplicates, that is, those names that vary only through punctuation, spacing, abbreviation, word variants and typographical errors. Figure 2.7 illustrates some of the problems that can be found in organizational names. Variations introduced by punctuation are omitted.

The Dialog Company Name Finder contains numerous examples that illustrate the difficulty of standardizing company names. For example, there are 9900+ records in CNF for K-Mart, K Mart and KMart. By applying the RANK command, it is easy to determine that there are 6100+ unique terms in this set of records. 'Unique' is defined as including variations in punctuation and content. The unique entries for KMart include store numbers, locations, abbreviations and typographical errors. Even a very distinctive name like Corning Glass Works with 400+ records has 46 unique terms in CNF.

Impact on searching

Examples of standardization problems abound in the literature and in every search that results in an answer set. Numeric data is another problematic area. Report, contract or patent numbers may be entered with or without punctuation and spaces,

- Inconsistent usage

Sisters of Charity Health Care
Sisters of Charity Health Care Systems Inc
Sisters of Charity Health Care Systems Corp
Sisters of Charity Healthcare
Sisters of St. Charity Health Care Systems Inc

- Non-standard abbreviations

Univ Queensland, Dept Chem Engn/St Lucia/Qld 4067/Australia/
Dep. Chem. Eng., Unv. Queensland, St Lucia, 4067, Australia
Univ of Queensland, Queensland, Aust
Queensland Univ., St Lucia (Australia). Dept. of Chemical Engineering ← *imbedded in author field*

- Variants introduced at time of entry

Note: Word, spacing and abbreviation variants found in the Mcdonnell Douglas Aircraft Co. name

Mc Donald	Douglas	Air	Co
Mc Donnell	Dougles	Aircr	Company
McDonnell		Aircraft	Corp
			Corporation
			Crp
			Div
			Ltd

Note: Word order variations found in the company's name

Douglas Aircraft Division McDonnell Douglas
Mc Donald Douglas Aircraft Co,
Mc Donnell Douglas Aircraft Co.
McDonnell Douglas Aircraft
McDonnell Douglas Corp. Douglas Aircraft Co.
McDonnell Douglas Corp. Douglas Aircraft Div.
McDonnell Douglas Corp. McDonnell Aircraft Co.
McDonnell Douglas Douglas Aircraft Co.

- Transposition of name elements, particularly those derived from personal names

A D LITTLE	ARTHUR D LITTLE RESEARCH INST
A D LITTLE INC	ARTHUR DLITTLE
AD LITTLE	ARTHUR DLITTLE INC
A LITTLE IN	ARTHUR DLITTLEINC
AD LITTLE INC	LITTLE A D INC
ARTHUR D LITTLE	LITTLE AD IN
ARTHUR D LITTLE & CO	LITTLE AD INC
ARTHUR D LITTLE ADL	LITTLE ADINC
ARTHUR D LITTLE CAMBRIDGE MASSACHUSETTS	LITTLE ARTHUR D
ARTHUR D LITTLE CO	LITTLE ARTHUR D CO
ARTHUR D LITTLE COMPANY INC	LITTLE ARTHUR D ENT
ARTHUR D LITTLE ENTERPRISES	LITTLE ARTHUR D ENTERPRISES
ARTHUR D LITTLE ENTERPRISES INC	LITTLE ARTHUR D ENTERPRISES INC
ARTHUR D LITTLE IN	LITTLE ARTHUR D ENTPR
ARTHUR D LITTLE INC	LITTLE ARTHUR D INC
ARTHUR D LITTLE INC CAMBRIDGE MA	LITTLE ARTHUR D INC CAMBRIDGE MA
ARTHUR D LITTLE INC CAMBRIDGE MASS	LITTLE ARTHUR D INC USA

Figure 2.7 *Characteristic variations found in organizational names*

ARTHUR D LITTLE INC UNITED STATES OF AMERI	LITTLE ARTHUR D INTERNATIONAL INC
ARTHUR D LITTLE INCOPORATED	LITTLE ARTHUR D INTL INC
ARTHUR D LITTLE INT INC	LITTLE ARTHUR D INTN
ARTHUR D LITTLE INTERNATIONAL	LITTLE ARTHUR D INTNL
ARTHUR D LITTLE INTERNATIONAL INC	LITTLE ARTHUR D LIMITADA
ARTHUR D LITTLE INTL INC	LITTLE ARTHUR D LTD
ARTHUR D LITTLE LIMITADA	LITTLE ARTHUR D RESEARCH INSTITUTE GB
ARTHUR D LITTLE LIMITED	LITTLE INC AD
ARTHUR D LITTLE LTD	LITTLE INC ARTHUR
ARTHUR D LITTLE LTDA	LITTLE RES INST ARTHUR
ARTHUR D LITTLE RES INST; US AS SEC	

Figure 2.7 *Characteristic variations found in organizational names (continued)*

as illustrated in the earlier patent example. Retrieval of sales data may be complicated by how the numbers are reported – in actual monetary units, in thousands or in millions. Monetary units may be converted incorrectly. Amounts may be miskeyed, or the data may simply be missing from the field. Physical properties such as boiling point may be reported in different units which are not clearly identified.

The more one looks into the issues of standardization, the more apparent it becomes that this is a Herculean task. We wish that someone had set a world standard early on and that everyone had followed it religiously. There is indeed evidence of attempts to set standards as we become more computer-literate. But the data problems are another story. It seems that everyone has an opinion on how data should be standardized to suit their particular needs or interests, without thought of the impact on others. Abbreviations, acronyms and individualized shorthand (sometimes known only to the writer) continue to proliferate. I often wonder, considering the obstacles that have been built into the search process, how searchers in non-English speaking countries manage to do online searching at all.

Part of the vision of standardization is to recognize that just because you know how the data is organized, abbreviated or whatever, the next person who needs it might not know, and a person looking for it ten years from now will certainly not know it either. We will have to define standards that will work across different disciplines and different delivery methods. As the Internet becomes everyone's data superhighway of the immediate future, the need for standards will become increasingly apparent. I worry that we will continue to ask the same question: Why didn't somebody standardize that before?

Standardization is a process that can be assisted tremendously by the computer. But it still requires the human thought processes that can distinguish what is appropriate, right or good. Rules can be written and software built, but human intervention is required to solve the problems that do not follow the rules. There is also the 'chicken-and-egg' question: do you standardize the query or the data? If the query, how do you get everybody to do it the same way? Humans are terribly independent; their analytical skills are different. We may never be able to solve all of the problems associated with standardization, but we have to try.

Further reading

Basch, Reva (1990), 'Database reliability: The black box', paper in: Proceedings of the 11th National Online Meeting, New York, pp. 31–6.

Basch, Reva (1992), 'Decision points for databases', *Database* **15** (4), August, pp. 46–50.

Basch, Reva (1990), 'Measuring the quality of the data: Report on the Fourth Annual SCOUG Retreat', *Database Searcher* **6**, (8), October, pp.18–23.

Basch, Reva (1992), 'An overview of quality assurance issues (online databases)', paper in: Database 2000. UKOLUG State-of-the-Art Conference, Guildford, UK, pp. 85–91.

Basch, Reva (1989), 'The seven deadly sins of full-text searching', *Database* **12** (4), August pp. 15–23.

Basch, Reva (1992), 'The seven deadly sins of online services', *Online* **16** (4), July pp. 22–5.

Chitty, Mary and Gelb, Linda (1986), 'Quality assurance and online searching: Empowering the searcher', paper presented at: Special Libraries Association, 77th Annual Meeting, Boston. 7p.

Dolan, Donna R., Craumer, Patricia and Anderson, Barbara (1992), 'Quality control at the system level' (includes related articles), *Online*, **16** (2), p. 30(6).

Ellingen, Dana (1991), 'Designing your first ... or your next ... database' (column), *Database* **14** (1), February, p. 90(4).

Gardner, Sylvia A. (1992), 'Spelling errors in online databases: what the technical communicator should know', *Technical Communication* **39** (1), February, p. 50(4).

Hudnut, Sophie K. (1988), 'Considerations in searching databases spanning 20 years', paper in: Online Information 88, 12th International Online Meeting, London, 1988, **2**, pp. 459–65.

Jacsó, Peter (1993), 'Searching for skeletons in the database cupboard. Part 1. Errors of Omission', *Database* **16** (1), February, p. 38(12).

Kesselman, M. and Perry, I. (1984), 'What online searchers should know about indexing and what indexers should know about online searching', Paper in: National Online Meeting, Proceedings, New York, pp. 141–8.

Mintz, Anne P. (1990), 'Quality control and the Zen of database production', *Online* **14** (6), November, pp. 15–23.

Norton, Nancy Prothro (1981), 'Dirty data: A call for quality control', *Online* **5** (1), January, pp. 40–1.

Pagell, Ruth (1991), 'It's Greek to me! Exchange rate translations and company comparisons', *Database* **14** (2), February, pp. 21–7.

Tenopir, Carol (1990), 'Database quality revisited', *Library Journal* **115**, October 1, pp. 64–7.

White, Howard D. and Griffith, Belver C (1990), 'Quality of indexing in online databases', *Information Processing and Management* **6** (8), October, pp. 18—23.

Chapter 3

QUALITY ISSUES IN INFORMATION RETRIEVAL: A PUBLISHER PERSPECTIVE

Anne Mintz, Director of Information Services at Forbes, Inc., publisher of *Forbes* magazine

Introduction

In the beginning, there was print. Bibliographic publishers and indexing firms created their products manually. But with the introduction of mainframe computing, an obvious application of the technology was to automate the publication of these types of products. The original use of their computers was for publishing in print, but some early online industry visionaries saw that the byproduct electronic file could be used for Boolean searching. This was pretty much the model in the 1970s – bibliographic files were the foundation, and some directory-type files followed. But in 1979, Mead Data Central fired a shot heard around the online world. The publisher of Lexis (legal texts which were fully searchable online), launched Nexis, a service with the full-text of newspapers, magazines and newsletters. Besides enabling a user to search on every word of every article in the publications it carried, Nexis allowed for the retrieval and printing of the entire article in ASCII format. While other services were experimenting with full-text in addition to bibiographic or numeric files, only Nexis carried all full text, cover to cover. This was a revolutionary, although pricey, entrant into the online arena. The rest, as they say, is history.

Why has full-text online caught on so dramatically? Its importance has become much more apparent since the spiraling cost of serials has undermined many institutions' ability to own and archive several years of various titles. *Access* to articles has overtaken the need to *own* them. Full-text online solves several problems, including space constraints, copyright compliance and royalty payments, and precision of searching. While ASCII full-text may seem to be the focus today, we can look to a future where exact images and searchable full-text will somehow be combined.

Today, most publishers of newspapers, magazines and newsletters are primarily in the business of producing print products, even if they are automating that process or using an inhouse desktop publishing system. These publishers must consider many factors when deciding whether and how to allow the public electronic access to their products.

Factors controlling availability

Among the factors controlling online availability are legal, financial and technological concerns, as well as data integrity and quality. While some of these may seem irrelevant to customers, they can determine if and where a title becomes available electronically.

Technological factors

Much to the amazement of some online searchers and end-users, for many publishers the technology is nowhere nearly as sophisticated as one would imagine.

Delivery of keyed vs. *electronic copy*

Automating the publication of print products was undertaken to get the product to press more productively. Thus, some publishers cannot yet provide electronic copy to online services due to complex coding in the copy which needs additional programming to strip down to ASCII. FORBES, as a primary example, is a large profitable title with a circulation of over 750,000. However, the company itself is rather small and does not have an excess of employees with time on their hands. Forbes is typical of many publishers in this regard. It currently has arrangements with about ten different search services and information providers to load text of FORBES onto their products, and that number grows each year. However, since each information provider has its own set of specifications on how the file is to be tagged and formatted and wants Forbes to do that work, there is little impetus to invest in expensive equipment or programming in order to accommodate them all. One major search service in particular has eight pages of file formatting specifications. FORBES is currently photocomposed electronically using Atex software, a fairly standard system for publishing. Atex was created to assist in layout, photocomposition and delivery to printing plants, not for creating machine-readable and text-searchable databases. Thus, the electronic copy has all the Atex photocomposition codes embedded in the files and would require a separate software routine to strip them out. It would then require programming for each of the ten different database producers to meet their specifications. With only one bi-weekly title, there is no economy of scale. Therefore, arrangements with seven of these producers call for a slightly lower royalty rate when electronic copy is not provided, meaning that seven companies *each* key the title in manually. Publishers take great care to make sure their publications go to press as error-free as possible, and have reputations riding on this commitment, so they are naturally concerned about errors made by others. These two realities come into conflict in the situation I am describing.

Let me make the implications of this perfectly clear. Keying means that, although the original magazine is perfectly spelled, it is possible for each of seven different companies to make separate but equally damaging typographical errors. This, in turn, means that you may not be able to retrieve articles from FORBES because someone else typed a name or company incorrectly – and different errors might be made on each system. To give an example of this, there are three places on one host system where Forbes had correctly spelled the name of Mr. Mitterand, but the name was keyed in wrong by the database producer. In two of these cases, it is a unique mention of the name, which means that neither of these articles would be retrieved when a searcher inputs the name correctly.

Where FORBES is accepted electronically by a database producer, such as Ebsco Publishing, the process (which is fairly low tech) is begun at Forbes. When an issue is released for publication, the files or 'stories' are downloaded from the Atex system onto a DOS platform. They are then copied onto floppy diskettes and mailed – not sent via modem – to Ebsco. At this point, the files are in Atex/ASCII format. Ebsco downloads the files onto its network, strips the Atex typesetting codes from the data, and adds special text tags which allow elements of the articles to be recognized electronically (in their case, on CD-ROM). Several software routines are run on the files to ensure accuracy, including, in certain cases, a visual comparison with the hard copy. Finally, the files are sent to Ebsco's production facility. This process can take up to two weeks, the span of one FORBES publishing cycle.

The process described is similar to that used by the other database producers to upload the text onto their systems. Forbes is in the process of implementing a new editorial system which will have the capability of providing better electronic copy, but this feature is one of the lower priorities in getting the new system up and running. This is true of a lot of publishers, especially in the past year or two, with new technology coming onto the market after extensive testing. It is expected that, within a few years, many more publishers will upgrade their systems from the bottom up, which will enable more sophisticated database creation.

Optical scanning is a technology spoken of with great hope by the electronic publishing industry. It has certainly come a long way in the past few years, but has not quite arrived yet. Quality concerns arise when publishers employ certain typesetting fonts that can 'confuse' the scanner. Consider the word 'modern'. When type is set tightly, the 'r' and the 'n' are quite close together; often, this causes the scanner to read the word as 'modem'. Since 'modem' is a word in the English language, a spell-check would not necessarily catch this error. When errors show up in articles from a reputable magazine, the reputation of the editorial product suffers, through no fault of the original publisher. As one can imagine, this is not an attractive scenario to most publishers.

Magazines with electronic delivery

Economies of scale have enabled some publishers to produce inhouse tapes for vendors. One publisher in particular, which has almost thirty titles available online, employs a license negotiator and technical staff to produce tapes according to the specifications of each online host they work with. Thus, you will find their combined file of publications on Dialog and Dow Jones News/Retrieval, and each of the titles as a separate file on Nexis. In this case, any "selected" full text will be decided by the original publisher, not by an intermediary database producer's editorial department. In this instance, the publications are online cover-to-cover. Each publication cycle, tapes are produced for each vendor. Any typographical errors in these files will be found in the print originals as well. The only 'quality' issue encountered here is making certain the right tape reaches the right vendor. A mistake will delay loading of the files and their availability within the advertised time period.

Of course, when the publisher does not have to pay an intermediary company a portion of the royalties paid by the host system for the file, this kind of venture becomes more profitable for them. Companies in this position will probably be quicker to adapt, in the future, to technology that allows for image transmission as well.

Delivery of newsletters

In the USA, newsletters are primarily found online in two places, NewsNet, a free-standing online service, and the Predicasts family of databases (on Dialog, Nexis and Data-Star). Each company approaches the business differently. In the case of Predicasts (now owned by IAC/Ziff Davis), the files are transmitted electronically to the database producer (Predicasts), which formats them for their own files, adds index terms, and then does the negotiation and loading with the search services. Publishers run the gamut of technical sophistication and Predicasts has several options for them. About 10 per cent of Predicasts newsletters are keyed in. Another 25 per cent or so are shipped on floppy disks in ASCII. If necessary, Predicasts will convert data into ASCII from a publisher's file. The remaining 65 per cent of publishers send the ASCII text via modem. Once the copy has reached Predicasts, it is tagged, coded, indexed and loaded onto the next release to each of the host services.

NewsNet, by contrast, is a search service in its own right. Like Nexis, it mounts each title as a separate file. Almost every file is created from full-text ASCII files telecommunicated directly to NewsNet's data center by the original publishers. These files are then processed by the publishers themselves through a proprietary error-checking program resident on the NewsNet mainframes. If the program detects errors, they must be corrected by the publisher and the file reprocessed until it is 100 per cent error-free. To this point, each publisher has control over file integrity. Once released by the publisher, the files are processed further by NewsNet. Any problems or errors that result after release by the publisher are handled by NewsNet. (As an aside, NewsNet has instituted a FIXIT command which allows searchers who find possible errors in the full-text to 'message' the publisher electronically to fix them.)

Daily newspapers online and ondisc

The availability of newspapers online has increased dramatically in the past several years. In the USA, DataTimes, Dow Jones, Dialog, NewsBank and Nexis carry the full-text of many newspapers, online and/or ondisc. In Canada, InfoMart and the Globe Information Services carry the texts of almost every major paper in Canada. In England, the *Financial Times* has been online for years, as have the *Independent* and other major newspapers. For information on which newspapers are available on what search services, reference can be made to BiblioData's *Newspapers Online*, which covers major international newspapers with articles online in full-text. As of the 1993 edition, international papers must be accessible through a US host in order to be included, but their entry will carry references to non-US hosts that also carry that title.

The primary reason that one can find newspapers online and ondisc in full-text is because the technology for producing the print copy – the publisher's primary business – was automated to enable the print product to go to press more easily. After a number of years, the hardware and software developed to allow for more sophisticated uses of this automation, and newspapers began using the technology to replace their expensive, labor-intensive clip files with an electronic inhouse 'morgue'. This enabled journalists and editors to perform research on their own newspaper electronically. In fact, both DataTimes and Vu/Text began as newspaper service bureaux which developed software specifically for the newspaper morgue function, not the searching function. As of the end of 1992, Vu/Text was relieved of the search service function by its corporate owner, Knight-Ridder, and now exists only as a service bureau. Dialog, another Knight-Ridder subsidiary, has taken over almost all the newspaper databases from Vu/Text. Generally, newspaper libraries have staff who index each article in every version of the paper, as part of the process of publishing the paper and storing it archivally. Field tags are consistent for internal and database publisher requirements, as are index terms. The index terms are created by each newspaper for its writing staff to use in retrieving past articles, rather than for external database searchers. There is little consistency from one newspaper to another, even on the same search service, which is why using index terms on this type of full-text file is usually not productive.

Newspapers are now engaged in developing or purchasing the technologies for their futures. This should produce even more changes in this sector of the text retrieval business. The transmission of data will probably be much faster than we could have imagined a few years ago. Data compression techniques will continue to be improved, and new infrastructures will allow for larger masses of data to be sent simultaneously. Many papers already transmit via satellite to remote plants.

Information intermediary companies such as NewsBank and Dialog have acquired license agreements for newspapers for CD-ROM products. When a title becomes available on CD-ROM in full-text, publishers are often apprehensive that the market for their online version will be cannibalized, but this has not yet come to pass. At this time, much of the major US press is available on CD-ROM in libraries, universities and corporations all across the country. While it varies from vendor to vendor, the searching of ASCII text at a customer-owned workstation is a fairly new concept. Financial, legal and business factors will determine how widely available such systems become. But once those factors are ironed out, the ability for a worker to search the full-text of a newspaper at a fixed price will begin to have the same type of effect that CD-ROM index products had; online publishers realized that people wanted predictable pricing options and created them.

Issues with graphics

One of the most intelligent advertisements I have seen lately is the one which UMI used for its Business Periodicals Ondisc product. It shows a page of ASCII printed out from a laser printer adjacent to a 'photocopy' of the article as it appeared in print. The caption says: 'Chacun à son goût'. Each to his own taste. When given a choice, people usually want to see the original.

Publishers and editors spend a great deal of time and money visually arranging the copy of a text, whether a book or a journal article. In many cases, the layout is actually part of the editorial content – a revealing chart, photograph or even an unusual page layout will have informational or entertainment value. UMI has put a lot of money into developing a product it hopes will be a harbinger of the future of document delivery. I used this as an example of a good advertisement, but it also happens to be the kind of product I wish to discuss. What UMI has done is develop a technology which they hope to parlay into implementation some time in the future, when the information infrastructure allows for quick, cheap and easy *transmission* of this digitized data. In the meantime, it is simply using a sophisticated technology to replace microfilm and reader-printers. What UMI probably intends is that, when the infrastructure allows it, they will have the product ready to transmit, already developed, with all the legal agreements in place.

In order to transmit graphics, however, some dramatic changes must occur. Depending on one's national government policies and on publishers' investments in new technology, some of these changes are closer to reality than others. The components which must come together are: fiber optic cable which will enable masses of data to be transmitted; exponentially faster transmission speeds (baud rates) and modems, since each digitized image page contains so much more data than ASCII; and optical scanners which recognize many typefonts, especially ones where letters are tightly placed.

With regard to transmission speeds, many newspapers and others are already using T1 telephone lines. These are high speed lines with more bandwidth, which allows for faster transmission of more data at one time. But not many customers for online products currently have access to such lines.

Optical scanning is close to reality, and in many places is being used successfully to digitize and store data. But the entire communications and transmission package is not as far advanced. In the USA, the proposed electronic superhighway which would serve as the backbone for this process is still being negotiated; the government and the private sector must work out the policies which will enable its implementation. Vice President Gore has proposed NREN (the National Research and Education Network), but the telecommunications industry, for the most part, would like this venture to be a private sector opportunity. Other countries will have their own models, like France, which has the Minitel model to draw from.

Image-based products with ASCII searchability

Once the product can be transmitted with graphics, what information practitioners, and probably most end-users, will really want is to be able to search the text as well. This is known as 'text-searchable image'. Sooner or later, it will be a part of our lives; whether sooner or later is the only variable. Images will be easier to digitize for transmission and/or storage. Instead of keeping physical copies of photographs or charts, the system will be able to store them digitally. With the correct indexing and location mapping, retrieval will be not only more accurate, but perhaps even enhanced. This will be part of the production phase of the publication itself, not an afterthought for which indexers and searchers will have to clamor. Customers are likely to see image-based, full-text searchable products for newspapers sooner than for magazines. Companies in the USA are very involved in automating the publication of journals and books with graphics, and it is likely that European and Far Eastern companies are in the game as well. The trade association for newspaper publishers and some newspaper librarians are working on standards for this image-based future, but the technology has moved so fast that many papers are not waiting to create their own files. What we will probably see is a UMI Business Periodicals Ondisc model, with an ASCII-based database front end which can be free-text searched, and an image file behind it for retrieving. They will be separate files but one will hook into the other for delivery purposes.

Other technological factors

Whether the file is prepared by an indexing/abstracting company or by the publisher, once it is sent to the host system, there may be further problems which affect the retrieval of the full-text. Some service bureaux used by publishers for processing data still are not equipped to handle tape cartridges, which have become the preferred way of storing files. This can cause delays in delivery to search services. Even though most providers have migrated from magnetic tape to tape cartridges, and most use overnight delivery services as opposed to the postal service, some tapes still arrive physically damaged. This is less common than it used to be, but it can still affect online availability.

Another factor might be the widespread availability of a file on many host systems, each of which has a different loading priority for that file. For example, it stands to reason that a Swiss newspaper database might have loading priority at Data-Star over a file with Australasian newspapers. However, on a US or a Japanese host, that Swiss paper might be very far down the priority list. A search service must rank the priorities of its clients. This reality, while not always on the mind of the seeker of information, certainly affects *perceived* availability. If one seeks to read the latest issue of FORBES online, one finds that it is available on certain services faster than on others, depending on whether that service accepts the electronic copy, and on how high a priority they think the title is for their customers. It would certainly be available sooner on US hosts than on European or Asian.

In a series of interviews performed in 1990, I learned of several other interesting matters concerning online host services which affect the timely availability of files. One host service reported that they load files around the clock, in three eight-hour shifts. This includes reloading entire files as well as updates. The loading queue is so long that the process is performed non-stop. The scheduling for this queue must be done fairly far in advance, which can have a negative effect on publishers who are considering backloading full-text to increase the coverage of a title. It also means that corrections to current full-text files may take longer to get online.

The other primary factor is the cost incurred by publishers. If the royalties collected do not cover the cost of maintaining and loading the files, the publishers will not get, or remain, involved in the online process. This was the case in 1992 when Knight-Ridder decided at a corporate level to load the Vu/Text newspapers onto Dialog, and discovered that about a dozen newspapers did not cover their own costs. Thus, despite customer protests, these newspapers did not move over to the Dialog system when Vu/Text ceased operating as an independent online search host.

One final matter concerning the availability of full-text online is the current state of technology at the major search services. The online literature is full of references to 'search engines' and how they must be revamped. The software on which Dialog, Orbit, BRS and so on run was written more than twenty years ago. The inherent limitations of this software have begun to hamper the implementation of full-text files. Since the software was designed for files with size-delineated fields, adding full-text does not allow for effective searching by limiting terms to the same text paragraphs. A capability that might normally be assumed by people seeking to search and print full text is not easily implemented by software that was originally designed to do something entirely different. There is a long way to go before we see the ideal search environment for full-text files.

Legal factors

License agreements

A publisher has to decide, first, whether electronic access is an area in which to invest resources. Most publishers are attracted by the promise of royalties from information providers and search services, but do not realize the overhead expenses involved in this business. License agreements must be drawn up which are practical for both parties. This is a time-consuming process, since many print publishers do not really understand the issues which must be addressed. Obvious issues include setting the royalty rate, the dates the agreement is in effect, and the embargo period from the time of publication until it can go online. It becomes even more difficult when one must consider whether to make the arrangement an 'exclusive', whether or not a contract can be assigned in case ownership of one of the parties changes, and when dealing with warranties and indemnifications, deletion and correction policies, and the delivery of electronic copy according to the search service's specifications. Questions like who is responsible for errors, whether there is to be a 'breach of contract' clause, and extent of coverage (cover-to-cover or 'selected') must be considered as well. This process can take a very long time. I have engaged in negotiations with three separate organizations, each of which took 18 months to complete, even though both parties were friendly to the deal and the negotiators understood the issues fully. One reason we sometimes see files come and go, or become spotty in coverage, has to do with poorly-written contracts entered into by parties not fully aware of all the relevant issues. The publisher has to decide whether the potential royalties are worth the time that must be devoted by the attorneys and the license negotiators.

Copyright

Copyright considerations are another area of legal concern. While online full-text delivery solves the users' copyright compliance problems, it may expose the publishers to additional liability, since they may not actually own more than first serial rights to the contents of a publication. Contracts in force may be so old that print rights are the only ones referred to. In some cases, the selective nature of the database may give rise to the argument that 'this isn't XYZ magazine, it's just five articles per issue', and that negotiations fall under rights and permissions per article, not generic publication rights. The publisher may have to renegotiate many contracts with individual writers and freelancers; in fact, the author community is catching on to a possible revenue enhancer for itself!

Intellectual property is the bottom line – 'Who owns the content?' will be a growing consideration in this arena over the next few years, and we may see changes in online file configurations as technology allows individuals and smaller publishers to bypass some of the current intermediaries.

Another set of copyright-related considerations has to do with other kinds of material the publisher does not own. This includes letters to the editor and syndicated columns. Two US examples are 'Dear Abby' and the columnist Jack Anderson. One would have to consult a print directory such as the *Editor & Publisher Annual Directory of Syndicated Services* to verify that this material may have appeared in print but will not, if the publisher is adhering to his syndication agreement, appear in the online version.

Financial factors

There has to be some financial incentive for a publisher to commit the expense and energy to bring full text online. There are several financial factors to consider.

Royalties

If the party publishing the database owns the contents (as is the case with Reuter Newswires or Dow Jones and the *Wall Street Journal*) online pricing is set by the same company that owns the data. In other cases, publishers will load their titles into one or more online files of their own and have the tapes loaded directly onto a second-party online search service. In most cases, information providers, such as Information Access Company or UMI/Data Courier, will act as intermediaries between the publishers and online search services such as DataStar, Dialog or Mead Data Central. Obviously, the more intermediaries between the original publisher and the customer, the less revenue the publisher will see, since the intermediaries take a share of the royalties. Royalties are set by publishers when they draft the original agreement to license the product to the next party, whoever it is. The information provider, if there is one in the deal, then charges the online host a certain royalty of its own, completely independent of the publishers, in order to recover costs and produce a profit. In most cases, the intermediary company has a license with the publisher to load other titles as well, and the publisher has nothing directly to do with the search service. Until Forbes finds that it is profitable or even cost-effective to produce the formatted product internally and absorb the costs involved, it will remain financially attractive to use such an intermediary. In an interesting twist, we are now seeing cases where search services are making arrangements with print publishers directly, but using an intermediary's electronic file of their title(s). I mention this simply to give an indication of how complicated this can get, and why one may or may not see certain titles in certain products online and on CD-ROM.

Pricing

A number of factors go into the pricing of a product, which may affect online or ondisc availability. These include, in addition to licensors' demands for royalties, the intermediary company's own business plan, the costs of the technology, various customer requirements (such as budget constraints) and the competition. Of course, pricing also depends on the market for the product, with differing levels for an online homework helper for students, a database mounted on the wide area network of a major research university, or a dialup system used by the technical information center of a multinational pharmaceutical firm.

Publisher priorities

If electronic publishing is not a primary business or a part of the future business plan of the organization, the company must consider long and hard whether staff time and technology is being put to good use in developing revenues in optical and electronic products.

Editorial factors

How full is full-text?

In 1987, Ruth Pagell, a well-known online journalist, wrote a seminal article entitled 'Searching Full Text Periodicals: How Full is Full?' for DATABASE magazine. She performed research on a title covered by Information Access Company and loaded on DataStar, Dialog, BRS, Dow Jones News/Retrieval and Nexis. Her results showed that the title had less than full coverage everywhere except Nexis, and that even IAC had different coverage on different services. Much of that inconsistency has improved in the last few years, but the problem still remains that some indexing/abstracting companies that load full-text onto their services are not including every article. In some cases, only articles covered by the intermediary's indexing and editorial policies are included in full text. In other cases, only articles longer than a certain length are included. Yet the fact remains that these databases are advertised as having full-text available. One solution to this problem is offered by *Fulltext Sources Online* (BiblioData, Needham Heights, MA). This book lists periodicals covered on the major hosts that are available in full-text, file names, numbers and/or acronyms, chronological coverage, and whether coverage is selective or cover-to-cover. Users must understand that each information provider and/or search service is making this editorial decision, and not the publishers. The criteria are usually financially-based: Will we generate revenue from all this full text or should we include only those articles we think will be useful?

Conclusion

While many database producers and original publishers are working hard at developing new technologies and search engines, there is a long way to go before we see easily searchable full-text linked with images. The structure of the publishing industry does not allow for smooth sailing into the full-text database business. Some publishers are still unclear on what they have signed license agreements for. Copyright considerations are in flux. Even if all the required technology were in place, the other factors affecting online availability and information quality that I have outlined here need to be resolved.

Note: A version of this paper appeared in *Database*, **16** (5), October 1993, pp. 24–31.

Chapter 4

ASSURING DATA INTEGRITY AND QUALITY: A DATABASE PRODUCER'S PERSPECTIVE

Earl Beutler, President, Research Information Systems, Inc., a CD-ROM publisher based in Carlsbad, California

Background

Since the dawn of the 'information age', companies and organizations have ventured into the marketplace to provide services to consumers and information professionals which allow the user to locate general or specific information on a wide array of topics. Such services, for the most part, are launched by compiling large quantities of original material from a variety of sources, usually in a particular subject area, into a single, searchable volume.

Until the middle 1970s, virtually all of these services took the form of printed volumes of information, such as *Index Medicus*, *Excerpta Medica*, *Current Contents* and the *Science Citation Index*. Usually, such secondary works contained one or more indices which provided access to the data in a variety of ways. Commonly indexed were title words, subject headings (in which indexers attempted to categorize each work in the compendium), and authors. Other indexes also existed, including citation indexing, which provided for searching by the contents of the bibliographies of individual works.

With the advent of the computer age, virtually all of these compendia or databases migrated to computer-based systems. When data was placed in electronic form and combined with appropriate software, users realized a number of obvious advantages. Primary among these benefits was the ability to locate material much more quickly, and from a combination of indexes. Limitations based on the logistics of printing and shipping were virtually eliminated. The ability automatically to transfer data into personal databases also became available.

Prior to the availability of low-cost computer systems and laser printers, the capital and infrastructure that was required to launch a printed information service was quite significant, providing a barrier which prevented any but the largest organizations from launching such a venture. Thus, the ability to publish databases in electronic form or without the need for expensive typesetting equipment or services opened the door for the development of many new database products, and today there are many thousands, in various electronic media.

One such new service was developed by a team which included the author of this chapter. *Reference Update*, a diskette-based biomedical current awareness service for microcomputer systems, was conceived in 1987 and delivered commercially in 1988. While this team had extensive experience in the development of microcomputer software applications, none of its members had any knowledge of the process of establishing a bibliographic database. While this lack of experience was in many ways a drawback, it also proved to be a boon by offering a fresh perspective on the subject. It is largely from the experiences of this team that the contents of this chapter are drawn.

Although databases may take many forms, including bibliographic, enhanced bibliographic (i.e. including abstracts or annotations), full-text, or images, most of the aspects of data integrity remain the same. For the purposes of this chapter, however, most illustrations will be based upon the author's experience with enhanced bibliographic databases.

The goal of this chapter is to assist the reader in understanding the challenges involved in the creation and maintenance of a database service, and to provide sufficient information to allow for objective evaluation of the data integrity of such a service.

The importance of data integrity

Although the importance of data integrity is somewhat obvious to the information professional, some discussion is warranted. There are two essential reasons why databases must be accurate and reliable. Because searching is generally based upon exact matching (although 'fuzzy logic' may provide for varying degrees of matching) of words or phrases from titles or abstracts, keywords, authors and other indexed terms, any errors may lead to failure to locate a key reference. It is also obvious that an article which has not been included in a service will never be retrieved.

The second reason that it is so important for the data to be accurate, especially in a bibliographic database, concerns the re-use of that data. Because the searcher (or the end-user of the data) may utilize this information as a citation in a future work, any errors may be propagated throughout the literature. This potential complication has sometimes been called an 'information virus' because the misinformation can spread and divide in much the same way as a real virus or a software virus. This situation has been aggravated by the increased use of bibliographic software in which electronic data is automatically transferred into a personal database and utilized in producing computer-generated bibliographies.

Data integrity, then, encompasses the following four areas:

1. Accuracy, which may be defined as being true to the original form of the data;
2. Completeness, which may be loosely defined as covering all material claimed by the providers of the service;
3. Consistency, defined as the uniform application of a standard set of 'rules';
4. Timeliness, which may be defined as the time lag between publication of the primary versus the secondary material, and which should be consistent with the stated definition of the database producer.

There is another aspect of data integrity, indirect in nature, which is beyond the scope of this chapter. In any electronic database, retrieval software is utilized to locate material of interest to the end-user. Features or 'bugs' in this software may have a very significant impact on the successful ferreting out of important data. Accordingly, studies of data integrity are highly dependent on the quality of the search software that is used for this purpose.

Accuracy of data

All database producers must develop a mechanism through which the original data is captured into their internal database. There are currently four different methods by which this primary task is accomplished:

1. Electronically, through material (e.g. computer-readable tapes) provided by the primary publishers;
2. Keyboard entry, using single input;
3. Keyboard entry, using keyboard input with separate keyboard entry for verification;
4. Scanning and optical character recognition (OCR).

Various aspects of these methods may be combined. For example, a database producer may choose to use OCR for one entry of the data, and keyboard entry for the verification step.

Selection of the method of entry of these data is based upon the methods available to the database producer, as well as on the costs associated with each method. Each method has its own costs and benefits, which we will discuss below.

As far as accuracy is concerned, obtaining the information in electronic format (in the form of typesetting tapes or other computer media) would be the preferred method for any database producer. This method virtually ensures accuracy (defined above as being true to the original form).

At the time of writing, most primary publishers are still unwilling or unable to provide electronic copies of their source information. This does appear to be changing, however, as the primary publishers migrate to higher technology solutions.

Capturing electronic information from such sources is not without its problems. A file from a typesetting system, for example, will most likely be filled with various codes related to the setting of type, including type size, fonts, indentation, margins, character spacing, etc. To utilize such a file, the database producer must either write software to interpret these codes properly, or assign an editor to accomplish the same task. In either event, the possibility of interjecting errors exists. Furthermore, obtaining such information is not without its costs. As primary publishers seek survival in the electronic age, they are investigating new sources of revenue. Accordingly, there appears to be an emerging (and, for database producers, somewhat disturbing) trend on the part of the major publishers to assess fees for providing data in computer-readable form.

Single-entry keyboarding is perhaps the simplest and the oldest mechanism of transforming printed information into a database. The limitations of this method, as it relates to accuracy, are quite obvious. Keyboarding is highly dependent upon the skill and dedication of the individuals who perform the task, and it is clear that entry errors will occur, even with the best of keyboarding personnel. The degree of error may be mitigated, to some extent, by a second step of reviewing and editing the hand-entered material. A non-scientific survey of major database producers indicates that, at present writing, keyboarding is the primary technique utilized for data entry.

Dual-entry keyboarding offers the second-highest degree of reliability (after obtaining computer-readable data from the primary publishers). In this method, the same data is entered twice, preferably by two independent keyboarders. Using a special software program, the two entries are compared, and any discrepancies are displayed for review and correction by an editor and proofreader. Ideally, this individual should have an original copy of the source material (or a scanned image) to use for comparison, rather than simply 'guessing' at the correct entry. The degree to which such a validation program allows for variation between entries in certain fields (author address, for example) may also impact the integrity of the data.

There are other, more subtle aspects to this process that may affect its reliability. For example, more errors are likely to occur if the proofreader is allowed to select between the two entries than if the erroneous data must be corrected.

Optical character recognition (OCR) technology has made great advances in the last several years, and has recently emerged as a viable method of accurate transcription of source material. Nonetheless, it remains an imperfect technique; the quality of character recognition depends on a number of factors. These include such things as the fonts of the original, the type of paper used, and the presence of font or typestyle variations within the same document. In the best of cases, 100 per cent accuracy may be achieved, but it is not unusual for a significant number of errors to appear.

There are other considerations when using OCR to input source material. Many databases, especially in the biomedical field, include only the author initials rather than first names. If the first names are indeed included in the source document, further editing or conversion using software is required if the data are to be consistent.

Per our definition of accuracy, however, there is more to accuracy than scarcity of errors. If a service is to be true to the original material, one must also include such aspects of the source document as capitalization, non-English characters (such as Greek letters, accents and umlauts), character attributes (such as boldface type, italics, superscripts, subscripts and underline), symbols, chemical formulae and figures.

In the pre-computer era, such considerations had far less impact on the accuracy of data, since the primary use of such services was research. Beginning in the 1980s, when users began to transfer material into personal databases for incorporation into bibliographies, these became important considerations, since it is customary to cite a reference exactly as it appeared in its original form.

The presence of such non-standard information further complicates the task of incorporating material into a useful database. It is most common for computers to use ASCII encoding (or EBSDIC on IBM mainframe systems) to represent the letters A–Z, numerals 0–9, and more standard characters (e.g. %, &, !, or @). No such 'universal' standard exists for other characters or character attributes, so that the database producer may need to develop its own coding system if this information is to be included.

Taken to the extreme, inclusion of non-English material may include dealing with completely non-English character sets (such as Japanese, Chinese, Hebrew, Cyrillic, or Arabic).

If the decision is made to cover such 'special' data, an additional burden is placed either on the searcher or on the software that will be used to retrieve information. For example, the Greek letter 'α' may be represented in some publications as its English equivalent ('alpha') and in others as 'α'. If one wants to locate all references which contain some form of 'alpha-interferon' in the title, the search process may be complicated by the presence of the original Greek characters.

In the end, each database producer must choose a method of entering information. The decision is based upon a standard cost–benefit evaluation which includes such factors as user demand, competition, and costs associated with ensuring accuracy.

Completeness of data

Various information services endeavor to employ different levels of coverage. In secondary bibliographic services, there are two essential types: selective and complete.

In a selective service, the database producer will generally select material that is relevant to the subject of the database. This may encompass an extremely narrow field (e.g. important papers on cytokines) or a more broad-based subject (e.g. papers of interest to those in biotechnology). For such services, completeness is totally subjective, since one person's key paper is worthless to another.

Complete bibliographic services, for the purposes of this chapter, may be defined as those which purport to cover the entire contents of a particular group of publications. The term 'entire contents' is subject to some variation as well, as some services may exclude items such as book reviews, obituaries, and/or letters to the editor. There are also several 'hybrid' services which cover the entire contents of one set of publications, and selective contents of others.

Since evaluation of the completeness of selective services is subjective at best, this chapter will discuss the challenges involved in compiling a complete database (or a hybrid database, to the extent that its coverage falls into the complete category).

In order to create a complete bibliographic database service, the database producer must establish a mechanism for ensuring that all material is indeed captured. There are two procedures that must be in place: one to verify that the source document is received, and the second to ensure that the received material actually appears in the database.

To anyone who has worked in a library, or indeed to anyone who has ever subscribed to a publication, it is clearly not adequate simply to assume that those publications that arrive in the mailbox constitute a complete set of information. The postal system, which remains the primary means of delivery of publications, is far from perfect, as are the internal subscription fulfillment systems of many primary publishers. Accordingly, it is incumbent on the database producer to establish a reliable tracking mechanism.

For those publications that appear regularly and reliably, this tracking process is relatively straightforward. A journal that is scheduled to appear each week is quite noticeable in its absence. On the other hand, many publications have a stated policy of issuance at 'irregular' intervals, which renders the tracking process extremely difficult. In between these two extremes are those publications that have regularly stated issuance (e.g. three volumes per year of four issues each) but which frequently appear far behind schedule.

Any tracking system should therefore accommodate all types of publications. For a regularly published journal, the database producer should be alerted if the publication has not been received within a few days of expected arrival. For those publications which are regularly scheduled but historically irregular in their issuance, the database producer may not be aware of a missing issue until the following issue is received.

Should a publication not be received, a procedure must exist for obtaining the data. This may include filing a claim with the primary publisher or seeking a replacement from another venue (such as a local library). In addition, an editorial policy must be in place as to whether the issues should be published out of sequence, or whether to wait for the 'missing' issue before proceeding to the next.

Once material is received by the database producer, the data must be captured by one or more of the methods discussed above. This generally involves a number of complex operations, throughout which there is a possibility that some material could be 'lost' to the service unless appropriate precautions are in place. Of course, the end-user of the information will not know if the information is missing because it never arrived at the database producer, or because it was mishandled internally.

Unless all material is actually included in a service that purports to be 'complete', it is virtually impossible for the user to rely with confidence on its content. The user should understand the policies of individual services before deciding how heavily to depend on their data. Some 'complete' services, notably certain Online Public Access Catalogs (OPACs) that also serve as bibliographic databases, include only material that has actually arrived in the library. This is consistent with the stated objective of such services, but the limitation must be known and considered by the searcher.

Consistency of data

In order to ensure consistent retrieval results, the searcher must be able to depend on the internal consistency of the data or, at a minimum, be fully aware of any inconsistencies. In the earlier example of author names, the searcher must know whether the database includes author initials, first names, or both.

The same applies to some of the other attributes discussed in the section on accuracy. If the database includes non-English characters, the searcher must be aware that it may be necessary to search for both 'α' and 'alpha'.

Consistency can also be crucial in areas such as the title of the source publication. Most publications are known by a variety of names. For example, the *Proceedings of the National Academy of Sciences of the United States of America* is colloquially known as *PNAS*; however, the 'standard' *Index Medicus* abbreviation is *Proc.Natl.Acad.Sci.USA*. If the database does not use a standard list of publication names (which is readily available to the user), retrieval by this criterion may be rendered useless.

Timeliness of data

Timeliness, like completeness, is somewhat subjective. Its level of importance is also highly dependent on how the data is to be used. A static database covering articles published during the 1970s will not be judged on the basis of timeliness. A current awareness service, on the other hand, which will be used to alert investigators and clinicians on the latest developments in AIDS research and treatment, must be as current as possible if it is to be of maximum utility.

Any database producer who is attempting to offer a current service and is concerned about the integrity of the database must be concerned about how quickly data appears in the file. There are a number of factors which impact this 'time lag', including how the source documents are obtained and the method of capturing information. If, for example, the data are available online directly from the publisher's typesetting files, it is possible that references will appear in the secondary service *before* the primary paper is published. If, on the other hand, the database producer simply waits for a journal to appear in the stacks of the local library, then photocopies references, mails them to India or the Philippines for keyboard entry, and waits for them to be returned for inclusion in the database, a time lag of several months is common.

Impact of the information provider

Many databases, probably the majority, are ultimately searched using vehicles other than those provided by the organization that produced the data. Such vehicles include online hosts, CD-ROM systems, OPACs, and diskette-based software. In many cases, a single database will be available through a variety of different providers. Thus, when one reviews the integrity of a database, one must also take into consideration the possible contribution of the information provider.

Following its preparation, the database is transmitted to the information provider in computer-readable form. From this point, it may go through any number of additional preparation steps before it is available to the consumer. Each of these steps introduces an opportunity for the interjection of new errors, or other transformation of the data.

For example, the *Reference Update* database produced by the author's organization includes, in its original form, major Greek and other non-English characters. These characters are preserved in the diskette-based version of the database. In addition, the same database is licensed to a CD-ROM provider. On this platform, the CD-ROM software is unable to accommodate these so-called 'extended ASCII' characters, and thus they are converted to their English equivalents (e.g. 'alpha' instead of 'α').

Evaluating databases

As the number of electronic information services continues to proliferate, it will be increasingly important for the consumer to evaluate their integrity based upon the various criteria discussed in this chapter.

To begin an objective review of a database, one can generally obtain factual information from the producer. For example, what publications does the service cover? Does it claim 'complete' or selective coverage of the publications? What are the producer's policies on inclusion of non-English characters and special text attributes? Are these preserved when searched through a variety of sources?

Checking the timeliness of a service is also relatively straightforward. Although most database producers maintain a policy for turnaround of source material, it may not always be adhered to. After determining the frequency of updating of the data files (which may differ depending on the searching venue), one can extract a relatively large sample of the latest material and compare it with the dates that the equivalent print publications were received in a local library (or with the retrieval from another database with known timeliness). Ideally, such an assessment should be made over a period of time, since database producers may experience periods of atypically rapid or slow turnaround, depending on the load of new material. In addition, one should attempt to select a wide array of publications, since many database producers assign a priority level to certain journals. A weekly publication (such as *Science* or *Nature*) might appear in a service within days of receipt, while other, lower-impact publications may not appear for weeks or even months.

Assessing the accuracy of a service, while relatively straightforward, may take a tremendous amount of effort. Although it is simple to determine the database producer's policy on inclusion of non-English characters and attributes, tracking the rate of errors will generally require a large sample of data which must be compared with the original materials. Top quality data services may have accuracy rates as high as 99.98 per cent, which would indicate that errors appear in only two out of 10,000 characters. Other services may have significantly higher error rates. In any case, a large sample is required if one is to obtain a statistically significant result.

Evaluation of consistency should include checking a sampling of records for such features as presentation of authors, consistent application of journal abbreviations and publication date entry.

Perhaps the most difficult aspect of data integrity to assess is that of completeness, particularly in the case of a so-called 'complete' service. Not only is it necessary to determine whether all issues of a large sample of publications have been included in the database, but whether all individual articles have also been covered.

Error correction

Needless to say, even the best of databases will have errors or omissions. It is therefore necessary for producers to have procedures in place for the correction of such material, and possibly for the notification of users, especially in the instance of more serious errors. In the case of services which are available through online sources, both of these can be accomplished fairly easily. Correcting databases on other, more static media can be much more problematic. An archival database on CD-ROM, for example, can be corrected only through the release of a complete replacement disk.

It is also important to keep in mind that it is not only the policy of the database producer that needs to be considered, but also that of the online host, CD-ROM producer, or other licensee of the data. Although the producer may send a correction to each vendor of the data, it may only appear in a portion of the data, or in some version of the database.

Other responsibilities of the database producer

As an additional mechanism of quality control, it is important that the database producer provides a simple, straightforward method for consumers to report the presence of errors in the data. Only in this way can the database producer track and improve accuracy. In addition, it provides a means to determine whether the third-party licensees of the data are preserving the data integrity as it is transported and installed on other media.

Conclusions and recommendations

With the rapid proliferation of sources of information in electronic form, the subject of data integrity has become increasingly important. Unfortunately, there is no mechanism currently in place to provide for consistent and objective assessment of the integrity of these databases.

Increasingly, there is significant overlap of the data contained in commercially available services. In such cases, the primary criterion in selecting a database may well be the integrity of the database.

The author suggests that a committee be established consisting of information professionals and representatives of the database producers. [See Armstrong, Juntunen, Quint *et al.*, for reports on recent progress in this area.] The role of this committee would be to establish clear and objective criteria for the evaluation of data integrity using some of the information contained in this chapter. On a regular basis, all significant databases should be reviewed, with the results published in a public document. In this manner, not only will information professionals and consumers be better equipped to choose their data sources, but the database producers will be encouraged to maintain high standards of data integrity, just as the publication of on-time performance rankings for individual airlines forced the adoption of more realistic scheduling and greater attention to timely departure and arrival.

Chapter 5

APPLICATION OF TQM TO THE CONTINUOUS IMPROVEMENT OF DATABASE PRODUCTION

Barbara Lawrence, Division Director, Technical Information and Tony Lenti, Manager, Editorial Operations, American Institute of Aeronautics and Astronautics Technical Information Division

Introduction

AIAA

The American Institute of Aeronautics and Astronautics (AIAA) is the world's largest and oldest professional society. Its membership comprises over 40,000 aerospace engineers. Its mission includes the words 'foster the dissemination of knowledge', a role that AIAA has long taken seriously by providing information services for the aerospace community. These services include primary publication, currently six journals, two magazines, Progress and Education book series, meeting papers and international conference proceedings. AIAA's history as a secondary service provider is equally extensive and historic, beginning with the founding of the library in 1936. AIAA began abstracting literature, including Soviet literature, in the 1940s, first published *International Aerospace Abstracts* (IAA) in 1961, and joined in a partnership for the acquisition, processing and dissemination of worldwide aerospace scientific and technical information (STI), with the National Aeronautics and Space Administration (NASA) in 1962.

The Technical Information Division is the core of AIAA's information services today, and remains a partner in the NASA STI Program. The Division houses the AIAA Library, a private collection of aerospace-related material acquired from the world's open literature. Principal products include *International Aerospace Abstracts*, a bi-monthly publication containing abstracts and indexes of selected papers taken from this literature, as well as the *Aerospace Database*, the electronic form of *IAA*, which also includes records of report literature processed at the NASA Center for AeroSpace Information (CASI), in Maryland, USA. We currently announce 45,000–50,000 records a year, which are formatted and cataloged consistent with the input from NASA CASI and NASA's international partners.

Why quality? Why TQM?

Quality assurance for database producers in general involves every aspect of the information handling process, from the time the data is acquired, to monitoring its implementation on the host system, and further, to customer service and user education. The perception of database quality is impacted by the information host hardware, the retrieval software, the database design, user support and education, and most importantly, the content of the data itself.

As a database producer, AIAA is responding to the emergence of quality as a major issue among information users. While the number of available databases grows, the variety of channels grows, the user base increases and becomes less intermediated, and so the definition of quality evolves. We have found that the marketplace is demanding fast turnaround of information in a consistent and easy to retrieve fashion. Scientists and engineers are relying more and more on electronic databases either as a personal resource or through information centers and libraries. These factors led us to reconsider our approach to quality assurance and continuous improvement programs. After some soul-searching, we realized that we could do better with an idea we always championed – quality. Our idea of quality was a little smug and misdirected at times. We still have a long way to go, but we have made significant strides. We are changing, and take comfort in the fact that one basic principle of Total Quality Management (TQM) is just that: Change = Continuous Improvement.

The guiding principles of TQM that have fostered a feeling of positive change throughout our organization have and continue to be as follows:

- Focus on customer satisfaction
- Organize work as a process
- Measure results
- Recognize that people, as teams and as individuals, are the key
- Foster a culture of continuous improvement.

The overall management of quality for us at AIAA has involved all these aspects, set within a framework of defining and meeting user needs, performance requirements and budgets.

First steps

How we started: rationale for first TQM team

At AIAA, we believed that we had a quality product and that we ran the operation in an efficient manner, but we realized that we could not show this either qualitatively or quantitatively. Therefore, one early step was to list existing quality control procedures as one way of rationalizing our quality efforts. After analyzing this list we noticed many repetitive and/or obsolete tasks and functions. This convinced us that TQM methodologies held promise for strengthening our service and our work environment. So we addressed the first findings and then established a structure for quality activities, one that fit within the existing organization.

Therefore, our next step into understanding and application of TQM, in May of 1990, was actually to assign the job of Quality Assessment to one of our production managers. As we had only limited notions of TQM concepts, we were pleased that the *Aerospace Database* itself proved a very valuable resource in retrieving documents relating to TQM. The aerospace industry had embraced TQM, and AIAA was already running an annual TQM conference. Interestingly, this literature helped AIAA managers appreciate that TQM techniques had meaning in service environments, and were not restricted to manufacturing environments alone. In fact, one of these papers, from Honeywell Space Systems Operations (SSO) says:

> This paper describes the application of TQM in an engineering dominated aerospace business, SSO. To a large degree, customer satisfaction is obtained by SSO through the quality of its non-hardware items, such as data item submittals, design reviews, engineering analysis, etc. As a result, SSO more closely resembles a service business than a product business.[1]

It was then decided to organize a Quality Assessment Team, something akin to a Quality Circle, which was quite in vogue at the time. The team was formed from members of the different work units, and designed as an open forum for the exchange of ideas, with the objectives of improving teamwork skills and moving decision-making to the appropriate level. The original group was composed of eight staff members representing document fulfilment, document analysis, descriptive cataloging, indexing, abstracting, editorial, micrographics and office services. Although cross-department teams are not an earth-shattering concept today, it was a change, and was met with some resentment and suspicion from some of the staff, and from some management as well.

We also had a (perhaps) subconscious objective to convert a stable work environment with strong functional boundaries into a more progressive, open-boundaried team. This idea was met with wariness and even resentment from the staunch believers in specialized work units and traditional methods of management and problem solving. Some believed that if you ran a tight ship there would be no need to discuss change or bottlenecks – there just wouldn't *be* any.

This initial approach, involving staff and using those responsible for the information as catalysts in analyzing the process, became the impetus to change the way we do business. We would apply quality principles and enable the staff to be part of the solution. As we evolved, we understood TQM as an approach to facilitate continuous improvement, reduce barriers between departments and broaden staff knowledge.

Evolving approaches

The first series of quality management teams worked on a 9–12 month cycle. Membership was changed based on the focus of the group and the desire to expand staff training. The first team, mentioned above, was a place to start involving staff actively in process change. We wanted to do better than the American average of 0 to 1 suggestions per employee per year, and to improve our own record, which was no better. We believed that staff had knowledge of details that probably eluded their managers. We were also aware that the Japanese average is 60 suggestions per employee per year.

So, this first team was chartered to capture the questions and comments of the staff at large, things one would hear employees say during conversations with each other: 'I wonder why we're still doing this?' 'I think it would be better if ...'.

The team members started by taking turns explaining procedures in their work groups and how they felt they could be improved. Since this cross-departmental effort was unusual, people were initially uncomfortable, and sometimes quickly added 'I'm glad my supervisor isn't here to hear this'. This was exactly what was desired, a chance for the worker to have some say, or at least to express views on current practices – and to offer solutions to problems in the other work units as well. We were now on the road to putting problem-solving techniques and responsibilities into the right hands – those with intimate knowledge of the work process.

Survey

A useful approach generated by the first team was the formulation and distribution of a staff survey on quality issues and interest in the organization in general. The survey was concise and to the point, and was meant as a catalyst for generating suggestions from the staff themselves. There was an 85 per cent return on the surveys, and the staff interest was refreshing. The desire to cross-train in other areas was overwhelming, and basic concerns were heard which had never before been expressed as openly. We were on the right track!

The survey in essence consisted of the following:

1. Are there procedures or functions within or beyond your own area that you feel warrant modification, elimination, or improvement? Keep in mind any cost- or time-saving procedures that might be instituted. Address backlogs, repetitive efforts, workflow, training practices, feedback, or anything else.
2. Is there an area within TID that you would like to know more about?
3. Would you be interested in cross-training in another function or area?
4. List any additional concerns or views you may have.

The completed surveys were used as a point of reference for the team to address areas of concern. It was the basis for an enhanced and augmented cross-training program, as well as the first step for additional task forces, spin-off groups, etc. The staff became proficient in writing up process analysis reports as well as being part of the solution.

Some of these early suggestions focused on employee benefits, such as 5-year service awards, and some on new products; others were about areas where the initiator had limited knowledge. While we welcomed these suggestions, we now encourage a focus on close-to-home matters, and we have tried to improve the analytical skills of staff to increase suggestion success. But all of the initial survey suggestions were evaluated by the team and by management, and two-thirds were implemented.

The second assessment team concentrated on process analysis, and used flow charting as a useful tool. It was so interesting that a few of the members could not wait for the next meeting. They hovered over the evolving flowchart with growing enthusiasm as our current process was recreated before their eyes.

Lively discussions ensued. Bottlenecks in the process, as well as superfluous tasks, were identified. As a result, certain steps were eliminated and others were moved to where maximum efficiency would be derived. Additional, more detailed flowcharts of each aspect of the process were designed as working tools for analysis. This has proven invaluable as we contemplate further changes in our workflow.

The third assessment team has been working with an expanding set of tools and measurements. One key principle of TQM is to measure everything. A Continuous Improvement Wall – full of flow charts, bar charts, pie charts, arrows and labels – was established in the conference room, where it was accessible to the whole staff. The Wall continues to be a tool for communicating progress, change and learning through the evolving flow charts and statistical measures.

One observation derived from the Continuous Improvement Wall was that our traditional measures had been statistics on output: number of abstracts per year, number of foreign countries covered, per cent of journal articles or conference papers, and so on. We watched the evolution of our thinking to incorporate process quality assurance measures, such as error rates. Then we realized that we had the foundation in place to address customer satisfaction – the driving force for TQM activities. Thus, a key task of the third team was using the criteria of the NASA Excellence Award for self-evaluation and for exploring additional measurements that would be useful in tracking our progress. Since NASA is a key customer for AIAA, anything learned in this evaluation could be shared with our program office

PERFORMANCE ACHIEVEMENTS
- Customer satisfaction
  - Customer Performance
  - Schedule
  - Cost
- Quality
  - Quality assurance (Hardware/software/service)
  - Vendor quality assurance and involvement
  - External communication
  - Problem prevention and resolution
- Productivity
  - Software utilization
  - Process improvement and equipment modernization
  - Resources conservation
  - Effective use of human resources

PROCESS ACHIEVEMENTS
- Commitment and communication
  - Top management commitment/involvement
  - Goals, planning, and measurement
  - Internal communication
- Human resource activities
  - Training
  - Workforce involvement
  - Awards and recognition
- Health and safety

Figure 5.1 *NASA quality excellence award criteria summary*

as well. A summary of the evaluation criteria is given in Figure 5.1.

Learning how to measure quality

Measure results

Measurement is the tool for tracking change; if you can't measure it, you do not know how you are doing. In fact, some have said, 'If you can't measure it, don't do it'. So goes the theory of quality management. Without formal statistical training, we were unsure about our success. But true to our approach to TQM as a learning process, we took stock of the traditional measures, and made an effort to move forward.

Traditional measures

One can measure the result, the quality, or the quantity. All are necessary to keep an organization on track. At AIAA we have traditionally measured the result and the quantity. These measures include the number of accessions produced, breakdown of accessions by country of publication for the different document classes handled (journals, books, meeting papers, etc.), and so on. Of course, we also incorporate financial measures: number of subscribers, profit and loss data, and budget data. Our library tracks usage data such as the number of documents delivered, online connect hours, reference queries and customer service calls.

The production process analysis, performed by the second quality assessment team, led to the requirement for production error measures. We knew that these measures should be easily graphed and posted to serve as tools in assessing the efficiency of a given process. These measures would also give us an indication of any area where improvement was warranted.

Using our process flowchart as a starting point, we identified areas in which data input was generated, validated, proofread and processed. A prime task of the team was to find ways effectively to measure and benchmark error rates. The first result was to create new feedback mechanisms between data creators and reviewers, in order to enhance data accuracy at the time of input. The team then concentrated on actually measuring error rates at various stages of the input process; we focused on the elements that make up each of our records.

Cataloging is the first input operation in our flow. This information makes up the citation portion of each record. It includes items such as source, publication details, authors, affiliations, financial support statements, and report, contract and grant numbers. Placing values on the errors caught at different proofreading stages, both within the group and at the final editorial stage, provided an understanding of what type and what quantity of errors were being made. This information was used by that department to provide individual and group training, to reduce error rates, and to allow all catalogers to feel responsible for the data they were creating. In some cases, as in reading galley proofs, a trend in error detection was found, as shown in Figure 5.2. An acceptable error rate was established; this is expected to decrease with further enhancements to input processing and desktop publishing capabilities. These error rates are currently monitored on a quarterly basis to maintain benchmarking measures. Measurements continue to provide invaluable feedback necessary for process analysis and subsequent improvement. Figure 5.2 shows the 'before' and 'after' results for two error checks in this process.

Customer satisfaction measures: currency

At this point, the team took its first real step toward developing user-focused measures. Prompted by an article that addressed database currency as one quality measure relevant to database users,[2] we selected one of the suggested methodologies to evaluate how AIAA input for journal data stood against other databases, to identify any problem areas, and to track results as we redesign the production process.

The initial approach was to search by publication date using our CD-ROM

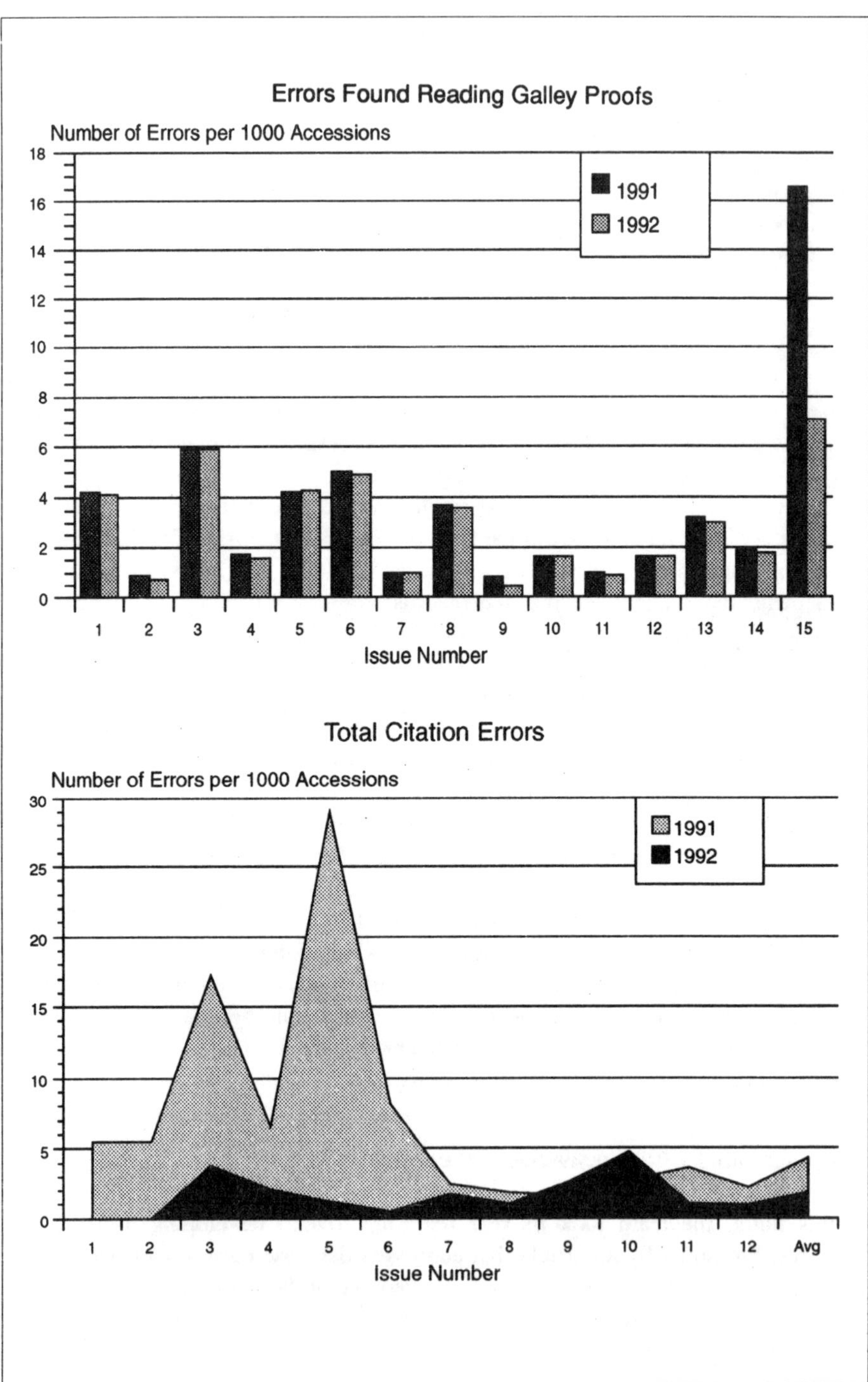

Figure 5.2 *Error measurements and improvements*

product. Although primary journals may be published before or after the issue date, and specific months may be omitted altogether, this approach – while not 100 per cent accurate – gives a good indication of the currency trends in our database updates. All journal records with a January publication date were selected and plotted against the month the item record was published in the database. Due to lags in receipt time, domestic and foreign journals were treated as separate sets. Results were compared, graphed, and used as indicators and tools in process analysis and quality assessment.

A simpler technique (Figure 5.3) was to graph a sample of 100 journal items for each month of update, choosing only journals in which the covers state a month of publication. The results proved to be about the same. The graph indicates the distribution of time lag (in months) between the cover date and appearance in our database. Results have shown that currency of items announced in the database falls well within average ranges for similar databases. Reducing time lags between cover and announcement dates continues to be a major goal in workflow design and a major factor in quality assessment. Especially important is the issue of working more closely with our foreign sources to ensure timely receipt of their publications.

Customer satisfaction measures: interlibrary loan

The preceding examples show how measurement can be used to locate problems. In the next example, measurement was used as the tool for problem-solving.

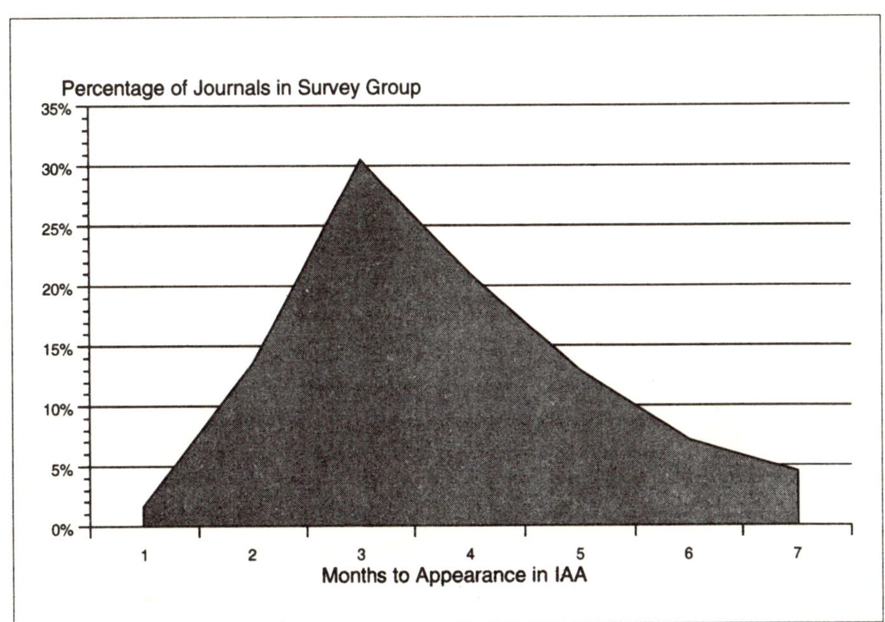

Figure 5.3 *Currency (based on 100-journal survey group) – 1992*

The AIAA Library is a resource for the NASA centers, so that each center does not have to build a complete collection. The Library has documents for every abstract in the database, and provides interlibrary loan services to the NASA centers. AIAA has always prided itself on shipping orders within 24 hours.

However, in the fall of 1991, NASA discontinued a microfiche service which had supplemented each NASA library collection. As a result, the volume of requests for interlibrary loan increased substantially. Suddenly, NASA librarians began to complain that service was slow, often 30 days or even longer. Fortunately, the AIAA librarian had just developed an interlibrary loan management system, using DBase III-Plus. This system would produce routing slips, overdue notices and mailing labels, while also tracking activity and timeliness. Library staff were just starting to input data when the complaints surfaced. They input several older months' data and then printed out the response time charts, as seen in Figure 5.4. The customer was right.

But now we had more problem-solving tools, and we established a process action team to review the work flow and improve the process. These process action teams are composed of staff involved in the activity, as well as staff from other departments who have been involved in some aspect of TQM learning. The analysis skills, plus the outside view, have been productive in designing process improvements. As shown in Figure 5.4, interlibrary loan responsiveness has returned to target. We learned that measurements must be continually monitored to be of value, that process improvement is not a one-time thing.

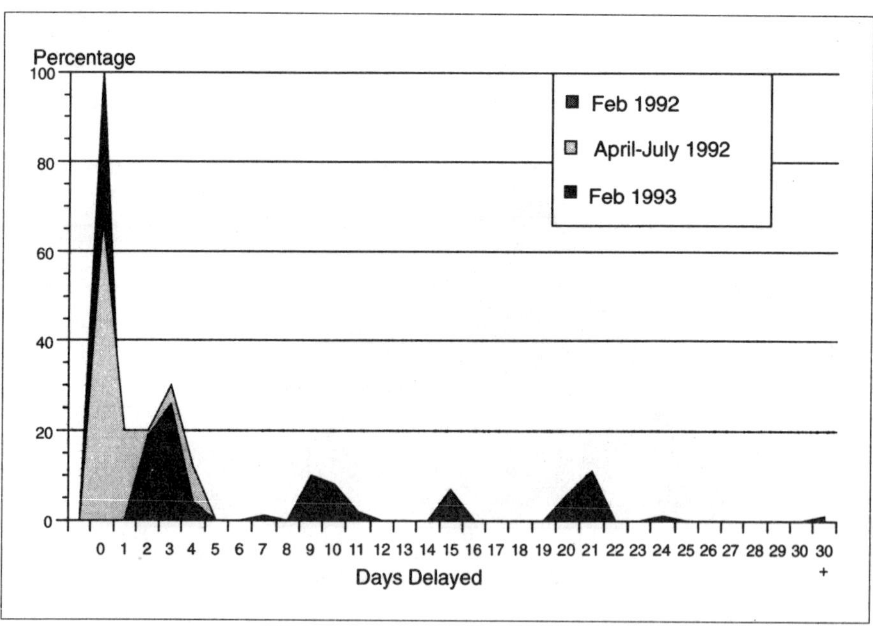

Figure 5.4 *Interlibrary loan response time (in days)*

What happens when you get involved: specific results foster a culture of continuous improvement

Almost 40 per cent of the staff has been involved directly with the various assessment teams, process action teams, and working groups. About thirty teams have proposed improvements, and two-thirds of those have been implemented and monitored. Implementation of ideas was achieved at minimal or no cost. The staff in general is more aware of customer requirements and more sensitive to interfaces within the operation. Communication is freer and barriers between work units have been reduced. AIAA saved at least $25,000 in annual expenses as a direct result of the team activity. Productivity improved 11 per cent in 1991, and 8 per cent in 1992.

The staff has been encouraged to offer suggestions. It was stressed that these need not be earth-shattering or save thousands of dollars. We were looking for the subtle pragmatic changes that make for an easier workflow, reduction in errors and enhanced quality of the information we provide our customers. This effort is supported by an Employee Incentive Program which rewards teamwork, achievement, and suggestions. The quarterly award nominations are evaluated by peers, the non-managerial staff. The executive director announces the winners at an all-hands meeting.

All suggestions, however, are reviewed and analyzed. While implementation is a requirement for an award-winner, winning is not a prerequisite for implementation. The New York management team considers each suggestion, offers guidance to the suggester, and arranges for implementation when an idea is approved. Every suggester receives an acknowledgement from the executive director and a response from the technical information division director, regardless of the outcome.

A sampling of staff generated ideas and their benefits to the organization are outlined below.

Suggestions: activities and quality improvements/benefits

Activity: automated document log

A staff-created, PC-based program has replaced a manual source log generated by the cataloging unit. Source information is entered, along with the unique accession number of each selected paper in our database. The automated log is used to track documents as they move through the production process. Statistics used in compiling status reports are now produced automatically instead of being compiled manually at different work stations.

Benefit: The implementation of this program has greatly enhanced activity in the cataloging department, achieving a 10 to 15 per cent productivity increase by the clerk, and allowing for the processing of more accessions, thereby enhancing the database. Time savings for statistics maintenance were realized in several departments, as there had been duplicate efforts elsewhere. Now the data can be shared or remanipulated as required.

Activity: online source list

An online source listing of journal titles was developed and implemented. This database of serial source titles was linked to the cataloging entry program. It allows the cataloger to access journal titles, country of publication and ISSN numbers, which can be picked from the window display.

Benefit: The online sourcebook reduces the amount of time involved in keying bibliographic information and the probability of typographical errors. It also saves editorial time by requiring less proofreading. Users of the database are assured of consistent and accurate journal title entries.

Activity: inhouse creation of proof copy of citations prior to printer's blue-lines

In the production of *IAA*, final proofreading of the citation portion occurred when we received galley proofs back from the printer. Thus, any changes had to be treated as costly author alterations at the printer, and required additional work to ensure that they were also made to the online file. A software program, run after photocomposition, now prints a final-version facsimile of the citation portion of a record. Final proofreading and corrections can thus be performed in-house, prior to sending the work to the printer and prior to transmitting the data to the database.

Benefit: Reduced error-correction printing costs, saved time in inputting changes to the system, and streamlined the work flow.

Activity: standardization of editing symbology and style of author abstracts

A standardized format and style guide for editing the author abstracts included in *International Aerospace Abstracts* was developed for the abstractors.

Benefit: The use of a standardized editing format helps to speed the flow of work among the abstractors, typists and proofreaders. It also reduces typing and proofreading errors due to the inability to understand abstractor's comments.

Activity: reduction in photocopying requirements

Published literature input to the NASA STI Database often includes publications, such as conference proceedings, which contain large numbers of papers. These are often photocopied so that the abstracting and indexing staff can complete work on the entire publication in a timely manner. After process analysis, a set of guidelines was developed that modified procedures and reassigned work flow, ultimately reducing the amount of time and photocopying required.

Benefit: A 30 per cent reduction in staff time for photocopying, with attendant reduction in photocopy supplies and maintenance. One step towards ensuring timely input of information for the database.

Activity: automation of duplicate checking

Previously, at the end of the production process, a printout was prepared listing all author names and titles. This printout was checked by the Analysis group in order to identify any duplicate entries. A program sub-routine was developed in-house, using the WordPerfect Office text-editing program. This sub-routine generates a master file, reviews the titles listed, and identifies duplicate entries.

Benefit: Eliminates duplicate entries in 15 to 30 minutes, versus a full day of intensive review by staff.

Activity: utilizing library order information for feedback in the document analysis department

Since November 1990, the document analysis staff has been actively using information from orders for documents received by the AIAA Library as a means of enhanced selection of items for inclusion in the NASA database.

Benefit: Through this activity the selection staff is aware of what topics are hottest in current aerospace research. Knowing which topics and publications are of most interest to the user helps to maintain a comprehensive and expanded database that meets changing needs.

These seven examples taught us that ideas for improvements can come from anyone on the staff, and that change need not be radical or costly to be beneficial. We also uncovered hidden talents among staff members, which has led to job reassignments in some cases.

Process action teams

The encouragement of suggestions allowed us to learn new skills in process analysis and measurement. In order to incorporate these techniques into the routine, we began to use process action teams for problem solving. Unlike the original three assessment teams, which were part of a training process, these teams have brief life-spans and very specific charters. Each team includes people from within the function being addressed and from other work units. Representatives of all interested parties, the creators and the users (customers) are included. Teams promote a sense of the whole, i.e., that we are all working toward common objectives.

Process action teams are chartered by management and given much more specific guidance than the early exploratory assessment teams. A team leader is identified, and this person is encouraged to keep the managers informed. The team reports to the senior staff, and all participants get recognition. Sometimes a first presentation sends the team back to work with a revised focus. But in the end, after a term of two weeks to two months, problems are solved and new approaches are installed. The solutions in the suggestion activity described previously were often systems-based.

Now, we often find that training, or retraining, is a useful solution. We also encourage people to think about lessons learned, be they about the problem-solving process, the function reviewed, organizational interaction, or anything else.

Process action teams have tackled a wide range of issues. Some problems seem mundane, such as how to keep library materials promptly shelved (unlike most reference-oriented libraries, which do not worry about having the documents in the library, we need to find documents for interlibrary loan or document delivery services). Other issues included a review of errata policy, and a major alternative work-flow initiative.

Projects/programs

As our organization gained in skill and vitality, we were able to address more ambitious programs more readily. Because we were not dependent on the available time of a few managers, but could use a larger resource base, we were able to bring a database upgrade project from plan to completion in less than two years, to study and implement telecommuting, to restructure our exchange agreements, and to add new technology. All of these efforts took place within the same time-frame, and all resulted in productivity and quality improvements. Yet AIAA did not add staff analysts or managers during this period, and the work was done without interrupting production. There are other projects as well, but the following are described because they have the most impact on the database product.

Database upgrade

The database upgrade project evolved directly from a meeting of the NASA STI Program participants. The project was initiated in July 1991. A working group first addressed the definition of database quality and identified several guiding principles. It then met twice to work through the STI Program's existing Data Element Dictionary, identifying subgroups of data elements for detailed study. It was agreed that the present effort should focus on data upgrade issues, that is, those affecting current input procedures and possible retroactive corrections. Issues affecting software capabilities would be identified for subsequent review.

Each data element was examined, the data element dictionary was revised where necessary, and specific issues and recommendations were formulated. A group of more general issues and recommendations affecting groups or 'families' of related fields were discussed as well, and a general strategy was developed for defining and categorizing the database upgrade tasks.

The guiding principles and goals for database quality as defined by the working group are summarized as follows:

- Consistency: the type and scope of data in each field and the format in which the data are entered should be the same for all input producers, and from year to year. If it is no longer possible to make past data consistent, differences should be noted in the user documentation.

- Granularity: each specific piece of information should be stored in a separate field to facilitate access for searching. Display formats combining different fields should be just that – display formats created by the system software - and not large amorphous fields in the database itself.
- Accessibility (Search and Display): the number of fields that can be searched should be expanded to meet user needs, and text-based searching should be made available whenever possible.
- Simplification of input: data element content and format should not be restricted by the limitations of input processing or of publication production software.
- Selecting the right kinds of data: database fields and retrieval software should meet the information needs of our customers: the users of RECON, the *Aerospace Database*, and other products of the NASA STI program and its partners. Fields no longer used should be eliminated; new fields should be introduced when necessary.

In addition to the data structure changes and revised data input guidelines, current index terms were added to over 400,000 records that had been entered in the STI database before 1968. Retrieval is now easier because searchers can use a common subject vocabulary. ISO (International Standards Organization) country names and codes were adopted, conforming to database searcher requests to use standards where they exist. These codes were revised retrospectively, as had been done for the index terms.

Error correction

The value of any database depends on both the breadth and depth of its coverage, and on the accessibility of any report using the database's navigation tools. Errors in indexing, typographical errors in abstracts, and missing or improper author and publication posting can make any record inaccessible, or cause it to appear incongruously in a data set for a totally unrelated search.

The AIAA has always had an ongoing error-correction program for its records on NASA's RECON database, but this program affected neither the *Aerospace Database* on DIALOG nor the *Aerospace Database on CD-ROM*. In the autumn of 1992, as part of the aforementioned database upgrade effort, the AIAA solicited DIALOG's cooperation in reloading its database from the original RECON files. The reloading, scheduled for late 1993, gave us an impetus for a concerted effort to search out and correct as many errors as possible in the time available. This error search included looking into previous error lists, locating typographical errors in the CD-ROM product, soliciting user feedback, and researching the original printed *IAA* journals and source publications as necessary. Under this program, over 1 000 errors were corrected in a six-month period at a significant increase over the error-correction rate of previous years. More importantly, these efforts have laid the foundation for a redoubled error-correction research program, which will increase user value by further minimizing the percentage of database errors.

Foreign acquisitions

AIAA exchanges its own journal publications with those of sister societies and research institutions worldwide. This is one avenue for obtaining publications for the library and the database. Since exchanges comprised a significant portion of the material abstracted, AIAA sought to control better the means by which exchange agreements were reaffirmed and maintained. A database was constructed to give focus to the exchange process and allow standard comparison of key elements such as time elapsed and contact personnel.

Structuring the reaffirmation process has provided staff with an accounting of which agreements might need renegotiation. This avoids costly lapses because of personnel changes or miscommunication of partner policy. Since NASA, our major customer, was conducting a similar exercise, it makes it easier to respond to their inquiries about the exchange effort.

Telecommuting

For several years, AIAA has had a 'flexible work hours' policy, in which an employee and his supervisor decide upon a personalized schedule, allowing maximum flexibility in meeting both corporate and employee requirements. In keeping with the production-side goals of TQM, i.e. increasing employee productivity, product quality and employee satisfaction, the organization has instituted a program wherein employees may work at home (telecommute) up to two days per week. Those who opt to telecommute consider this an advantage, as they do not have to spend an hour or more each way in transit, and are not restricted to working during the company's normal business hours.

Telecommuting is treated as a privilege reserved for employees in good standing with more than one year's experience, whose job functions do not require them to be physically on-site. Telecommuters are further required to provide their own computers and maintain or exceed on-site production levels. In the first six months of the program, participating employees' productivity during telecommuting hours has increased approximately 20 per cent over their on-site productivity.

OCR and document scanning

As of early 1993, neither *International Aerospace Abstracts* nor *The Aerospace Database* offers full-text search-and-retrieve capability, but the contemporary information industry environment may make this feature a competitive necessity. Offering this service will require quick and efficient entry of greatly increased amounts of text into our computer network. Even without such a product, the company has a sizeable need for text entry: about 40 per cent of the AIAA's abstracts are taken from the original authors' abstracts, either verbatim or edited to fit *IAA*'s style. It would be difficult significantly to increase database coverage without incurring the substantial costs of adding additional data entry and proofreading staff.

Current document-scanning and optical character recognition (OCR) technologies, although not perfect, have matured sufficiently to be cost-effective in this environment. AIAA has acquired a flatbed scanner and OCR software, with the goal of reducing the time typists spend entering abstracts, and thus freeing them to do additional proofreading and typographical error correction. This ability will also allow the Institute the flexibility to develop full-text and/or image-based database products as the market for them, and the technology to produce them, matures.

Lessons learned

AIAA learned many lessons, some mundane and some radical, as we engaged in the change of organizational style described here. At times we found ourselves just affirming management truisms. But overall, we have become believers in the simple precepts of continuous improvement.

The local-level lessons were these:

- One can obtain positive results during the learning process. This quick return on time investment helps maintain forward momentum.
- Staff has hidden skills and talents, which in a compartmentalized environment would have stayed hidden. In an open environment, contributions increased as staff learned that they were recognized, and that senior staff would listen.
- The more effort by management, the more results will be obtained. The relief for managers was that they did not have to do it all. But they did have to listen, to coach, to make organization-wide decisions and (the hardest part) to release control.
- Formal training in statistical process control, benchmarking, and other relevant methodologies would be useful, but more so after an organization begins to internalize the overall TQM concepts.
- Measurement techniques and graphics can be simple. Most winners of last year's NASA Excellence Award used line or bar graphs. But the results, the measures and their messages, must be shared with the organization. Let everyone take pride.
- Finally, tie the continuous improvement process to the goals, and let these goals be user-driven. This redefinition of goals is where AIAA stands now. We are optimistic about our potential.

Thus we have found that the generic quality model of input (resources), processes and output (products and services), as shown in Figure 5.5, holds up for information

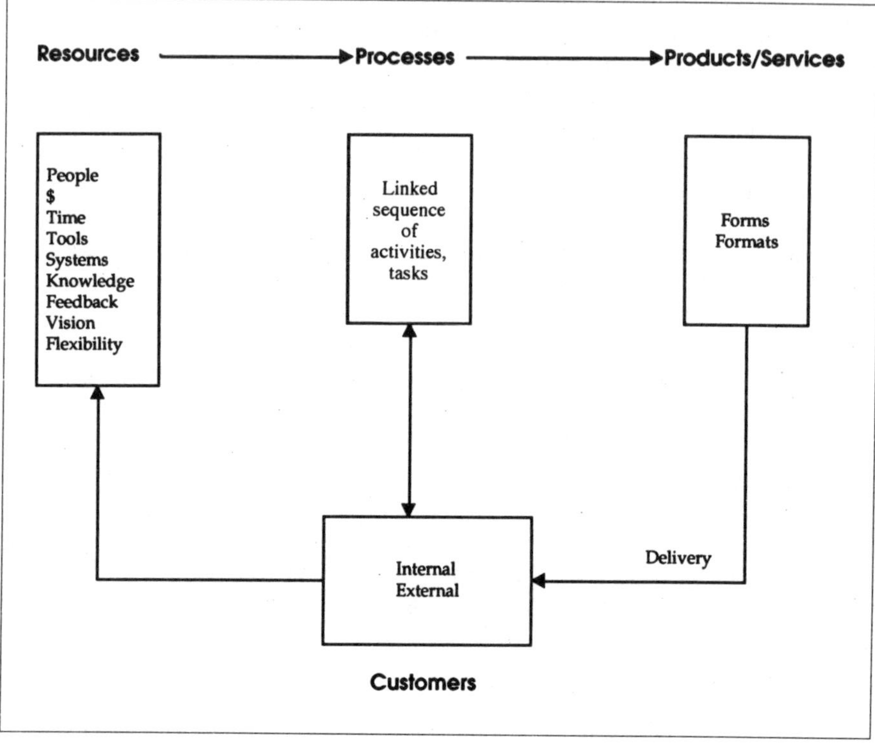

Figure 5.5 *Generic quality model*

service organizations that are concerned with delivering a value-added service. Our experience reiterates that the people are the critical resource, that process analysis and measurement are the major tools, and that customer focus breeds success.

Conclusion

An information service organization can change its culture and increase its value without slogans, elaborate programs, or expensive resources. What is needed is a progressive attitude, a sense of humor, a well-tuned ear and commitment from the top – nothing radical, just thoughtfulness.

Quality management is, in fact, a learning technique that can help us:

- Ask questions about why we do what we do
- Focus on the customer
- Design and implement change
- Continually improve.

In today's environment of outspoken users, increasing database competition and expanding end-user access, the user definition of quality is not static. AIAA expects that, using the methods of TQM, our information service will continue to provide quality and value – as defined by the user at any given time.

Acknowledgments

The authors wish to thank staff who have been particularly engaged in our change process and who have contributed to this report: Brenda Bell, David Purdy and Igor Vesler. We also thank Bonnie Midnica, who helped us put the manuscript together. This work was part of AIAA's partnership with the NASA STI Program, under contract NASW–4373. An early version was presented as part of an National Federation of Abstracting and Information Services course, Total Quality Management in the Information Environment, on October 1, 1992, Washington, DC.

Notes

1. Wilford, R. Poe and Jackson, M. Freeman (1989), 'Excellence through Continued Improvement', AIAA Paper 89-3186. In AIAA/ADPA/NSIA 1st National Total Quality Management Symposium, Denver, Co., November 1–3, Washington, D.C., AIAA.
2. Jacsó, Peter (1992), 'What is a(n) (up)date? – Currency Test Searching of Databases,' *Database*, June.

Part II

ROLE OF THE SEARCH INTERMEDIARY

Chapter 6

QUALITY ASSURANCE IN THE INFORMATION SERVICE ENVIRONMENT

Kristin K. Oberts, Technical Manager, 3M Information Services, St Paul, Minnesota

Introduction and background

Much has been written recently about total quality management (TQM), particularly as it applies to American industry. In fact, total quality management principles can also be applied quite effectively to a library setting. Libraries strive to improve service and meet customer needs better; both of these goals are directly tied to total quality management. This paper addresses the methods employed within 3M and the Information Services department of 3M to assure quality of services and resources.

It is important to provide a brief background on 3M and the Information Services department before launching into the quality assurance discussion. 3M is a diversified manufacturing company serving industrial, commercial, health care and consumer markets worldwide. 3M has operations in 57 countries with headquarters in St. Paul, Minnesota.

3M's library organization, Information Services, is a network of 14 US-based libraries and information functions that provide information support to all parts of the company – business, sales and marketing, engineering, and research and development. A staff of 80 people responds to requests and provides information to 3Mers globally. There are also sister 3M library organizations in various countries, including Germany, Japan, England, France and Canada. The groups work cooperatively, addressing overall information needs for all of 3M. The mission of

Information Services is to be the primary, worldwide technical and business information resource for all 3M personnel. Its purpose is to strengthen 3M's global competitive advantage by providing answers to information requests, access to information materials, bridges to internal technical knowledge, and leadership and expertise in the effective use of information.

The quality program

Quality management is alive and well at 3M. As a recognized leader in innovative management, 3M strives to produce high quality products which focus on customers' needs. 3M's current quality program, Q90s, is built on the framework of the Baldrige Quality Award. The Baldrige Award incorporates many of the concepts of total quality management, including employee involvement, customer input and measurement of customer satisfaction.

The Q in Q90s stands for Quest, underscoring the continuous improvement that is an essential part of the program for the 1990s. Q90s, as the pursuit of global excellence, is built around the implementation of a global quality management system that strives for excellence in each business unit of 3M. The focus is on understanding customers' present and future needs and then empowering employees to meet those needs.

The typical tools used in the process are:

- Benchmarking
- Customer Satisfaction Surveys
- Problem-Solving Teams.

The key objectives of the program are: to exceed customer expectations; to increase global market share; to develop innovative products and services; to recognize employees as the most valuable resource; to meet 3M's financial objectives; and to be an exemplary corporate citizen with sensitivity to public concerns.

With this corporate program as background, the focus can now shift to the use of its components to realize total quality management in the 3M Information Services environment. The emphasis here will be on the processes as opposed to the actual outcome of the processes, though specific outcomes may be highlighted to emphasize a point.

The schematic (Figure 6.1) represents processes used to implement the Q90s total quality program within Information Services at 3M. This is a staged process which builds on information at each stage. However, the schematic could also be drawn with arrows going in many directions. It is true that information gained at one juncture may, in fact, cause the organization to rethink an earlier step in the process. In general, though, the flow indicated on the schematic is what actually takes place.

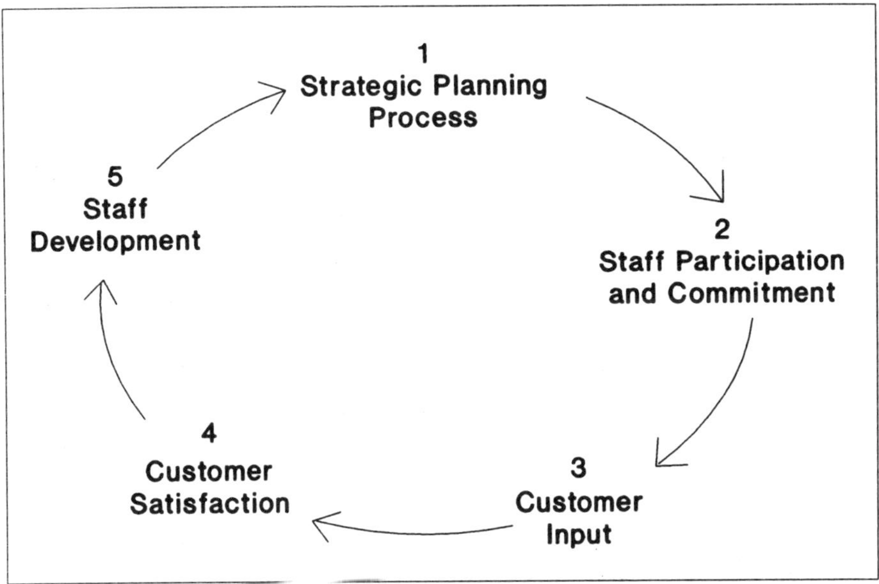

Figure 6.1 *Quality Assurance in process in 3M Information Services*

Strategic planning process

The first stage in the process is development of a strategic plan. The strategic planning process at 3M is made up of the following components:

- Operating units and costs
- Business and current status
- Trends
- Alternative sources
- Mission statement
- Key success factors
- 3M information services in 2006
- Critical issues, strategies, and programs
- Risk assessment
- Investment requirements
- Indicators of success.

The Information Services strategic plan is written with the Q90s program in mind. Current status is reviewed, and consideration is given to the likely changes in the next five years, inside and outside of 3M, that would impact on Information Services. The organization is evaluated against both internal and external competitors, and the process looks 15 years into the future. The mission statement is updated to reflect current and future positioning.

Key success factors

In the identification of 3M Information Services key success factors, the word 'customer' appears, not surprisingly, nine times:

- The services we provide are the ones that best meet our customers' needs
- Customers know what services are available
- We answer customers' requests accurately
- We meet customers' time requirements
- We deliver information in the form that customers want
- We deliver services cost-effectively
- We make it easy for customers to request or find information
- We provide an atmosphere that makes customers feel welcome
- Customers believe we are knowledgeable and will deliver what is promised
- We ensure confidentiality of 3M information
- Customers feel that we make customer service our highest priority
- 3M management supports Information Services and encourages information use.

The critical issues identified include the fact that there is an increasing demand for our services, and there are higher expectations for our services and resources. At the same time, the costs of those services and resources are increasing faster than funding. There are a number of strategies for responding to the critical issues, including: increasing the organization's knowledge of customers' expectations; measuring customer satisfaction with services provided; and strengthening the electronic delivery of information. Finally, indicators of success are defined and measures for success are agreed upon.

Staff participation and commitment

An organization's strategic plan does not become important or realistic until it is accepted and implemented by every member of the organization. Staff involvement is a critical part of a successful TQM program.

To make that happen within Information Services, other Q90s concepts are employed, including communication and employee involvement/empowerment. A copy of the plan is distributed to every staff member in advance of a department-wide meeting, at which time the plan is discussed and questions are answered.

Every staff member is then encouraged to contribute ideas for implementation of the plan by participating in small cross-functional brainstorming meetings. This process results in many ideas, which are then narrowed to between 10–20 priority programs. Again, the results are communicated to the entire staff. Many of the programs have organizational homes; the remainder are turned over to volunteer task teams. Information Services' staff continue to be kept informed about progress on programs at department-wide quarterly meetings.

Customer input

Gathering customer input is a major focus of the quality management program. Printed surveys and focused interviews are very effective methods of gaining user input about specific issues, ranging from services for a particular location, to the use of a resource such as *Chemical Abstracts* by bench chemists. Recently, in an effort to gather information on how the network of technical libraries is being used, a one-page survey was sent to 4 540 3Mers who work in the various laboratory buildings in St Paul. In addition to learning that 3Mers visit libraries most often to use reference materials and current journals, it was learned that more than a third of the respondents did not have their own terminal or personal computer (an important factor as Information Services migrates to more and more electronic delivery of information). Responses to several open-ended questions provided feedback on the need for more CD-ROM resources and online journal contents services.

Focus interviews are another effective method of gathering customer input. In the focus interview arena, teams of two Information Services personnel interviewed 3M laboratory directors. The directors were asked their opinions on library service priorities, both existing and potential, in light of limited financial resources. One specific electronic service that was requested frequently was an online journal contents service. Our most important resource, they felt, was our staff of highly trained information professionals.

3M traditionally has had a large number of subscriptions to Chemical Abstracts' printed products. Two years ago, Information Services surveyed the technical community to determine their use patterns of *Chemical Abstracts*. Based on the data, two of the subscriptions were eliminated and one was relocated to a higher-use location in 3M Information Services.

In all of these examples, the information gathered provides a tool for the strategic planning process to ensure that Information Services is providing the services and resources that its customers want. The questions asked are critical to the success of gathering relevant information.

Customer satisfaction

The fourth critical component of the quality assurance process is the assessment of customer satisfaction. A survey provides an effective method of assessing satisfaction, provided that questions are direct and responses can be measured. Since December of 1990, on a six-month basis, all 3M users of in-depth reference services have been queried about their satisfaction with the service they have received. The number of surveys sent out each time has ranged from 356 to 494, and the response rate has ranged from 72 to 77 per cent. Each user receives a computer-generated one-page survey form which is individually addressed and includes the name of the library which provided the service and the subject of the request. On a scale of 1 to 5, with 5 being most favorable, the average overall rating was 4.58 for all time periods surveyed thus far. In addition, each survey has asked the requester to estimate the amount of time saved as a result of receiving the information. It is the answer to this question which has been of greatest interest to 3M senior management. The average answer has been between 19 and 26 hours. This is a useful piece of data to aid in justification of the service Information Services provides.

Information Services provides a number of electronic services through a menu available on a VAX computer and accessible to the 3M community via the corporate network systems. In order to get feedback from the users of the resources on the menu, an electronic survey is conducted every six months. Users are asked if they have found what they were looking for; how often they use the resource; if they found the software easy to use; if they are likely to use the resource again; and if the online help is useful. They also have the opportunity to provide open-ended feedback. There are more than 3 000 users of the menu resources each month.

Staff development

Finally, and most important, is staff development. This begins as part of the hiring process and continues all the way through the performance feedback and long-term career discussions with each individual staff member and his/her supervisor. People are hired who are well-qualified not only to carry out the job for which they are hired, but who also appear to have the flexibility in skills and attitude to move into a variety of positions within the organization. Position descriptions have been developed for both support staff and librarian/information specialists. Staff see that with additional responsibilities and success in their current job, they have the potential to move through the organization. There is an annual performance review process which involves job expectations set by the individual along with his/her supervisor. Quarterly reviews of performance progress are held, at which time one or both people can modify the list of expectations based on new priorities. The annual review is an opportunity for the employee to get feedback on the past year's performance, and also to discuss short- and long-term career potential. There is also a discussion of educational opportunities, which is critical to the continued success of the organization. If people have proper training, they are better able to deliver a quality product. This is an area on which Information Services places a great deal of importance, since information tools and technology change so rapidly. The staff needs to be up-to-date and knowledgeable about the latest developments. On average, Information Services' staff participate in 80 hours of continuing education per year.

Summary

The process described above is continuous, and the steps overlap. The Q90s process is iterative and ongoing. Each fall, Information Services re-examines its strategic plan and updates the organization's direction based on the information gained throughout the quality process. None of this can happen successfully without good communication – communication with customers, with staff, with management – in a form that all can understand. It is also important to note that the process described above works in the 3M culture; this may or may not be the case in another corporate environment. Quality is a strategic advantage and continues to play an integral role in 3M's success.

Further reading

Anderson, Kristin and Zemke, Ron (1991) *Delivering Knock Your Socks Off Service*, New York: AMACOM, 1991.

Berry, Leonard L., Zeithame, Välerie A. and Parasuraman, A. (1985), 'Quality Counts in Services, Too', *Business Horizons*, 216–25 (May/Jun.).

Brockman, John R. (1992), 'Just Another Management Fad? The Implications of TQM Total Quality Management for Library and Information Services', *ASLIB Proceedings* **44**, 283–8, (Jul.–Aug.).

Brockman, John R. (1991), 'Quality Assurance (QA) and the Management of Information Services', *Journal of Information Science*, **17,** 127–35.

Leonard, Frank S. and Sasser, W. Earl (1982), 'The Incline of Quality', *Harvard Business Review* **60**, 163–71 (Sep./Oct.).

Mackey, Terry and Mackey, Kitty J. (1992), 'Think Quality! The Deming Approach Does Work in Libraries (14-Point Total Quality Management Plan)', *Library Journal* **117**, 57–61 (May).

Riggs, Donald E. (1992), 'TQM: Quality Improvement in New Clothes', *College and Research Libraries* **53**, 481–3 (Nov.).

Chapter 7

BETTER SEARCHING THROUGH BETTER SEARCHERS

Barbara Quint, Editor, *Searcher: the Magazine for Database Professionals*, founder of the Southern California Online Users Group (SCOUG) and principal in Quint and Associates, an information consulting firm in Santa Monica, California

From a consumer perspective, the online database industry has always relied heavily on the skills of searchers to produce a quality product. Pick your analogy: If online data is food and drink to many corporate and government research staffs, supermarket search services satisfy appetites with data ranging in edibility from raw commodities, to microwave-ready packages, to fast-food selections from the deli counter. Search services rarely, if ever, provide data on a plate. If online data is the cure for humanity's ills, database producers serve as pharmaceutical houses developing, marketing and distributing specific alternatives. Searchers still serve as the physicians needed to connect specific illnesses in specific patients to specific therapeutic alternatives. The database industry sells the online consumer the right to ask questions instead of answers, though answers are what the consumer seeks and hopes to buy.

Extracting answers from most databases requires extensive searching skills. 'End-user' search services may boast that menus, intuitive interfaces, or extensive online help screens can substitute for extensive search skills. Even so-called end-user services usually pre-suppose extensive training and knowledge of the field in their targeted market. For example, the simplest of online interfaces – those used in library online public access catalogs (OPACs) – still prompt for last name first, assuming awareness of the ancient (though no longer necessary) traditions of bibliographic construction. Legal search services such as Mead Data Central and Westlaw cover case law and statutes that an educated layperson should be able to read and understand at some level. However, searchers would do better to have a strong legal background, a library science degree, or lots of discounted connect time if they hope to use the systems to retrieve cases and statutes competently. And not everyone who buys a share of stock can expect to use Dow Jones News/Retrieval's databases reliably without first investing some serious learning time.

Traditional search services that market to professional or intermediary searchers place even more reliance on the sophistication and dedication of their users. Services like Dialog Information Services and its sister company Data-Star all circulate regular monthly newsletters, extensive 'quick look' handouts, and major multi-binder background documentation to keep their searcher clienteles busy learning databases and software commands. Most 'supermarket' search services index their databases under file numbers or exotic mnemonics which searchers must master before they can even reach a specific file. Few services integrate different databases based on content and consumer needs, though many offer cross-file searching features. In fact, few search services or database producers integrate changes in the construction of single large databases over time. For example, they rarely consolidate changes in subject headings by re-indexing earlier records. In most cases, the industry simply provides searchers with warnings and hope they hear and remember them when the need arises. Rather than move mountains of data, the database industry generally prefers to forward more and more maps to the mountain guides.

Other chapters in this book address challenges and attainments in quality from the database industry's viewpoint. This chapter will focus on the searcher's perspective, in particular, the view of professional searchers who make a living locating answers in databases for clients. If remarks grow a trifle acerbic at times, let me justify the vinegar by quoting myself, 'Searchers must be the only profession in the world dippy enough to pay in advance for something we have to fix on the fly'. Professional searchers – the online database industry's final quality control team – agree in advance to pay for accessing information resources whether or not their skills can extract the answers dormant in the system. Usage-based pricing rewards the industry for lengthy searches, even when the length of stay reflects floundering for an answer.

The prime directive: users define quality

The most important principle in studying quality issues for databases is to remember that the user defines the quality of information products. Only the questioner knows if a source has provided a satisfactory answer – if the 'answer vending machine' has earned its coin. No matter how diligently a search service or database producer may follow quality control standards or recommended practices, if the final product does not match reasonable expectations generated by marketing of the product, then the product has failed the ultimate quality test. In the final analysis, the professional searcher must accept responsibility for the failings of industry product, just as a physician cannot defend against malpractice by deploring general problems in the pharmaceutical industry. Professional searchers have an ethical responsibility to warn clients about the inadequacies or failings of databases and the searches they generate in relation to specific client information needs. In the final analysis, the end-user searcher must live and die under the banner *caveat emptor*.

However, 'reasonable expectations' tests allow the searcher community to know when to shout at the industry, and how loud. The first major corollary that flows from the principle of user-defined quality is that the customer does not and should not care about who fixes flaws, as long as flaws get fixed. Most database problems allow for more than one solution. For example, database producers may bear primary responsibility for misspelled words in a database, but if a search service offers a 'sounds-like' software feature to compensate for misspellings, the customer may find the substitute adequate. If certain fields contain unsearchable terms, e.g. company names filed under the initial word 'the' as in most leading online company directory databases, the database producer could ask the search service to ignore the term in searching, or to provide records with double company name fields – one with 'the' and one without – for the problem records. Fixes at the search service level do not always mean changing the database in a single file. Better solutions may lie in integrating data from multiple files, e.g. matching addresses from directory databases with institutional listings in bibliographic files. As long as buyers get what they need and expect, the product works effectively; as long as they don't, it doesn't.

Search services bear the brunt of responsibility because they cash the checks. 'I didn't know the gun was loaded' has always been a weak defense. Fair or not, blaming the database producer ('I knew it was loaded but they're not my bullets') is an unacceptable defense, certainly to most end-user searchers. In this instance, professional searchers should learn resentment from the amateurs. If search services know that a database producer has severe problems with quality, they should put whatever pressure they can on the producer to fix the problems. Very wise, far-sighted search service executives, however, might prefer to fix major problems at the search service end. If a database performs markedly better on one service than on another, two events might occur: first, many searchers could opt to switch to the higher quality service; second, a database producer could not risk leaving the search service, no matter how successful their database became, without assuming the burden of installing substitute fixes. In the competitive world of online search services – a world of CD-ROMS, growing network tape leasing of databases for OPAC networks, and so on – such bonds would corral 'cash cow' databases and prevent them from stampeding to greener pastures.

The other major corollary that flows from user-defined quality judgements involves industry motivation. Quality control is an expensive process in the database industry. Often, valiant souls fighting for quality inside a database company meet resistance from revenue-oriented colleagues. If an industry player does not have unlimited resources for repairing any and all flaws in a database, applying user-defined quality standards can correlate the expenditure of scarce quality improvement funds with the fixes most desired by customers. In such cases, information providers may find themselves generating higher sales, or at least favorable consumer press, by responding to customer concerns.

A case in point: Anne Mintz wrote an article in *Online* magazine ('Quality Control and the Zen of Database Production', **14** (6), pp. 15–24, November 1990) that suggested that search services provide searchers with an easy electronic mail route for reporting errors or problems with data. Mintz called the recommended feature the 'Fixit' command. In 1992, NewsNet, the leading newsletter online search service, installed the new feature and received a Product of the Year Award from Online, Inc., as well as other prizes and laudatory press coverage. The president of NewsNet reported that the cost of initiating the Fixit feature was relatively trivial and the reactions of customers very complimentary. In fact, it turned out that Fixit became a means for providing customer support to foreign clients without investing in overseas operations. If the industry listens to customers, they can find what customers want fixed most and first. Such fixes can justify expenditures as marketing opportunities.

Concentrating on final product as perceived by the customer can also improve the efficient coordination of quality improvement programs between database producers and search services. For example, if a search service plans to install a deduplication command for removing duplicates at the time of the search, database producers might better invest quality improvement funds in something other than duplicate reduction in initial data tapes.

Obviously, every searcher, end-user or professional, must compose a basic search strategy to deal with specific information needs. However, one might expect the database industry to provide certain basic support, depending on tasks that their marketing has promised to perform for specific user groups. Search services marketing to end-users should and usually do provide more invisible fixes or hand-holding guidance than services targeting professional searchers. A feature that might benefit professional searchers as a convenience or bonus might constitute a minimum standard for end-users. For example, end-user services should support automatic singularization and pluralization of search terms, while professional searcher services might not require the feature. On the other hand, lots of fixes that search services offer end-users would be wonderfully useful to professionals, too.

Database producers that specialize in a specific category of information should be held to a higher standard of performance than producers whose files carry scattered fields with similar data. For example, bibliographic megabases often include as a field the author's place of work. Sophisticated searchers often use the field for directory checks. Omission of complete addresses and telephone numbers might be acceptable for a bibliographic data supplier but totally unacceptable for a directory database producer. On the other hand, if the bibliographic database producer began to market directory-checking of the institution field to end-users, such promises would change the quality standard.

See how it works? Whatever the industry sells, it ought to deliver – and deliver to the right address. One product design approach might satisfy a dedicated, knowledgeable, expert consumer, and another tempt a casual, less skilled, amateur consumer. But both types of consumer pay their bills, and both deserve to get what they paid for.

What do searchers fix?

What flaws or inadequacies do search services and database producers either tacitly or overtly expect searchers to correct through adjustments to search strategies? What fixes do they expect searchers to provide? What types of fixes do current information industry practices indicate that searchers are expected to provide, rather than the product itself already having in place? Obviously, these will be difficult and debatable judgement calls. For end-user searchers, we might try to apply the standards of an intelligent layperson interested in responding to industry advertisements. For professional searchers, we might look at the training classes, search manuals, database guides, online help screens and other forms of documentation. We can assume that such instructional material reflects industry assumptions about what constitutes the searcher's responsibility, and not the industry's, in satisfying a typical search for typical material.

Let us take a look at each phase of the search process as outlined in 'Inside a Searcher's Mind: The Seven Stages of an Online Search' (*Online*, **14** (3), May 1991, pp. 13–18; **15** (4), July 1991, pp. 28–38). This article provides a good review of searcher decision points, though modesty forbids my recommending it too highly.

Reference interview

Search services expect the searcher to understand and supply all the relevant components of the question. As a rule, they do not supply advice on how to think through a question online, though occasionally search aid software or menus may address this deficiency. Monthly newsletters often discuss general approaches to different types of questions, and connect announcements of new databases, or changes in old databases, to specific search needs. Searchers must read and remember such connections or look them up at the time of the search. Only a few end-user services walk searchers through a menu of reminders. In fact, most online services do not make a basic collection of documentation available online. Supermarket services that do supply such instructional material online often charge for search time, though at low rates. In some services, the cost of looking for help online can vary radically depending upon the approach chosen for getting the online instructions. For example, using a Help command while in a database will carry the full connect-hour charges for the file, while searching for the same information in a separate 'housekeeping' database will drop costs to a minimal level.

In most cases, confused searchers can also contact customer service desks for advice. In the USA both search services and database producers usually supply tollfree numbers. Some end-user services, such as STN International, Mead Data Central, and Westlaw, hire specialists – chemists or lawyers, for example – to staff customer support desks. However, the only general attempt to supply professional searcher advice to any end-user, anytime, anywhere, on any subject and at no charge was the S.O.S. service from Telebase System's Easynet Knowledge Gateway. Unfortunately, the S.O.S. service cut back hours severely in 1991–1992 in the face of recession-based revenue losses. A few search services have installed 'house broker' services that allow a requestor to discuss information needs with a searcher on staff – or an information broker on retainer – and receive an intermediated search for a fee. In general, customer service desks faced with a 'Do-It-For-Me' request refer the requestor to a nearby library or to a list of information brokers which they maintain.

Descending into mundane matters, not all search quality issues have to do with the higher ends of wisdom and scholarship. Mercenary matters also arise. Who will pay for the online search? Nothing so depresses the quality of the online search experience for a professional intermediary searcher as getting stuck with the bill. In general, search services supply professional searchers with sufficient billing information to deal with billing on their own after the search is conducted. Few search services attempt to predict the cost of a search, although Dialog and OCLC have introduced features that allow searchers to place a cap or not-to-exceed limit on all or part of their search expenses. End-user search services often take credit cards to verify their own direct billing. However, in general, search services do not support third-party billing plans or supply credit checks on clients for professional searchers. When it comes to gauging the client's ability to pay, and predicting how much the search will cost, searchers are generally on their own.

Educating the client about the content of databases and the nature of the online search process forms an important component of most reference interviews. In general, search services supply basic file explanations online. On request, they will usually supply searchers with handouts that explain and advertise the general search process as well as some specific databases. With some exceptions, such as custom screens for boutique search services or mandatory screens preceding use of some specialized files, most end-user services expect searchers to know what they want and what the search process will get for them. Professional searchers bear primary responsibility for educating clients about the elements of the database and the search process that relate to the quality of the final output.

Smart information consumers who decide to use a professional searcher should conduct an interview of their own to determine the prospective searcher's qualifications. How much experience does the searcher have on the specific database and/or search service? What is the searcher's educational and employment background? Has the searcher conducted similar searches for other requestors? What does the searcher charge for his or her time, and/or for any overhead costs? What baud rate does the searcher use for searching and retrieval? What is the estimated maximum cost of the proposed search? Can the searcher suggest any ways to reduce that cost by changing search conditions or parameters, e.g. delayed delivery of results? Will the searcher supply value-added services such as document delivery or critical evaluation and synthesis of results? What qualifications and/or charges will adding such value cost the requestor? In general, requestors do not want to get stuck with poor searches which cost as much as good searches. Nor do they want to spend their search budgets on the education and training of the professional searcher.

Tactical overview

Reverting to medical analogies, professional searchers are like physicians. Their judgements form the diagnosis and therapeutic recommendations for specific patients. End-user searchers are like patients. In the final analysis, they make the decision to swallow the pills or sign the surgery permission form or start an exercise course based on the doctor's advice. Clients and searchers together define success and failure. The tactical overview stage is where searchers judge the overall approach to a search. Using three basic criteria for judging research – Speed (delivery time), Quality (relevance, accuracy, currency, coverage in terms of both dates and sources, etc.) and Cost (total charges to the client) – the searcher and client must define relevant parameters of success and failure. The searcher must decide whether to conduct the bulk of the search online, or to use online databases to find offline resources. The searcher must decide when the online search should stop, and determine the impact of a decision to stop on the quality of search results.

The database industry will almost never tell a searcher the worst news: 'You have wasted your money and your time. These search results are totally inadequate because you did not know enough to assess what databases to use or to construct a correct search strategy, or even to comprehend the meaning of any results you might have stumbled across, assuming you got very, very lucky.'

That kind of 'Shoot-the-Messenger' news is something that searchers can only get from other searchers and then only after the fact. Several major online search services support electronic mail or bulletin board systems, but almost without exception, their features and pricing do not allow searchers to share their experiences or create workgroups. Online computer coaching does not exist except for Easynet's curtailed S.O.S. service and some exotic specialized systems. The online trade press provides some assistance for the 'big picture' judgements, but searchers must purchase or have access to, and remember to consult, the appropriate publications. In general, searchers are on their own when it comes to overall strategy formation. End-user searchers, though often more aware of the exact nature and quantity of information they need, often lack the background knowledge needed competently to evaluate the relevance of individual databases and the effectiveness of alternative search strategies. They also lack the discipline of a third-party observer to prevent rationalizing results as better than they really are.

Speaking of bad news, this stage of the search process may force ethical searchers to consider their own qualifications to continue. If a searcher lacks basic skills for conducting a complex search on a specific subject or in a specific database, he or she should consider passing the assignment on to another searcher. At the very least, the ethical searcher should warn the client of personal inadequacies. In some cases, the searcher should even refuse to conduct a search rather than do a very bad job. For example, with years of experience on dozens of search services and literally hundreds of databases, I warn all clients never to use me for chemical searches. As for patent searches, I absolutely refuse to conduct one. The databases in these fields have such specialized technical requirements and such ingrained complexities that a client would just waste money if I were to conduct such searches. By the same token, sometimes a client wastes their time and money conducting an online search at all. Clients who have more time than money might do better using print sources in a library or conducting a telephone survey. Calling experts can prove to be a bargain even for clients who do have the money for a database search. Staying offline is always an option for the ethical searcher.

Database selection

Before searchers select a database, they must first find it. For professional searchers, this may involve checking database directories to locate databases that may not reside on immediately accessible search services. Most end-user searchers – and many professionals – rely on database documentation supplied by the search services they already use. Some end-user services provide question-driven assistance for selecting databases. Search services marketing to professional searchers may provide full-text searchable versions of some database documentation. For example, Dialog Information Services has a full array of searchable tools including the menu-driven Homebase, basic file descriptions in the BlueSheets (File 415), and back copies of the Dialog Chronolog newsletter (File 410), plus Help screens for specific file information such as basic database description, available fields, output formats, prices, etc. Not all of Dialog's extensive print documentation is available online, however. For example, the lengthy chapters that provide detailed field descriptions and sample searches for individual files remain offline, as does the list of full-text titles available in various multi-title collections throughout the service.

Unless a service provides lists or collections of databases by subject category or type, searchers may need to know database names or even file numbers and mnemonic tags before they can request background information on specific files. For example, the Help (?) command in Dialog will provide file descriptions, field structure, limit and display format options, and rates for every file – but only if you already know the file number. For less experienced searchers, the problem is compounded by the compulsion of some database producers to give databases exotic trade names, turning Says-What-It-Does/Does-What-It-Says titles like *Engineering Index* into head-scratchers like *Compendex Plus*.

After locating candidate databases, searchers must evaluate them individually to determine their relevance. Details such as currency, dates of coverage, content, format, source coverage and so on usually appear in printed, or sometimes online, documentation. However, with rare exceptions, information on what might negatively impact search results is hard to find. Searchers can sometimes reconstruct critical developments using old newsletters. Changes in source coverage, varying formats (citation only versus abstract, abstract versus full-text, etc.), new coding schemes, new descriptor terms – all these factors can invoke the dreaded Mummy's Curse, in which changing the rules of inclusion, with little or no warning, drastically limits the scope of the search.

Usually, database producer documentation provides the fullest available background information on a specific source. In rare cases, such as Mead Data Central's NEXIS Product Guide, a full-text search service will take responsibility for title-by-title documentation of database producers' rules of inclusion. For recent or emergency changes in file status, searchers may find the information only after they have already logged onto the database, e.g. in on-screen bulletins or banners. Searchers may not learn that a file has ceased updating, for example, until they scrutinize the latest update information online.

In any event, searchers must proceed as best they can to evaluate databases before committing their funds, whether or not the industry has supplied them with cheap, accessible avenues to the kind of reliable information they need to make informed judgements.

At the database selection stage, the searcher should have begun recording deficiencies or questionable areas for the databases being considered, and tallying the value that might be lost by omitting certain databases from the search. This information will feed into the final evaluation of search results.

Some searchers need to decide which search service to use for access. In most cases, they will go with the service to which they have immediate access and/or the one they know best. However, in some cases, different approaches in handling a specific database, or serious cost differences, may warrant an effort to acquire access through a different search service.

Search strategy formulation

Designing an effective strategy for specific databases on specific search services is clearly the searcher's responsibility. In earlier phases of the search process, the searcher analyzed the client's needs and evaluated the resources available for answering those needs. They should also have rated their own skills and experience in dealing with the subject at hand. Hardworking searchers will have educated themselves whenever necessary to insure a reasonable level of skill. Based on their judgement of sources, client needs, and their own knowledge and skills, the searcher will then choose a basic strategic posture – 'pearl-growing' around a central core of relevant references, a modular 'building block' approach, successive approximations, samplers, etc.

Underlying all search strategy formulation lies the great truth of getting information from machines: computers do not understand concepts; they track terms. Once the reference interview and tactical overview stages have established the parameters of the search, and the database selection step has arrayed the resources, searchers must come up with the terms the computer needs to retrieve information relating to the concepts.

End-user search systems usually lean toward one of two approaches – either total free-text or strict reliance on indexer-created subject headings and thesauri. The free-text approach, typified by Mead Data Central, generously adds terms invisibly – usually at least automatic singularization and pluralization, sometimes even synonyms or equivalencies (e.g. Russia = Soviet = USSR). Recent developments on several search services allow for natural language searching using English language sentences rather than programmer-style lists of terms linked by Boolean or phrase-making operators. At the other end of the spectrum, many end-user services, e.g. the medical PaperChase service, restrict or at least encourage searchers to use clearly defined fields. They may prompt the user for an author or company name or a key date. They may assume that subject terms must match an indexer's thesaurus of approved descriptors. Some of the more helpful interfaces may expand subject coverage by tapping the reference links that thesauri build between terms.

In composing strategies, end-user searchers must understand their subject and generate synonyms to cover it. They should also provide the system with parameters needed to focus the search on the most relevant factors, such as major authors, key companies or research institutions, preferred journals, dates of interest, etc. If the service does not prompt for such data, the searcher should dig into the manuals or the help screens or call customer support. In short, the end-user searcher should find some way to get all the data that matters to them into the search strategy. They should not let their lack of experience with computerized retrieval leave them with a bunch of building blocks lying loose at the end of the search strategy formulation process.

Professional searchers should insure that they have, or acquire, any background information they may need to compose an informed search strategy. The experienced online searcher usually prefers to use a free-text approach that offsets possible indexer failure and provides more flexibility in realigning terms after the search commences. Professional searchers use some indexer-assigned subject descriptors and thesauri to identify synonyms during initial strategy formulation and to hold in reserve for limiting search output after the session starts. Terms are not always obvious. Sometimes individual sources – authors, institutions, journal titles, etc. – or the inherent focus of an entire database can substitute for broad subject terms and fundamental concepts. One of the most important lessons professional searchers first learn, and one that end-users must learn, is the undesirability of entering broad, high-use terms in databases devoted entirely to a subject.

Besides dealing with synonyms, searchers must array the terms in a logic that matches computer system and database structural requirements. They should tie terms together using phrase operators with word order and distance between terms reflecting the way the database is constructed. For example, searching an index with assigned subject or title words as the primary fields of interest may call for much tighter word order proximity than searching natural language full-text databases. When the search software or the database design fail to respond adequately to simple requests, the searcher has to remember to compensate for the failings. For example, they may have to analyze the number of letters past the word root that would still retrieve meaningful synonyms, and insert that number in their strategy. They may have to calculate which files use which form for author's names. 'Last name first' is usual, but is there a comma between the last name and the first? Is there a comma and a space? Is the first name an initial or a full name? Does that vary from record to record in the same file? And so forth, and so on.

The online search/feedback or reviewing results

Most searchers operate from a broader service mandate than just online searching. In judging the efficacy of a search, searchers consider the full ramifications of different approaches to client welfare. For example, a perfect search may wipe out the budget for acquiring documents identified by the search, thus invalidating the exercise. Full-text retrieval of key documents may cost more than a bibliographic search, but the immediacy of the return may warrant the investment in cases where retrieving documents more economically would take too long. In conducting a search, the searcher is responsible for saving the client time and/or money to the best of his or her ability, within the client's budget and information needs. For example, a searcher may choose an appropriate money-saving approach, such as running a search strategy through cross-file indexes first, rather than paying top dollar for direct database access. The most critical decision most searchers make is when to stop searching and, if necessary, how to re-group before resuming the search.

The skilled searcher forms a bottom line expectation of what the output will be from key sources, and uses this expectation to evaluate the success of strategy. Success is one side of the coin. Failure is the other. Searchers are responsible for scanning output from a search to revise and adjust the search process. Output from one database may eliminate the need for, or wisdom of, searching similar files. Searchers may gather new terminology from retrieved records and use that new knowledge to re-execute a revised search strategy or generate an entirely new search in still another file. Failure to find useful material can be an indictment of the searcher's performance, or the database industry's. Most 'dirty data' is discovered by tight-lipped searchers mumbling 'This is ridiculous. I know it's in here somewhere'. When search services fail to provide obvious data to competent searchers, there is almost always something wrong with the database or the search software. On the other hand, failure can also indicate a poorly designed or poorly executed search strategy or an incorrect database selection. For these judgements, the searcher stands liable.

Presenting final search results

Upon completion of the search, the searcher should usually edit the search, remove irrelevant material, and provide minimal sorting. Under severe time or money constraints, 'rip and ship' may do. However, minimal editing is advisable if only to guarantee that the searcher gets one last chance to check for errors in the search strategy. On some searches, or for some clients, searchers may perform considerably more value-added functions. They may choose to sort, classify, and/or comment on retrieved items. They may package the search with full-text documents retrieved separately. They may analyze statistical or financial information or synthesize a number of studies into a single overview. They may also provide machine-readable copy ready for entry into a document processing or spreadsheet program.

Each of these improvements places its own quality demands on searchers.

However, even with minimal value added, all searchers should provide a verbal or written critical assessment of the search's value. In particular, they should warn the client of what the search does not do. In self-defense, they may choose to identify the culprit in 'dirty data' situations. No matter whose fault it is, however, the client must know what they have gotten for their effort and money. At the same time, the searcher should inform the client about alternative strategies still open to them, and earnestly request client feedback after review of results. In fact, good searchers continually perform conscious or subconscious reviews of completed searches as part of their regular professional learning process.

What help do searchers get?

How can you make good searches? Make good searchers. How can searchers learn to search better? Study hard and apply what you learn. How can a search operation manager guarantee quality? Hire good searchers. How can search operations improve their quality? Learn from their past to change the future. How can searchers get better products and services from the online industry? 'Bitch and switch,' as I've said before.

Training

The database industry provides most of the training that professional and end-user searchers receive. Dialog has considered a certification program for searchers of its system. Library schools offer some online training for professional searchers. Career-focused educational programs offer access to end-users. In general, the online database industry is very generous in supporting curricular access to databases. For example, Dialog, Chemical Abstracts Service/STN International, Mead Data Central and other services provide free or dramatically discounted access (85 per cent off or more) to students and faculty. Most services offer training files online, computer-based tutorial diskettes, videos or some combination of these. Prices may vary significantly. In general, the online training databases are cheaper than the other media, probably because the material needs less preparation and less marketing, and costs less to produce, update and distribute.

As a rule, large supermarket search services and high-priced, successful boutique search services conduct a lot of training in person. Major database producers may piggyback their training with that of their host services, or may conduct separate programs, or both. End-user clienteles impose a substantial burden on services. Training programs do not always succeed. End-users may be too busy to attend or to conduct the follow-up searches needed to embed the skills taught by trainers. They may not recognize the importance of apparently trivial search software grammar. In general, both professional and end-user searchers have trouble changing old habits. In recent years, search services have added many new commands and features with which experienced searchers sometimes find it difficult to keep up. At the same time, services have re-priced, changing the cost of doing things the old-fashioned way, and thus rewarding professional searchers who are capable of change and penalizing those who are slow to adjust.

Professional searchers should also attend major conferences, to network and learn from other searchers and to examine vendor products and services. At this juncture, the dominant conferences in the online arena are Online Inc.'s Online/CD-ROM conferences (usually rotated among Washington DC, Chicago IL, and San Francisco CA), the National Online Meeting and IOLS (New York City), and the International Online Information Meeting (London, England). Professional society conferences, e.g. Special Libraries Association, Medical Libraries Association, may also offer considerable support. Searchers interested in CD-ROM can attend special seminars and conferences. However, the more established conferences usually have substantive tracks covering the newer technologies. Dialog also holds major conferences called Dialog Updates for its searcher community. Database producers often schedule special presentations and training seminars around major national conferences.

Documentation

Search services provide online and print documentation for their software and files. Documentation usually includes annotated database catalogs, handy overview sheets and regular newsletters, plus lengthy guides to general search software and to searching specific databases. End-user services usually emphasize online documentation over print. They want the searcher to stay online even to learn how to search. Services oriented toward professional searchers may also provide special targeted material, usually developed in conjunction with applications oriented training programs.

Online documentation and support can differ significantly in scope and quality. Searchers inexperienced in the basic conventions of a service's software may find it difficult to traverse online documentation at all; they protest, 'If I knew how to do it, I wouldn't need to ask'. On the other hand, some professional search services leave masses of file-specific user guides offline, although their experienced users would have no trouble accessing them online. Search services usually supply the most basic information online – a list of available databases with file tags, specific database field structures, search prices and brief database descriptions (producer name, file content, sources and/or type of material covered, dates of coverage, etc.). Help screens are usually used to educate searchers about system software and features. Very few services offer any online instructional programs in basic commands or utilizing 'walk-through' search demonstrations. To the extent that instructional lessons are available in computerized form, they tend to take the form of 'canned' searches on computer diskette.

Not all documentation comes from the search services. Database producers often supply basic kits explaining to end-users how to search online, and more detailed documentation for professional searchers, e.g. thesauri, code books, title-by-title rules of inclusion for full-text compilations. Many search services offer online thesauri for major files with exceptionally informative or authoritative subject heading structures. Though many search services have the capacity to offer full thesaurus display of cross-references and annotations, they usually require considerable justification before offering such valuable augmentation to a file. Most thesauri are published in print by database producers. Some producers also conduct detailed seminars for searchers, and provide substantial hand-outs.

Charges for database documentation – online or offline – vary. Online documentation usually involves some minimal fees, if only hourly connect charges for telecommunication. Basic background and command language 'cheat sheets' might be free, or included with the start-up charges for joining a search service. Database producers usually charge for extensive documentation, though some offer brief material and newsletters free of charge as part of a marketing effort.

Not all searcher improvement tools lie in formal documentation. Search aid software from independent software houses often attempts to short-cut the learning process. In general, search aid software has not prospered. Most has targeted the elusive end-user or inexperienced searchers, promising to eliminate the need to learn long lists of details about individual databases, or to master sophisticated search software interfaces. Unfortunately, end-user searchers often do not discover that such software aids exist until they have already learned enough to do whatever they want to do, or have given up on the entire process. At base, end-users are a tough sell, because they have trouble seeing the logic of paying money to pay money. Search aid software that has endured usually focuses on assisting the professional searcher for whom marketing costs are not as expensive, and who can see the long-term value of the package in terms of enhanced productivity.

For example, Personal Bibliographic Software developed Pro-Search, a front-end search aid, and Biblio-Links, for downloading data from databases into manipulable files on Pro-Cite, a bibliographic database management package; they then compiled all three products into something called the Searcher Tool Kit. Pastel Programming announced a sophisticated post-processing tool for handling search results from several major search services. Some major end-user services like CompuServe and Mead Data Central also offer search aid software or autopilot front-ends. Search aid software may be on the rise again.

The professional press is another important source of documentation for online searchers. The most influential trade journals are produced by a few key publishers. The major periodicals for professional searchers are: *Online* and *Database* from Online, Inc., and *Online Review* and *Searcher: the Magazine for Database Professionals* from Learned Information. Other sources with material of interest to professional searchers and information industry professionals include Learned Information's *Information World Review, Information Today, Link-Up*, and *Monitor*, as well as Online, Inc.'s *CD-ROM Professional* and Meckler's *CD-ROM Librarian*. CD-ROM databases often receive extensive reviews in these as well as in more general library publications. The *Gale Directory of Databases* is currently the major directory available for identifying electronic databases in all media – dial-up, CD-ROM, diskette, handheld computer devices, and batch-processed. BiblioData's

Fulltext Sources Online provides essential details on the availability of individual periodical titles on major full-text search services. Both of these directories are available online as well as in print.

The only major source targeted specifically at end-user searchers is *Online Access Guide*. Other general trade publications, particularly the computer magazines, carry occasional articles on online searching. As a rule, these tend to include inaccuracies or unrealistic hype on the online search process, although they may offer excellent coverage of search equipment such as modems.

Management issues

Not all issues relating to searcher quality concern individual searchers. Search operations, particularly those with several searchers on staff, require skilled and experienced management to insure that clients get the best service. Managers have several responsibilities – hiring, on-the-job training, monitoring searcher skills, managing search expenditures, negotiating arrangements with vendors and marketing search services. With the arrival of CD-ROMs and network tape licensing, some search operation managers make database acquisition decisions almost like a search service manager. In the publishing field, many search operation managers also act as their companies' database production staff; they arrange deals with larger database producers and/or search services, create documentation and marketing programs, design specialty services for their own management, and so on.

Hiring policies and procedures create the basic searcher staff. Standard personnel hiring techniques may serve for selecting new employees already experienced with online searching. Selecting new staff without searching experience but with potential talent for the activity, is a little trickier. In general, one should look for a person with verbal talents, a good general education, any appropriate subject field expertise and a comfort level with computers – or at least an open and inquiring mind. Candidates should also have persistence, love challenges, have a talent for talking to people and a desire to serve. Personally, I have always thought one could trust a person who works a daily crossword puzzle to possess at least the basic verbal and general education skills. Managers can motivate workers to enjoy computers and to develop a service orientation, but the talent for generating alternative terms for the same concept seems to be innate. The ability to get people to confess their ignorance in detail, i.e. to conduct a good reference interview, also seems to require a certain type of person, though experience can improve techniques considerably. Interestingly enough, special subject field expertise seems to be the least successful predictor of future searcher merit. Many top searchers, no matter how technical their search areas have become, seem to have a liberal arts background.

On-the-job training and monitoring searcher skills are difficult but essential challenges for search operation managers. More searches make better searchers, but by inference, this method of making better searchers means assigning some searches to less capable searchers. Some managers organize search staff assignments around key subject areas or specific search service skills. Others choose to remain flexible in staff assignments and therefore less reliant on any single searcher. Some turn to information brokers or external search operations for specially difficult searches or overflow work load. Training classes and coaching for end-user searchers put additional burden on searcher staff.

Where did the money go? What did we get for it? Could we have done better? To answer these basic management questions, search operation managers must gather and analyze data from invoices and/or logs maintained by searcher staff. Such data sources already supply the billing information used in charging back search expenses to individual clients. However, it requires different analytic techniques to convert the same information into management decision data. Managers also need feedback from clients on the success of individual searches.

Recently, my company, Quint and Associates, began to develop quality audit procedures with a multiple module approach to analyzing a busy search operation. The initial beta test involved a division of a Fortune 100 company. The company chose a selection from the eight-module package: evaluation of existing monitoring procedures, data source and search service evaluation, staff skills and performance evaluation, equipment assessment and recommendations, evaluation of post-processing presentation to clients, marketing plan, organizational barriers assessment, and strategic plan including negotiation recommendations. To produce the audit, we relied on three primary data sources: a detailed analysis of past invoices from major search services (provided in electronic format if possible); a two-month sample of searchers' work produced by matching downloaded session records with searcher and/or client evaluation of output; and general staff discussions including an on-site visit, communication with staff, and review of general statistics and procedures for the operation. For a complete quality audit, the beta test showed that a survey of clients, and possibly of management, would be advisable.

The initial beta test proved fascinating. The data from invoices and the review of working searcher techniques pointed immediately to some key procedural changes that searchers could make to reduce costs substantially. The invoice data proved particularly useful in identifying which databases dominated the search operation's budget. Most of the major files were available from a number of vendors, leading to recommendations on negotiating better deals – a task made easier by having expenditure data in hand. To me, the most fascinating result lay in discovering that our final recommendations were for more searching, not less. More value from the search dollar means better service to clients and, in the long run, better relations with vendors. In the future, we hope to beta test remaining modules and to follow up with quality audit sites.

We suspect that changing searcher behavior is the hardest task in improving a search operation. Proficient searchers operate like trained musicians, using the keyboard to play ideas instead of music. As search software and databases evolve, it puts tremendous pressure on searchers at a very basic hand–eye coordination level. Major productivity improvement could depend on installing needed changes in search aid software, replacing the need for multiple-step alterations of technique with a push-button approach.

Negotiation can achieve substantial advantages for search operations. The online dial-up industry is under more and more pressure to move away from usage-based pricing to flat-fee or subscription pricing. Many search services have begun negotiating fees with clients on an individual basis. The split nature of the online industry – where data comes from one source and the searching from another – creates a natural environment for consumers to achieve advantage. When lions fight for market share, jackals eat the meat. Smart search operations managers have also learned to link forces with other search operations in company-wide, regional, or subject-based consortia. In many cases, search operation managers can trade access to their end-user communities, or even publicity value, for solid cost savings.

Searcher community activism

We end this chapter as we began – focusing on data products and services that fail to fulfill their promise. For the good of clients, the searcher profession and the long-term welfare of the information industry, searchers continue to lobby the database industry to improve their products. Most of the lobbying occurs at an individual level, but some searchers have banded together. The Southern California Online Users Group holds annual weekend retreats that invite searchers and information industry professionals to meet and discuss the real problems and potential of databases. In 1990, the Fourth Annual SCOUG Retreat developed the core framework for evaluating databases in terms of searcher perceptions. (For an article on the topic, see Reva Basch, 'Measuring the Quality of the Data: Report on the Fourth Annual SCOUG Retreat', *Database Searcher*, vol. 6, no. 8, October 1990, pp. 18–23.)

The SCOUG rating scale guidelines recommended that searchers build standards according to type of data and type of user. The 'reasonable expectations' test would apply. A directory file should meet higher standards on providing address and contact information than a bibliographic file. An end-user service should provide more transparent search aid features than a professional searcher service. Each scale would build around certain basic components: consistency, coverage or scope, timeliness, error rate or accuracy, accessibility or ease of use, integration, output, documentation, customer support and training, and value-to-cost ratio. The group recognized that one could not judge a database's quality independent of the search service's role in presenting the data. It also understood that if the industry markets to end-users or new user communities, the quality in terms of deliverables may sink unless special preparation is taken. By the same token, quality control procedures that work fine for one kind of data may not suffice when the database producer or supplier expands to other sorts of data.

Where stand the SCOUG scales and searcher community activism at this point? Unfortunately, the volunteer nature of these activities make them difficult to sustain over time. SCOUG-inspired efforts by European and Finnish groups, reported on elsewhere in this volume, have taken up the torch. First and foremost, searchers need to develop cost-effective tools for remaining in touch with each other, and with the online industry, on an ongoing basis. Today, most such discussions occur on electronic bulletin boards or teleconferences on information utilities like CompuServe, on private networks, or on the Internet. Unfortunately, professional searchers have been slow to develop their use of such tools. Many searchers do not even use the electronic mail and bulletin board services offered by leading supermarket search services. This is changing, however. Mead Data Central has implemented a searcher board on CompuServe. Dialog's acquisition of Data-Star finally provides it with a full-featured electronic mail service in Data-Mail, instead of the weaker DialMail. STN International may expand its powerful e-mail service, STN Mail, to allow for searcher bulletin boards. SCOUG itself is in the process of establishing an Internet presence. After that, watch out, information industry! Quality control is on the way.

Conclusions

Searchers must follow a multi-phase strategy to improve search quality. At the personal level, they must develop individual searching skills, knowledge and expertise, and stay on top of new vendor offerings and changes in familiar files. At the institutional level, they must manage search operations with rigorous procedures and managerial skills, carefully monitoring value received for each search dollar spent, and accept responsibility for training and maintaining a reasonable level of efficiency among their end-user searcher communities. At the professional level, they must lobby the database industry for better products and services and better value. Only with a combined strategy can we insure the welfare of clients and the future of the information age.

Part III

QUALITY TESTING

Chapter 8

PRIORITIES OF QUALITY

Carol Tenopir, Professor at the University of Hawaii at Manoa School of Library and Information Studies

Introduction

Many groups and individuals are looking at ways databases can be evaluated for quality in a consistent way. Several have developed detailed checklists of database quality to help with this evaluation process.[1] Three of the best are those developed by:

- the Southern California Online User's Group (SCOUG)[2]
- the Finnish Society for Information Services[3]
- Peter Jacsó, in his 1992 book on CD-ROM evaluation.[4]

SCOUG's proposed rating scheme for bibliographic, full-text and directory databases focuses on evaluating the results or outputs from an online search. They identified 11 main components by which a searcher can rate quality: consistency; coverage/scope; timeliness; value in terms of cost; accuracy/error rate; accessibility; system performance/ease of use; integration with other databases; output; documentation; and customer support.[5]

Because these factors will vary with the system that loads a database, SCOUG recommended that every system should be evaluated separately. Thus, for a database such as ABI/INFORM that is available on multiple online or CD-ROM hosts, multiple SCOUG evaluations and ratings are required.

The Finnish Society for Information Services' rating scheme focuses just on bibliographic databases, proposing five main categories of evaluation. The five categories to evaluate are: connecting to system and communications; search language and other technical aspects of the search; contents quality; aids to information retrieval; and costs.[6]

'Contents quality' in the Finnish scheme includes over 30 separate points. These can be roughly grouped into points covering: update policies; coverage policies; indexing and abstracting and other value-added fields; consistency of word forms; errors; and standardization of abbreviations.

Jacsó's book, although focusing on CD-ROM databases, contains evaluation criteria applicable to any electronic medium. His criteria are separated into four broad categories: software, dataware, database and hardware.[7] Under dataware he includes scope, content and quality; under database he includes accessibility, documentation/user support, installation and terms (including costs and licensing).

Each of these three proposes a checklist approach that will lead to consistent and systematic evaluation. SCOUG and Jacsó recommend computing a numeric 'quality' score, so similar databases can be compared and database producers and system vendors will see how their offerings rate.

Such checklists are valuable because they help codify, clarify and compartmentalize various aspects of quality. They ensure that consistent criteria are used when evaluating and comparing different databases, no matter the electronic medium.

What such checklists do not usually do is prioritize on a general level, although Jacsó's evaluation forms let each consumer set a weight for each factor to be evaluated. Most checklists make all quality issues appear equal, from a poor telephone connection, to a typographical error in the abstract, to a date field missing in many records in a database, to inadequate search software.

The other thing checklists often do is focus on *comparison* rather than on *quality*. For example, the size of a database is listed as one component of quality in some lists. *Size* is a comparative factor, not a quality one. One database may be described as having more records than another, but that says nothing about the quality of either. Bigger is not necessarily better. Comparison factors are relative to another database, quality is not relative.

This chapter builds on the recent checklists with a focus that is a bit deeper and narrower. It will examine what is *most* important in both defining and making a quality database and will concentrate on those things that are absolute quality factors, whether an evaluator is comparing databases or just looking at a single database.

Aspects of quality

As these various checklists illustrate, there are many different aspects that contribute to a quality experience in a database search. Martha E. Williams presents the aspects as an information generation–database use chain that focuses on the people responsible for quality at each link. Her seven-link chain includes: author/originator, primary publisher, secondary publisher (database producer), tertiary publisher (online vendor), gateway, searcher/analyst, and enduser/requestor.[8]

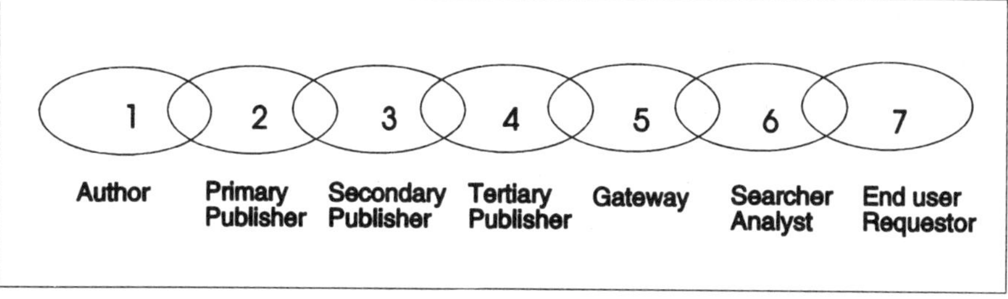

Figure 8.1 *Information generation – database use chain*

A more common way to look at quality is by component parts. SCOUG saw just three parts: the data itself, the database structure and organization, and the system on which it is loaded.[9] Jacsó calls these three dataware, database, and software.[10]

Figure 8.2 diagrams the components of a database system and where they can be separated.[11] The information content is the information that is gathered or created by the publisher or producer. Secondary publishers of indexes and abstracts arrange

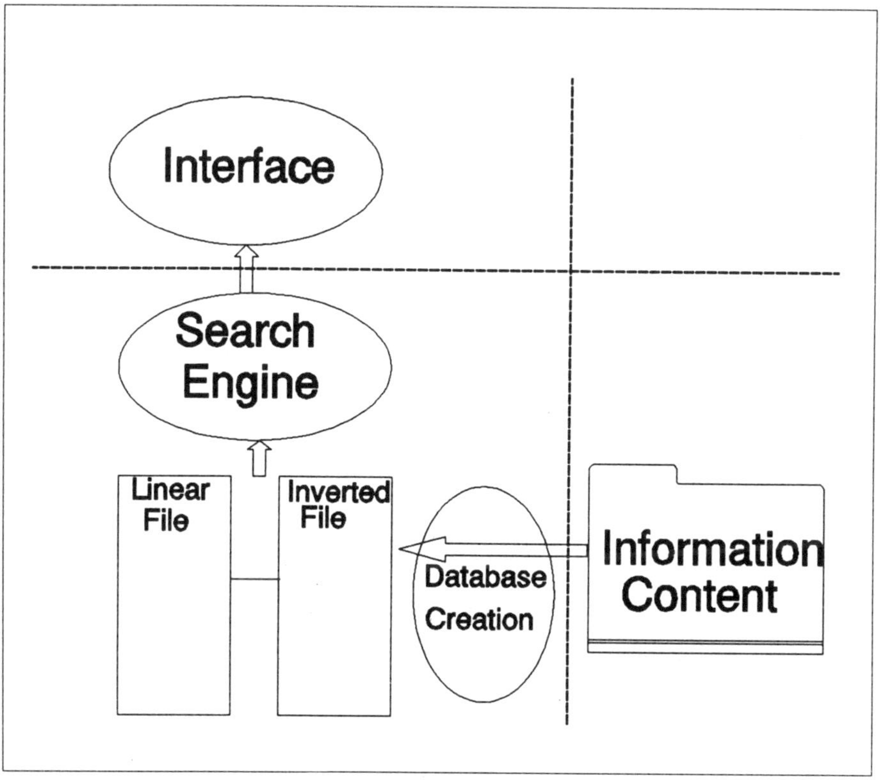

Figure 8.2 *Separation of the components of a database system*

bibliographic information and add value, such as abstracts or descriptors, to it. The information content is independent of software and of the distribution medium (print, CD-ROM, online or other). Content may be evaluated separately, as the dotted line indicates.

System software transforms the information content into a database by making the information searchable, creating inverted indexes (dictionary files) for searching with pointers to the linear file that is used to display records.

The retrieval software, also called the search engine, contributes search features that allow the database indexes to be searched. The power of retrieval software varies from system to system, a major reason that SCOUG recommends evaluating each system's version of a database separately.

The final component of a database is the user/system interface. It is how the user interacts with the retrieval software to use the database. The interface may use commands, menus, icons, templates, function keys, or a combination of these. Because several online and CD-ROM systems offer a choice of interfaces, the interface can be evaluated separately from the other database aspects.

Components or aspects of quality can also be categorized by function, as the Finnish Society for Information Services did with its five main functions.[12] Functions can also be viewed as logging on, searching, printing, and evaluating or using results.

Core of quality

The quality database searching experience depends on reliable telecommunications links, good, powerful (and easy) search software, predictable and acceptable response time, and a competent searcher, but all of these may be present without the total adding up to quality. One factor is central, without which quality cannot exist. At the core of all aspects is content – the information itself as created by the author, secondary publisher or database producer. Without quality content, the other aspects become unimportant. In that sense, content is the highest priority aspect.

Responsibility

Who is responsible for database content quality? Williams's chain implies that all seven links are equally responsible, but a perusal of the online system terms and conditions-of-use that include database producer disclaimers suggests that *no-one* is responsible!

Here are excerpts from a few typical disclaimers in Dialog's terms and conditions:[13]

> BIOSIS does not guarantee the accuracy, adequacy, or completeness of any information. ... BIOSIS disclaims all liability for errors or omissions ... .

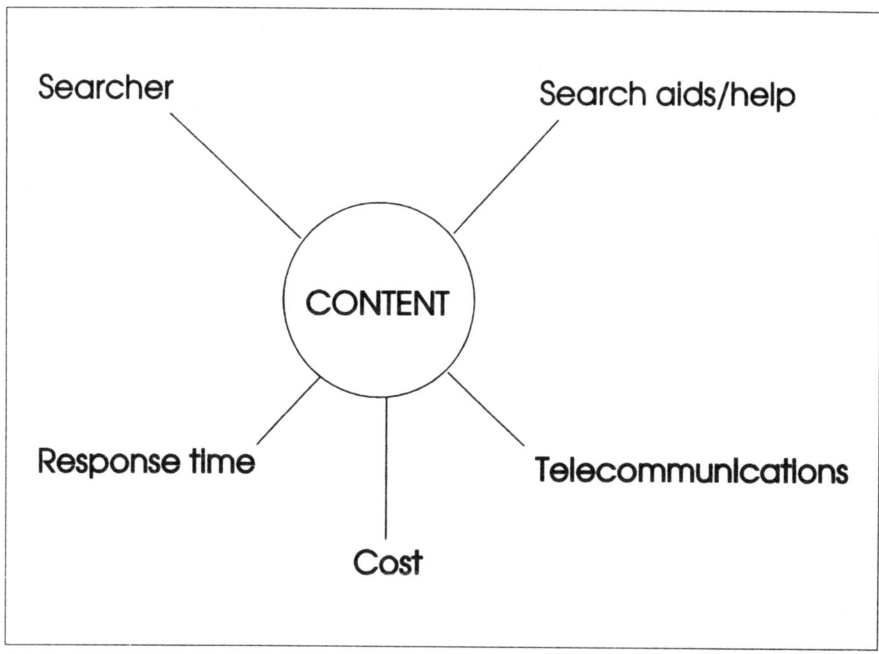

Figure 8.3 *Content is the core of quality*

> The [Information Access Company] databases are provided 'as is' without warranty of any kind. Neither IAC nor any of its data suppliers make any warranty whatsoever as to the accuracy or completeness of any of the databases or the results to be obtained from using the information contained therein and neither IAC nor any of its data suppliers shall be responsible for any claims attributable to errors, omissions or other inaccuracies in the information contained in any IAC database. The entire risk as to the results and performance of any IAC database is assumed by the user of that database ... .

Some producers warn users directly that their information may be of poor quality:

> INVESTEXT database users are advised that the electronic conversion and transmission of textual and numeric data may cause errors and/or omissions that are beyond the control of Thomson Financial Networks. You should also note that there is a delay between preparation of the research reports and their inclusion in the INVESTEXT database and the reports may therefore not be up-to-date.

> Teikoku Databank customer acknowledges that the type of information contained in the database will contain a degree of error. ...

> Elsevier Science Publishers does not warrant the scientific accuracy or

> completeness of the information contained in SEDBASE nor does it warrant the suitability of this information for any particular use or application. ... Because of rapid advances in the medical sciences, we recommend that independent verification of diagnoses and drug dosages should be made.

Let the poor buyer beware.

Disclaimers or not, database publishers such as Information Access Company, BIOSIS, Thomson, Elsevier and Teikoku are ultimately responsible (at least morally) for the quality, or lack thereof, of their content. Online hosts such as Dialog, Mead Data Central, Orbit and BRS are responsible too, only less directly so. They are responsible if their correction procedures are so awkward or expensive that they make it prohibitive for database producers to correct known errors. They are responsible if their loading programs do nothing to smooth out inconsistency of formats among and between databases.

Finally, searchers are responsible as well, if they continue to pay for junk data, or let errors go unreported, or fail to spread the word about content quality (both good and bad) of specific databases.

Content quality

What affects content quality? It is more than just typographical errors; as the Finnish Society for Information Services found, these may be relatively rare.[14] Here, the details from the individual quality checklists are helpful.

Analyzing the various checklists reveals that content commonly includes five things: (1) scope (also called coverage), (2) structure, (3) accessibility, (4) accuracy and (5) consistency. These five factors will be discussed in turn.

Scope

In a purely comparative list, *scope* can include many aspects, such as size, geographic coverage, language coverage, etc. In terms of quality, however, the SCOUG report summarized it best: no matter what a database has as its scope, quality in this regard means publishing a clear editorial policy and following that policy.[15]

A bibliographic database can restrict its coverage by only indexing journals in specified languages; a full-text database can be highly selective in the choice of articles it includes; a business directory database can set narrow criteria for which types of companies to include.

Narrow or restrictive scope does not mean poor quality, just as small size does not. Poor quality comes when the database publisher does not admit to those restrictions or does not clearly state the limitations. From the user's perspective, poor quality comes from not being told, or being told incorrectly.

For example, the BIOSIS database claims 'comprehensive worldwide coverage of

Trade & Industry ASAP
Journal Coverage

- Arkansas Business, 1/89--
- Association Management, 1/92--
- BC Business, 1/89--
- Communications Daily, 1/91--
- Canadian Business Review, 1/89--
- Canadian Labour, 1/90--
- Food in Canada, 1/91--
- Journal of Accountancy, 1/90--
- Mass Transit, 1/91--
- PC Magazine, 1984--

Figure 8.4 *Trade and Industry ASAP: journal coverage*

research in the life sciences' and *Compendex* claims 'coverage of the world's significant engineering and technological literature.' Yet a study revealed that scientific and technical journals published in Japan are only included in these two databases if the Japanese journal was written in English or another Western language or had English language summaries.[16]

Trade & Industry ASAP claims coverage of over 200 journals and a coverage timespan of 1983 to the present, but only 100 titles are covered for this entire period. As new titles are added, they are not added retrospectively, so some of the 200 titles begin coverage only in 1992 or 1993. Selected titles with their starting dates show this range (Figure 8.4).

National Newspaper Index's policy states that it 'provides cover-to-cover indexing of America's most important national newspapers,' yet it leaves out advertisements and some syndicated columns, not to mention the exclusions it does acknowledge, such as weather charts, stock market tables, crossword puzzles and horoscopes.

Very few, if any, bibliographic databases really do cover-to-cover indexing, although many claim they do. H.W. Wilson Company's advertising brochures claim cover-to-cover indexing for *Business Abstracts, Readers' Guide Abstracts* and other indexes, but their system documentation admits that their policy is to select articles only. They do not index or abstract advertisements, most letters to the editor, calendar announcements or short items.

Structure

Structure, the second component of content, can be viewed in a similar way. Structure includes what, and how many, fields are in a database. Whether and how these fields can be searched is dependent on the loading and search software, but they must exist in the first place in order to be searchable. Lack of certain key fields has a strong negative effect on the quality of a database.

For instance, *Library and Information Science Abstracts* (LISA) has no article/document type indicator, so a search cannot be restricted by type of literature. *Dissertation Abstracts* indicates only the university that awarded a degree, not the department from which it came. Many databases do not include ISSN numbers or CODENs for the journals they index. Only some business databases include value-added fields such as SIC codes, stock market ticker symbols, etc.

The bottom line of structural quality, like that of scope, relates to honesty. In this case, honesty refers to what per cent of the records contain the promised fields. Jacsó's chapter in this book provides details on how to test field completeness.

If a database promises that one can search by language, but fewer than 5 per cent of the records have a language code, as Jacsó found for *Books in Print*, it is a misleading claim, to say the least.[17] If Library of Congress Card Number is advertised as a value-added feature (as *Books in Print* does), but this field appears in only 31 per cent of the records, using LCCN as a search element limits that search immediately to less than a third of the file.

Jacsó also found that 20 per cent of the records in *Disclosure* lack number-of-employees and net-sales-per-employee, and 15 per cent lack gross profits and net income.[18] Maybe that information could not be obtained from the companies, but nearly 15 per cent of the records are missing Standard Industrial Classification codes, something that could be added by the *Disclosure* staff.

ABI/INFORM has four fields that represent journal titles. Lest a searcher think that these fields can be used interchangeably to restrict a search to a specified journal, he or she should know that, while Journal Name and Journal Code appear in nearly 100 per cent of the records, and ISSN in 97 per cent, CODEN appears in only 62 per cent.

If certain fields appear only in some records in a database, the database producer has an obligation to report this. It should be clearly stated in all the documentation that describes field structure. No user should have to guess what per cent of the records can be expected to include a particular field. Failure to document such omissions is one of the worst quality transgressions of all – users miss items without knowing it because the database producer withheld information.

Accessibility

Like structure, *accessibility* varies according to the loading procedures and software that make a database searchable. But again, the core of quality – content – must be of high quality first. Where structural quality relates to the consistent availability of standard fields, accessibility extends to what potential additional access points are present in the database records.

MESH TREE STRUCTURE

HORMONES, SYNTHETIC	D6.597
ANDROGENS, SYNTHETIC	D6.597.100
ANABOLIC STEROIDS	D6.597.100.194
5-ANDROSTENE-3,17-DIOL	D6.597.100.194.50
ETHYLESTRENOL	D6.597.100.194.239
FLUOXYMESTERONE	D6.597.100.194.289
MESTEROLONE	D6.597.100.194.400
METHANDRIOL	D6.597.100.194.429
METHANDROSTENOLONE	D6.597.100.194.464
METHENOLONE	D6.597.100.194.500
NANDROLONE	D6.597.100.194.590
NORETHANDROLONE	D6.597.100.194.637
OXANDROLONE	D6.597.100.194.686
OXYMETHOLONE	D6.597.100.194.723
STANOZOLOL	D6.597.100.194.893
TRENBOLONE	D6.597.100.194.930

Figure 8.5 *MESH tree structure*

'Value-added' is the key to accessibility quality. In a textual database, either bibliographic or full-text, the presence of controlled vocabulary descriptors from a hierarchical thesaurus can improve both recall and precision.

For example, in *Medical Subject Headings* (MESH), the term Anabolic Steroids is a descriptor. Using this term will make a search more precise (it ensures that the searcher does not retrieve all the other types of steroids), and will increase recall because it will also pick up articles that refer to anabolic steroids by their chemical constituents only. In the MESH hierarchy, all of the specific anabolic steroids are displayed under the broad term 'anabolic steroids', so they can all be searched in a comprehensive search. They can be searched by name or by classification code (Figure 8.5).

Without descriptors or descriptor codes assigned from a hierarchical thesaurus, such sophisticated search features as Boolean OR, thesaurus viewing, explode (to retrieve automatically all of the narrower terms under a broad term) and truncation are unworkable, or far less useful.

As another example of how controlled vocabulary helps accessibility, hard-to-define concepts can be searched more easily with good controlled vocabulary. Consider a search on how things have changed for the people of Guam in the last decade. The user does not want everything on Guam, just information on how lifestyle, customs, income level, attitudes and outlook have changed. Those are difficult concepts to search free-text, but several databases, including *Sociological Abstracts* (Figure 8.6), contain the descriptor 'QUALITY OF LIFE', which sums up all of these ideas in one heading.

Luckily, database designers are rediscovering the value of thesauri as knowledge bases, after speculation by some that controlled vocabulary would become obsolete with full-text. Thesauri and controlled vocabulary indexing are not obsolete. Good indexing provides additional accessibility, improved results and additional database quality.

Other value-added fields can also improve accessibility. In bibliographic databases, abstracts provide increased retrieval points and help relevance judging. In full-text, abstracts bring all major concepts into focus in a single paragraph. Quality abstracts adhere to national or international standards, are as informative as possible, well written, and of an appropriate length (generally between 100 and 500 words).[19]

In directory databases, codes such as SIC numbers, Dun & Bradstreet (DUNS) numbers, Chemical Abstract Registry Numbers, etc. all aid the user if they are applied consistently. Authority control of company names, states, countries, etc. can greatly improve accessibility in directory databases as well.

If timeliness and comprehensive coverage of large amounts of information are essential to a product's value, a database producer can add even more value. After many years of development, the Institute for Scientific Information (ISI) began adding extra retrieval points to its records in the *Science Citation Index* and *Social Science Citation Index* databases.

These are both huge databases created almost completely by machine. ISI felt it could afford neither the time nor the cost to add human-indexed descriptors or

Quality of Life

SN Subjective evaluation of an individual's or group's way of life, lifestyle, or living conditions, usually using an explicit inventory of factors.

BT Quality
NT Quality of Working Life
RT Affluence
Deprivation
Disadvantaged
Everyday Life
Family Life
Humanization
Life
Life Satisfaction
Living Conditions
Social Conditions
Social Status
Socioeconomic Status
Standard of Living
Well Being

Figure 8.6 *Quality of life*

abstracts. Their Keywords+field does so automatically, by assigning keywords to records based on computer examination of the titles of articles listed in the footnotes of the article being indexed. Abstracts are added if the original article contains an author-written abstract.

Accuracy

The two final categories of top priority quality run throughout the other three categories, but also contain some unique properties of their own. *Accuracy* and *Consistency* are implied in high-quality editorial selection policies, field structures and indexing. The application of scope, structure and accessibility must, of course,

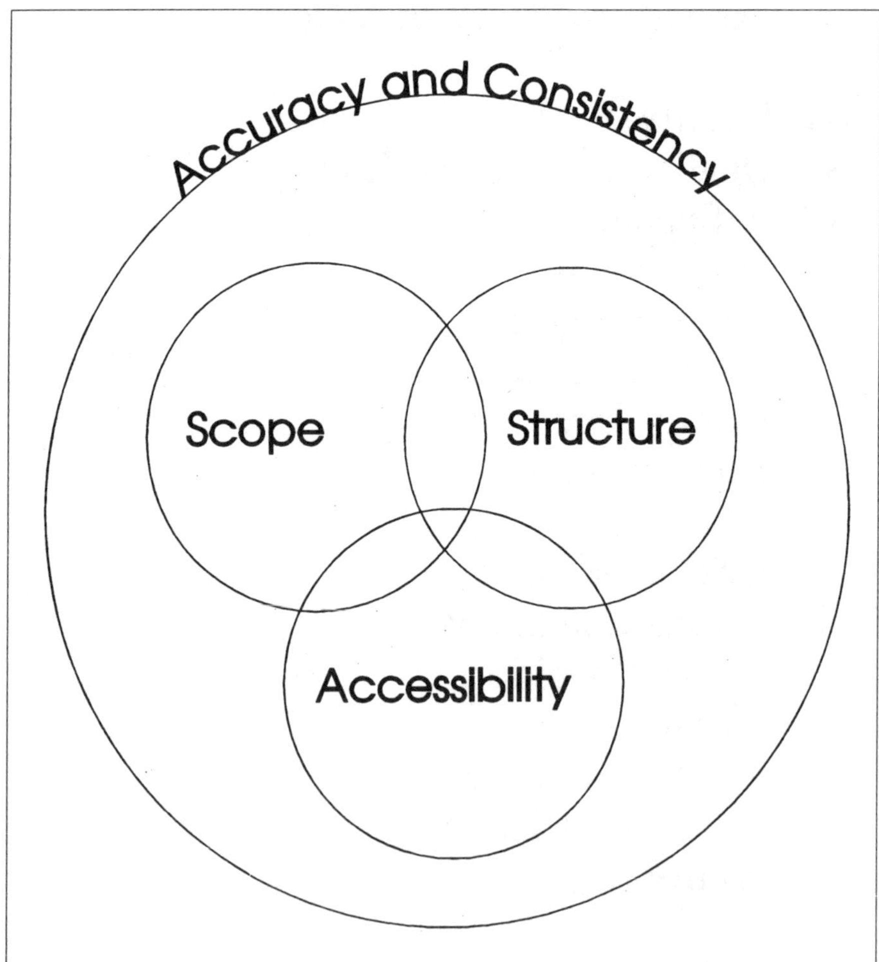

Figure 8.7 *Five aspects of content quality*

be both accurate and consistent to be of any use. Rather than a five-point list, the five aspects might be pictured as a Venn diagram (Figure 8.7), with accuracy and consistency included in all other content aspects. But accuracy and consistency are worth considering on their own. Accuracy is where typographical errors come to bear in the evaluation of content quality.

Accuracy is more important in some fields than in others. Factual and content-loaded fields should be double-checked for accuracy by database producers. Numeric fields, address fields, phone numbers and source fields, in particular, should be validated and verified, because the potential for problems in retrieval and use are so high if they contain errors.

For instance, Jacsó found that *Ulrich's International Serials Directory* listed the price of both *Biological Abstracts* and *Mathematical Reviews* as only $4 per year! Quite a bargain, but highly suspect.[20]

Typographical errors in text fields such as titles, abstracts, or full-text are unsightly, but do they impact search results adversely? Database producers claim that it is too expensive and time-consuming to spell-check and proofread to the degree necessary to get better accuracy. How devastating are typos in these fields?

Part of the answer to that question has to do with statistical probabilities. The more information there is in a database record, the higher the probability that the error will not be devastating. Thus, in a full-text database, the odds that one or two

Vacuums in INSPEC

```
17915 VACUUM
    2 VACUUN
    1 VACUU
    1 VACUUJM
    2 VACCUMM
    1 VACCUMS
  106 VACCUUM
    1 VACCUUMS
    1 VACUUMJ
    5 VACUUMP
  737 VACUUMS

S VACCUUM? AND VACUUM? ▪ 31
S VACCUUM? NOT VACUUM? ▪ 76
```

Figure 8.8 *Vacuums in INSPEC*

typos will adversely affect the search results is small, since the words are likely to be repeated elsewhere in the record.

This redundancy factor, or its lack, can be easily illustrated. Figure 8.8 shows a list of the variety of spellings of 'vacuum' in INSPEC. Out of the 107 misspellings *Vaccuum* or *Vaccuums*, 31 of the records also contain the word spelled correctly. This means that 76 of the records do not have any redundancy and would therefore be lost in a search if the searcher did not first check the index and choose all incorrect spellings along with the correct one.

A 1977 study by Charles Bourne pointed out that forcing a searcher to do such checking increases the cost of the search and necessitates more time to do a comprehensive search.[21] He noted that, even then, only errors that begin with the same word stem are likely to be retrieved, either from an index display or from truncation. Words with the first letters wrong are likely to go unnoticed by users.

Generally, redundant errors will adversely affect retrieval only if the user is searching with proximity operators and the word pattern is not repeated anywhere else in the document. Publishers are often willing to take this risk with searchers' results.

Imagine walking into a bookstore and seeing a sign: 'Books with errors and typos $20 – Proofread books $50'. Consumers would not stand for it, but database producers get away with such practices regularly. Many database producers claim that users cannot afford to pay what it would take to have cleaner databases, so they must be satisfied with the products as they are.

Non-redundant errors are especially problematic. These occur more often in short fields than in lengthy texts or abstracts. The 'parent country' field in *D&B – International Dun's Market Identifiers*, shown below (Figure 8.9), contains just one value. Someone looking for all records about England will be bound to miss many directory listings. An even more serious accuracy problem, especially with directory and numeric databases, is the reliability of the source information. In a company database record, if the name of the president, the phone number, or the gross sales are inaccurate because of poor data-gathering techniques, the record, and by implication the entire database, is worthless.

The Supreme Court case of Dun & Bradstreet (D&B) *vs*. Greenmoss Builders has been widely reported. A student hired by D&B to go through and interpret legal documents mistakenly reported that Greenmoss had filed for bankruptcy. Greenmoss sued D&B and won.[22]

Another well-known example is when the *Dun & Bradstreet European Market Identifiers* database was found to have used inaccurate currency conversion formulas. They alternately reported three Yugoslavian and three Greek companies as being the largest food companies in the world.[23]

Dun & Bradstreet's reaction to these problems was, in part, to revise their disclaimer. On Dialog, the *D&B Dun's Financial Records Plus* disclaimer statement reads in part: 'You acknowledge that D&B does not warrant or guarantee the timeliness, currentness, accuracy, completeness, merchantability or fitness for a particular purpose of the information. You also acknowledge that every business decision involves the assumption of a risk and that D&B, in furnishing the information to you, cannot and will not underwrite that risk in any manner whatsoever. You therefore agree that D&B will not be liable for any loss, damage or injury caused in whole or in part by D&B's negligence in procuring, compiling, collecting, interpreting, reporting, communicating or delivering the information... ."[24]

If the wrong information is reported, no amount of data input checks and double checks will ensure accuracy. Unfortunately, it is difficult for consumers to verify this aspect of accuracy, unless the correct information or source of the information is already known to them.

Because of this uncertainty, searchers must always question the factual information they retrieve. If a directory database includes large numbers of records with information listed as NA (not available), one must question the database's techniques for data verification. If something looks suspicious an experienced searcher will try to verify it in another source.

A corporate librarian in an oil trading firm reported that she always spot checks the worldwide oil price data they download every day. After doing this for 15 years, she recognizes when a price 'just doesn't sound right.' For those, she calls other sources, then adds a note to the price on their in-house system, alerting the traders

England in International Dun's

```
    1 PO=ENGELAND
    7 PO=ENGLAND
    1 PO=ENGLETERRE
51137 PO=UK-ENGLAND

ALSO

    1 PO=LONDON
    1 PO=DEVON
    1 PO=SURREY
```

Figure 8.9 *England in International Dun's*

to the verified information. Since no other companies bother to do this, hers has an advantage on the trading floor, because only her traders know the real price. Unfortunately, there is no better way to verify this type of data.

Consistency

Finally, probably the single most important measure of quality is consistency. A user can live with a database of limited scope if the producer publicizes the limitations and follows the statement of scope consistently. He or she can live with a database that has few fields if all are consistently present in the records. There may even be some merit in consistently making the same error.

Consistency allows predictability. Consistency helps users realize what they will and will not get in a database search. It makes search aids, such as manuals and help messages, meaningful.

Consistency cuts across all parts of a database. For example, a researcher who is running updates to a search on a regular basis needs to be able to rely on consistency in such matters as when a database is updated, the approximate number of records added at each update, the terminology used to index the subject, and the fields available for searching.

INVESTEXT is supposed to be updated semi-weekly on Dialog. Sometimes it is; other times there is as long as a three-week lag between updates.[25] Articles in ERIC about how schools can help prevent child abuse consistently use the descriptor *Child Abuse*, but variously use *School Role*, *School Responsibility*, *Teacher Role*, *Teacher Responsibility*, *Prevention*, and others, to index the other concept.

All of these are consistency problems. All greatly impact the quality of search results.

Advice to database producers

Database producers can improve content, the most important aspect of quality, to make quality products. Database producers have an obligation to provide an acceptable level of content quality while maintaining currency. It may not be easy, but at some point users are not going to continue to accept excuses.

Here are some fundamental techniques for improving database quality at the producer end. Some customers may be surprised that these are not being widely employed already:

1. Use spell-checkers with verification to correct scanning and data input errors
2. Use data validation on structured fields
3. Spend time on thesaurus development, maintenance and adding value
4. Hire qualified personnel to gather, index, input, check, etc.
5. Put pressure on online services to improve their error correction procedures
6. Add easy mechanisms for customers to report errors (such as Mintz's FIXIT

command, first adopted by NewsNet)[26]

7. Develop, print, and publicize editorial policies *and follow* them
8. Believe that users need and want content quality, and understand that poor practices cannot go on forever
9. If you can not manage a reasonable level of content quality, get out of the business (searchers should help by refusing to buy poor quality products).

Certainly, there are trade-offs. Time lags may be a problem already, without spending even more time and care in preparation. But as more products become available in electronic form, and as a wider base of consumers uses them, poor quality will not continue to sell. Better software for scanning, error detection, validation and automatic indexing can help with many of these quality issues, although not with all.

Finding out about quality

All searchers share the responsibility for testing and reporting on the quality of database content. If searchers do not make it their job to test quality, they will end up having to issue the same sort of disclaimers as database producers – but theirs will read 'let the client beware'.

Testing is not as difficult as many searchers imagine; not everyone need become a full-time quality control officer. There is a continuum of testing, from simple to complex, from quick to more time-consuming, from inexpensive to potentially quite expensive. Many more searchers will find a role for themselves on the quick or simple end than on the complex end. Each searcher can decide where on the continuum to draw the line of direct involvement (Figure 8.10).

Jacsó's chapter provides methods and details of many quality tests along all points of the continuum. The simplest technique, however, is one that every searcher can perform routinely for every database he or she searches. This technique is simply to see if someone else has already tested the quality of the database and written a review. Every searcher should be in the habit of regularly reading database reviews. Of course, one must be careful of who writes the reviews – an employee of the database producer is hardly likely to be unbiased. Some journals label these product reviews in some way, such as 'First Look', but with others the reader has to check author affiliation to make sure the review is objective. There are many good sources of database reviews. A selected source list is included at the end of this chapter.

A consortium such as the Finnish Society for Information Services, SCOUG, or any other group of concerned users, is a good avenue to accomplish systematic database tests on a large scale. Large-scale testing is prohibitive for most individuals, due to the time and money required to test a database rigorously. Working together, however, searchers could create a regular and consistent database reviewing vehicle. Some groups have proposed a sort of international *Consumer Reports* of databases.

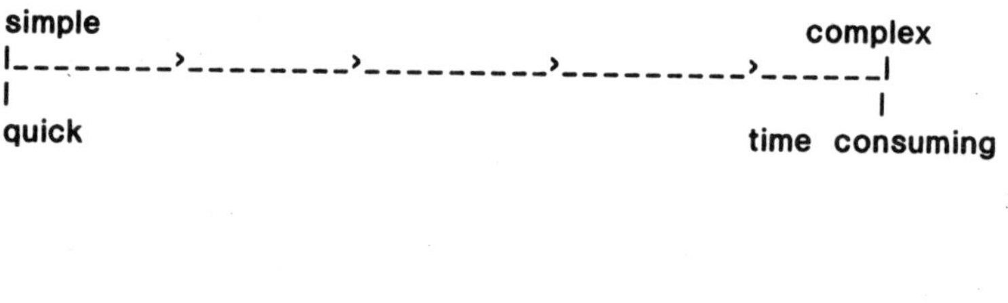

Figure 8.10 *Continuum of listing*

Internet is a natural distribution vehicle for such reports. Reports could be built incrementally, with many searchers from all over the world adding their input for each database. The development of a consistent checklist and standardized testing methods would assure some uniformity.

Conclusion

Content, made up of consistent and accurate scope, structure, and accessibility, is the top priority for quality. All quality is not created equal: without quality content, no amount of fancy programming, nifty interfaces, or clean telecommunications lines makes any difference. Database producers can create higher quality databases if they are convinced that customers care. Often, poor content quality is hidden, because it is never tested systematically. Jacsó's chapter provides several systematic methods for tests that measure database quality and that can help uncover some of the hidden dirty secrets of database content.

Selected sources for evaluating databases

Gale Directory of Databases. Detroit, MI: Gale Research, Inc. 2 volumes. Twice yearly. January 1993–. This merges and replaces three popular directories: *Computer-Readable Databases: A Directory and Data SourceBook*, Martha E. Williams, Founding Editor; *Directory of Online Databases and Directory of Portable Databases*, founded by Cuadra Associates. Volume One covers online databases, Volume Two covers CD-ROM, diskette, tapes, handheld, and other 'portable' formats.

Fulltext Sources Online. Ruth Orenstein, editor. Needham Heights, MA: BiblioData, twice yearly. A directory of periodicals (magazines, journals, newspapers, newsletters, and newswires) available online in full-text from major international vendors.

Jacsó, Peter. CD-ROM Software, *Dataware, and Hardware: Evaluation, Selection, and Installation*. Englewood, CO: Libraries Unlimited, 1992. Examples are for CD-ROM databases only, but the many useful techniques to test and evaluate databases work for any electronic distribution medium.

Database magazine (Online Inc., Wilton, CT). Probably the best source for comparative reviews and techniques for testing.

Online magazine is the companion to *Database* (they are published every other month by the same publisher). It has fewer database reviews, but many system reviews and discussions of broader issues of quality.

Online Review (Learned Information, Ltd., Oxford, England). Publishes reviews of databases and systems and research articles, as well as database news.

Information Today (Learned Information, Inc., Medford, NJ). Industry news, columns and some database reviews. Good for announcements of new databases and movements to improve quality.

Searcher: The Magazine for Database Professionals. Barbara Quint, editor (Learned Information Inc., Medford, NJ). Quint is an outspoken proponent of quality searchers and the guiding light of the Southern California Online Users Group.

RQ (American Library Association, Reference and Adult Services Division, Chicago, IL). Includes reviews of online and CD-ROM databases.

Notes

1. For a summary, see: Tenopir, Carol (1992), 'Evaluation criteria for online, CD-ROM', *Library Journal* **117** (March 1): 66,68; Tenopir, Carol, 'Database quality revisited', *Library Journal* **115** (October 1), 64–5, 67.
2. Basch, Reva (1990), 'SCOUG retreat addresses data quality issues', *Online* **14** (November), 81–2.

3. Juntunen, Ritva *et al.*, (1991), 'Quality requirements for databases – Project for evaluating Finnish databases', in *Online Information '91*, 15th International Online Information Proceedings, London, 10–12 December 1991 (Ed. David I. Raitt), Oxford, England: Learned Information Ltd. 351–9.
4. Jacsó, Peter (1992), *CD-ROM Software, Dataware and Hardware: Evaluation, Selection and Installation*, Englewood, Colorado: Libraries Unlimited.
5. Tenopir, 'Database quality revisited', 64.
6. Juntunen, 357–9.
7. Jacsó, *CD-ROM Software, Dataware and Hardware: Evaluation, Selection and Installation.*
8. Williams, Martha E. (1990), 'Highlights of the online database industry and the quality of information and data', *National Online Meeting Proceedings*, 1990, New York, May 1–3 (Ed. Martha E. Williams)/Medford, New Jersey: Learned Information, Inc.
9. Tenopir, 'Database quality revisited', 64.
10. Jacsó, *CD-ROM Software, Dataware and Hardware: Evaluation, Selection and Installation.*
11. Tenopir, 'Evaluation criteria for online, CD-ROM', 66.
12. Juntunen, 357–9.
13. Database Supplier Terms and Conditions (Palo Alto, California, Dialog Information Services, Inc., July 1991)
14. Juntunen, 354.
15. Tenopir, 'Database quality revisited', 64.
16. Ikushima, Keiko and Tenopir, Carol (1988), 'Availability of Japanese scientific and technical periodicals in major English language databases', in *National Online Meeting Proceedings*, 1988, New York, May 10–12 (Eds Martha E. Williams and Thomas H. Hogan), Medford, New Jersey, Learned Information Inc., 115–22.
17. Jacsó, Peter, Workshop held at National Online Meeting, New York, May 1992.
18. Ibid.
19. Tenopir, Carol and Jacsó, Peter, 'Quality of Abstracts', *Online* (May 1993), 44–55.
20. Jacsó, *CD-ROM Software, Dataware and Hardware: Evaluation, Selection and Installation*, 136.
21. Bourne, Charles P. (1977), 'Frequency and Impact of Spelling Errors in Bibliographic Databases', *Information Processing and Management* **13**, 10.
22. Mintz, Anne (1985), 'Information Practice and Malpractice', *Library Journal* **110**, 15 September, 43.
23. Pagell, Ruth (1990), 'Sorry, Wrong Number: Exchange Rates and Sales Figures', *Online* **14** (November), 20–1; Ruth Pagell (1991), 'It's Greek to Me! Exchange Rate Translations and Company Comparisons', *Database* **14** (February), 21–7.
24. Database Supplier Terms and Conditions, op. cit.
25. Tenopir, Carol and Hover, Katie (1993), 'When is the same database not the

same?' *Online* (July), 20–7.
26. Mintz, Anne (1990), 'Quality Control and the Zen of Database Production', *Online* **14** (November), 17.

Chapter 9

TESTING THE QUALITY OF CD-ROM DATABASES

Peter Jacsó, Visiting Associate Professor at the University of Hawaii at Manoa School of Library and Information Studies

Introduction

CD-ROM technology has brought us not only the advantages of unlimited searching of databases for a set fee, but also the chance to make extensive quality checks of databases with little effort and no extra costs, apart from labor. Analysis of data quality in printed publications has been an arduous job. The scope of manual quality testing is limited by the amount of time required to scan and evaluate randomly selected records. Online databases have offered the ability to automate most of the quality tests, but these require spending real money, as do real searches. CD-ROM users, on the other hand, can do comprehensive test searches without paying for them. Even better, many databases allow these test searches to be carried out during a trial period before committing oneself to subscribing to or purchasing it.

If such an opportunity is not offered, test searches during the operational period are still valuable, because subscribers may change to another database after the license period (typically one year) if the findings are not satisfactory. The fact that a new customer receives a cumulative database on starting a subscription gives teeth to the motivation for testing. Even if one has purchased, rather than subscribed to, a database, the test searches can be valuable as preparation for educated and effective searching.

Test findings can reveal the weak spots of the database, and save the user from falling victim to misleading claims by the file producer and/or database publisher, or even by independent reviewers. As CD-ROM databases enter the mainstream of library materials, more and more library journals are publishing CD-ROM product reviews. Regrettably, many of them sound more like TV testimonials for liquid detergents. Testimonials for CD-ROM databases may become even less trustworthy as users find it hard to resist writing 'testimonials' in exchange for the chance to win a $100 dinner coupon, as one publisher offered in an advertising campaign.

The beauty of computer-assisted searching can turn into a beast if the records are entered and/or indexed incompletely, inaccurately or inconsistently. While it might be tempting to refine a subject search by several additional criteria, too many relevant items may be excluded if a database is weak in terms of these criteria.

Elsewhere in this volume, Carol Tenopir and others discuss the major implications of database quality issues. In this chapter, we will look at three types of quality problems, and how to explore them through some model test searches. The adaptability of the techniques to a particular database depends both on the capabilities of the search software and on how the database indexes were created. Many of the techniques can be also used in the online environment, if one has the budget for it.

Incompleteness

Incompleteness of records is the most serious type of quality problem simply because it is invisible. While errors of commission are usually obvious to the naked eye, and may not be detrimental to the search, errors of omission – by definition – do not show up in database records. Yet they can drastically compromise a search without one's being aware of it.

To add to the problem, publicity materials sing siren songs about the numerous data elements by which one can search a database. Technically, records may indeed be searched by those proudly advertised data elements. But the unwary user who assumes that all the records in the database will contain some value (hopefully a valid one) in a field offered as an access point might be grossly mistaken. Records with blank or missing data elements are often missed in searches that specify these elements as search criteria.

For example, the *Standard & Poor's Directory* of publicly-held companies offers over 50 access points to the database of 10,000–12,000 records. What is not revealed is the significant volume of omissions: fewer than half the records contain information about operating income, total income or net income. Information about total current assets or liabilities is available in two-thirds of the records. Even such basic data as the date and place of incorporation, the type of corporation and the exchange where the company's stock is traded are absent from several hundred records. These criteria are routinely used for screening companies. Yet, due to the volume of missing information, a searcher who attempts such a screening will get very distorted results.

Similarly, a search by Library of Congress classification code for textbooks in the *Children's Reference Plus* database cannot validly be done, nor can a search be qualified by grade level – a natural in a textbook search – because only 11 per cent and 42 per cent of the textbook records, respectively, carry such information. In the *Encyclopedia of Associations*, only 50 per cent of the records contain membership data, and many other basic data elements are missing from 40 per cent to 85 per cent of the records.[1]

None of the help files or printed documentation provide even the slightest hint of the level of incompleteness of these databases. On the contrary, terminology like 'universal search criteria' and 'Each ... record is a complete listing of an organization' may mislead most searchers.

Of course, the scope of data elements present in each record is database-specific. In abstract databases, these fields typically include descriptor, classification code, document type, language and country code, and publication year. In directory databases, type of organization, area and zip code, SIC or similar classification codes are standard data elements.

This category of quality problem deserves special attention from the testing point of view. Completeness tests can be run on the entire database, not just on sample records.

But the easiest way to learn about the absence of data elements is when the database itself volunteers this information in an obvious way. The *TFPL CD-ROM Directory* is commendable for its straightforward solution and fair advice. Selecting a data element for searching produces a window that lists the possible values in the field. Those records which are not assigned any of the possible values are readily identifiable by the index entry 'not listed' (Figure 9.1). Selecting such entries in the different indexes indicates the degree of incompleteness in the database.

The *Directory of Library and Information Professionals* claims to have 45,000

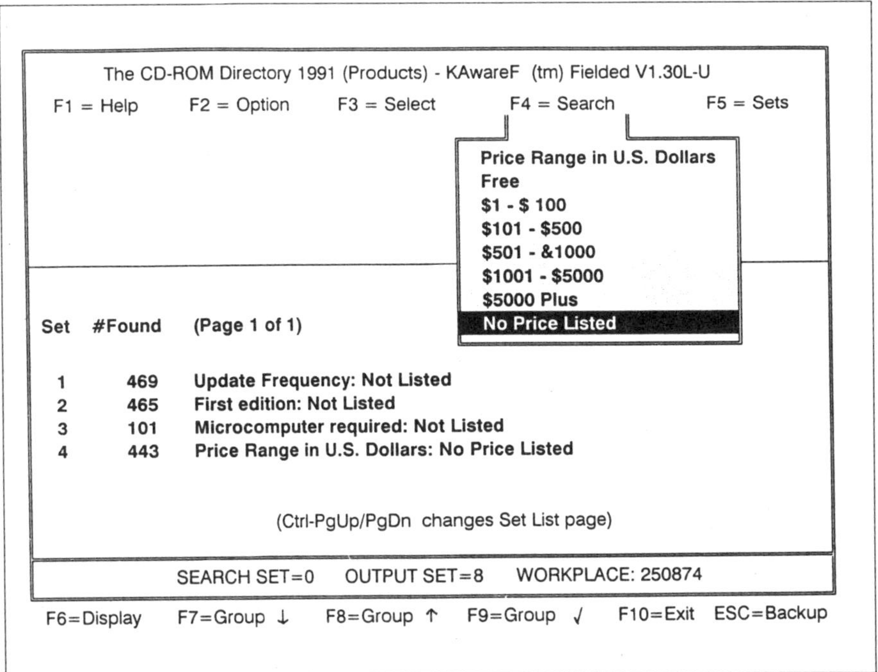

Figure 9.1

records. It uses the same software as in the previous example, and the same technique could be applied to advise the user about the database's high level of incompleteness. However, the publisher chose not to use it. When one searches by gender (e.g. to find out how many male and female deans there are in library schools) the search window shows the two options (Figure 9.2). What it fails to show is that 47 per cent of the records do not carry this information. After a couple of unsatisfactory searches, the lack becomes obvious. The manual admits this serious omission, but only for this field, not for others where lack of data is a problem. This poker-faced, business-as-usual approach is like that of the restaurant manager who does not sound the alarm when his establishment catches fire, to make sure that guests will pay the bill before they flee.

An easy way to test completeness is when the database 'surrenders' on first notice.

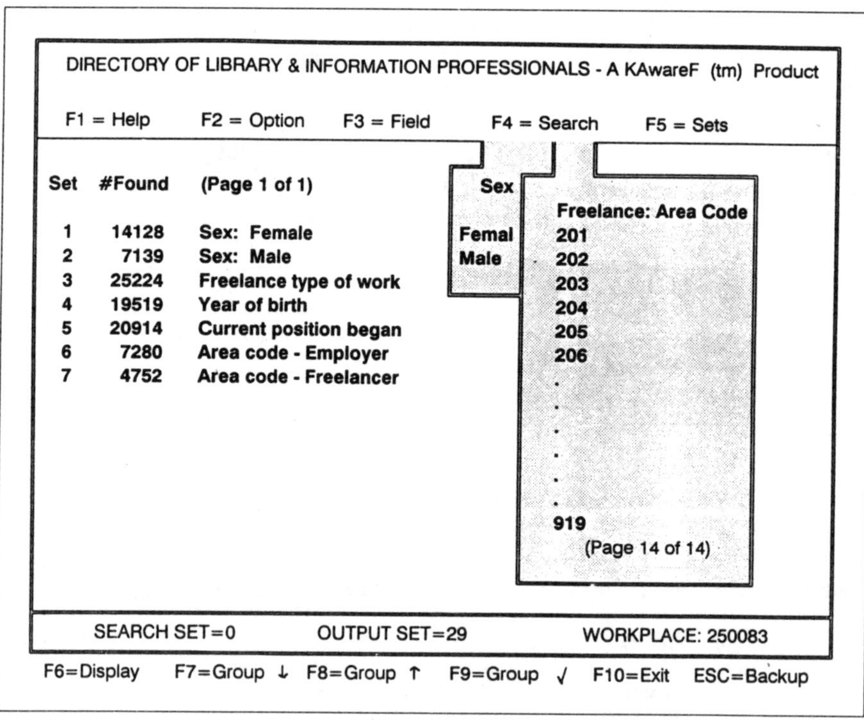

Figure 9.2

The user types the word 'none' in the appropriate cell on the search template, and for each of the chosen data elements the number of records that contain no data in that field is displayed (Figure 9.3). Unfortunately, this technique works only with databases that use the CD Answer software (*America: History and Life, Historical Abstracts, Computing Archive*, etc.).

A similar 'surrendering' notice consists of a specific code or character string

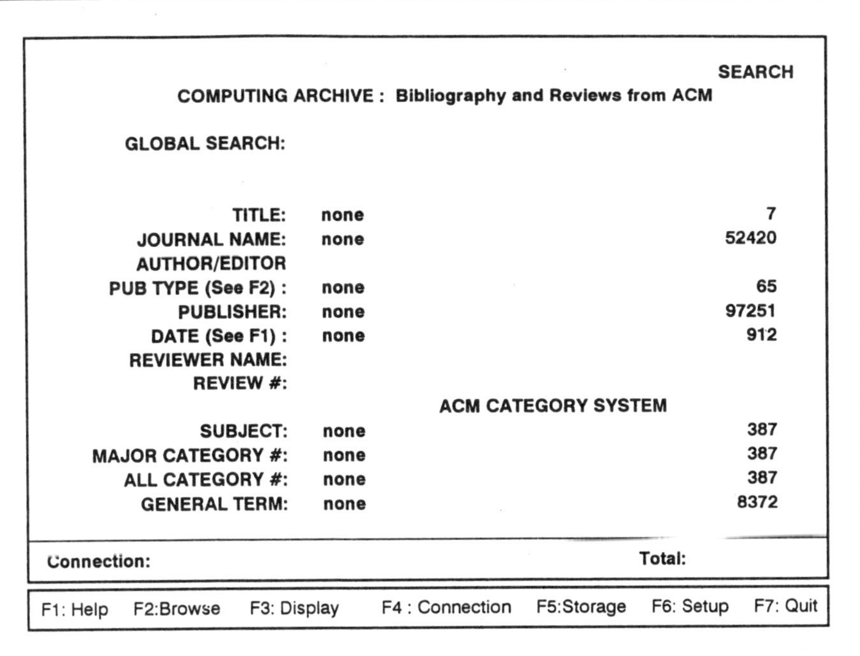

Figure 9.3

indicating that the data element is not available. Catalogers often use special terms or codes when a mandatory data element is missing, such as 'S.l.' and 's.n.' when the location or name of the publisher are unknown, or '19uu' when the decade and year of publication have not been determined.

Other special codes may include acronyms or spelled-out notations such as 'undetermined' (LISA), 'not available' (*Disclosure*), 'no abstract' (*Information Science Abstracts*), or something similar. These notations were not originally meant for aiding retrieval. The knowledgeable user can, however, explore the incompleteness level of the database either by browsing the indexes (Figure 9.4), or by searching specifically for such codes or notations (Figure 9.5).

A problem arises if such incompleteness indicators are only halfheartedly and inconsistently used, as they are in *Standard and Poor's* and *Books In Print*, for example. *Standard and Poor's* occasionally uses the code 'NA' or 'not available' if a data element is absent. Figure 9.6 shows a search to find records where the total current asset data is, and is not, available. The total number of records retrieved by this search is still far less than the number claimed in the database help file (12,000) or estimated by this author (10,328).

One encounters this halfheartedness problem again in *Books in Print Plus*, which claims that 'books without dates have an indexed year of 9999'. In fact, some do and some don't, as illustrated by Figure 9.7. Other searches show that there are nearly a

```
COMPACT D/SEC       SEPT-1991        (C) Disclosure

      Set  Items  Description
      ---  -----  -----------
? e ag=not

Ref     Items Postings       Index-term
E1          6        6       AG=NORWEST CAPITAL RESOURCES
E2          2        2       AG=NORWEST STOCK TRANSFER
E3        566      566      *AG=NOT
E4        566      566       AG=NOT REPORTED
E5          1        1       AG=OCE


Ref     Items Postings       Index-term
E1          1        1       CU=0009899171
E2          1        1       CU=0009899201
E3        960      960      *CU=NA


Ref     Items Postings       Index-term
E1          1        1       DN=75-317-0117
E2          1        1       DN=85-360-0393
E3      4,640    4,640      *DN=NA



Ref     Items Postings       Index-term
E1          1        1       FB=MV499
E2          1        1       FB=MV500
E3     10,171   10,171      *FB=NA
E4          1        1       FB=PR001   (Forbes 500 ranked by Profits)

Ref     Items Postings       Index-term
E1          1        1       FO=L050
E2     10,032   10,032       FO=N
E3     10,032   10,032      *FO=NA
E4         48       48       FO=R   (Fortune 50 Retailing)

Ref     Items Postings       Index-term
E1          4        4       PC=MUSICAL INSTRUMENTS  (3931)
E2          4        4       PC=MUSICAL INSTRUMENTS  (ALL 393-)
E3      1,831    5,493      *PC=NA
E4          2        2       PC=NARROW FABRIC MILLS  (2241)

Ref     Items Postings       Index-term
E1          2        2       PD=910601
E2          1        1       PD=910630
E3        182      364      *PD=NA

Ref     Items Postings       Index-term
E1          1        1       TE=929
E2          4        4       TE=972
E3        194      194      *TE=NA
```

Figure 9.4

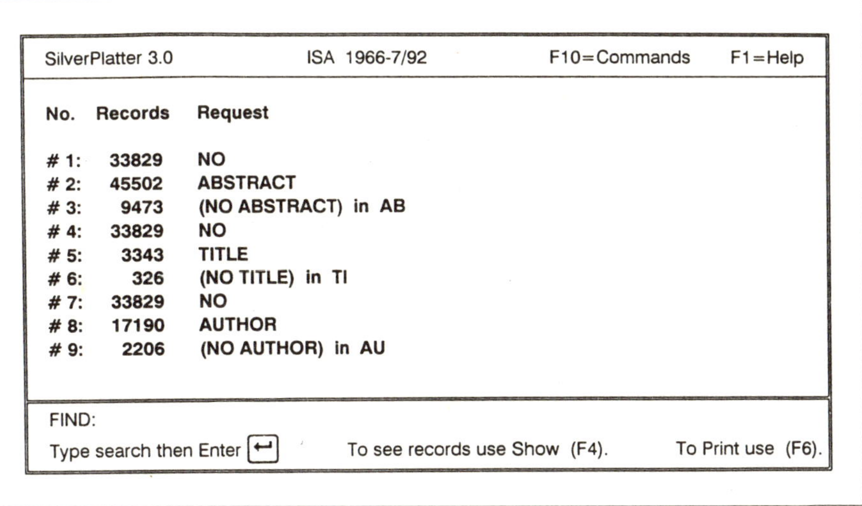
SilverPlatter 3.0 ISA 1966-7/92 F10=Commands F1=Help

No.	Records	Request
# 1:	33829	NO
# 2:	45502	ABSTRACT
# 3:	9473	(NO ABSTRACT) in AB
# 4:	33829	NO
# 5:	3343	TITLE
# 6:	326	(NO TITLE) in TI
# 7:	33829	NO
# 8:	17190	AUTHOR
# 9:	2206	(NO AUTHOR) in AU

FIND:
Type search then Enter ↵ To see records use Show (F4). To Print use (F6).

Figure 9.5

million records in the database. Still, when we search for records which have a publication year with *any* value, the resulting set is less than the total number of records.

The method used here to verify completeness is the fully truncated prefix indexing technique. A large number of databases can be tested in this way since it is supported by two very widely used search software packages, Dialog OnDisc and OptiWare. The first step in this procedure is to learn the total number of records against which the postings of the test searches will be compared. The database publisher may provide this information (often with an upward estimation that backfires when the completeness test is run). In many databases, doing a fully truncated search for a field which is known to be present in each record will indirectly show the total number of records. For example, in the *Canadian Bibliodisc*, the National Bibliography (nb) number is such a value. The subsequent searches show the incompleteness, which is undocumented, of other fields (Figure 9.8).

For numeric fields which are treated as numbers (e.g. price) one may have to use the arithmetic operator (>) to find out how many records include the chosen fields. A numeric search is also a good way to find the total number of records. In almost all the SilverPlatter databases, the update date (when the record was entered into the database) is automatically generated, and therefore is always present. It can be used to find the total number of records (as illustrated in Figure 9.10).

If arithmetic operators and full truncation are not supported by the software (as is the case with Wilsondisc and ProQuest), one may use partial truncation with field qualification for at least some of the fields. For example, in the Wilson databases one may use the **(DA) 8: OR 9:** command to find the total records added to the database in the 1980s and 1990s (identified in each record in the form of yymmdd) and then compare it with the result of the search for records with publication year data **(YR)**

```
FILE: PUBLIC COMPANIES

STANDARD & POOR'S CORPORATE DESCRIPTIONS plus NEWS provides
comprehensive strategic and financial information and current news on
approximately 12,000 publicly held companies.  These firms trade
securities on the New York, American, and regional stock exchanges; the
NASDAQ system; Over-the-Counter in the U.S.; and on various exchanges
in Canada and abroad.  The file provides access to capitalization,
corporate background, and financial data, including annual report
financials and recent interims.  Annual financials include both
"as reported" data and their standardized fielded elements,
several of which can be used for financial screening purposes.

     S&P PUBLIC COMPANY FILE February, 1993

      Set  Items  Description
      ---  -----  -----------
?S PC=?

      S1  10,328   30,554  PC=?

?S CA=NOT AVAILABLE

      S2      24       24  CA=NOT AVAILABLE

?S CA>0

      S3   6,957    6,957  CA>0

?S S2 OR S3

              24       24  S2
           6,957    6,957  S3
      S4   6,981    6,981  S2 OR S3
?
F1-Help  F2-Search    F4-Format  F5-Sort
```

Figure 9.6

19:.

Fields like document type, which have only a limited number of possible values, are good candidates for completeness testing. UMI's ProQuest software allows partial truncation with prefix for dates, but not for material types or for document length. One can test the completeness of these data elements by displaying the indexes, then marking and searching for all the terms (Figure 9.9).

In Wilsondisc's Wilsonline mode, one cannot mark the terms, but can expand a field-specific index and use the **GET X-Y** command to include all terms currently displayed. If the field has more than 20 values, the select-and-search process must be repeated.

If the software does not allow full, or even partial, truncation with field qualification, and prevents one from browsing many of the indexes (like SPIRS does) one can still conduct known-value test searches if the fields have a limited number of possible values and one knows what they are. Figure 9.10 shows that in

Search Browse Format Action Options Databases Books In Print Plus
au= Author
bn= ISBN
Search Workspace
SEARCH
SEARCH - Search category Notes
pr - price
Example: au= Jones and pr<20
(for all books by Jones under $20.00)
Note: Prices above $.50 are indexed to next highest dollar.)
py - Publication Year
Examples: py = 1969
py< 1969 (for all books before 1969)
py> 1969 (for all books after 1969 including those without dates)
Books without dates have an indexed year of 9999.
SEARCH page 18 of 19
ECS --► Program
PGDn --► Next Screen
PgUp --► Prev Screen
Esc --► Return to your search
Search Browse Format Action Options Databases Books In Print Plus
au = Author
bn = ISBN
kw = Keyword
kw = Keyword
l c = LCCN
pu = Publisher
su = Subject
ch = Children's Subject
t c = Title Code
t i = Title
se = Series Title
a t = 4, 4, Author, Title
t k = 3, 2, 2, 1, Title
cs = Combine Set
ac = Audience
gr = Grades
s i = Special Index
l a = Language
p r = Price
py = Publication Year
Search Workspace
1. t i = $ 981916
2. pu = $ 981915
3. su = $ 727122
4. py = 9999 9157
5. py = 1$ 908655
6. py = $ 917808
F1 --► Help
ESC --► Menu Bar
Enter new Search Statement and press ENTER
F10 --► Brief Citation
Search Completed

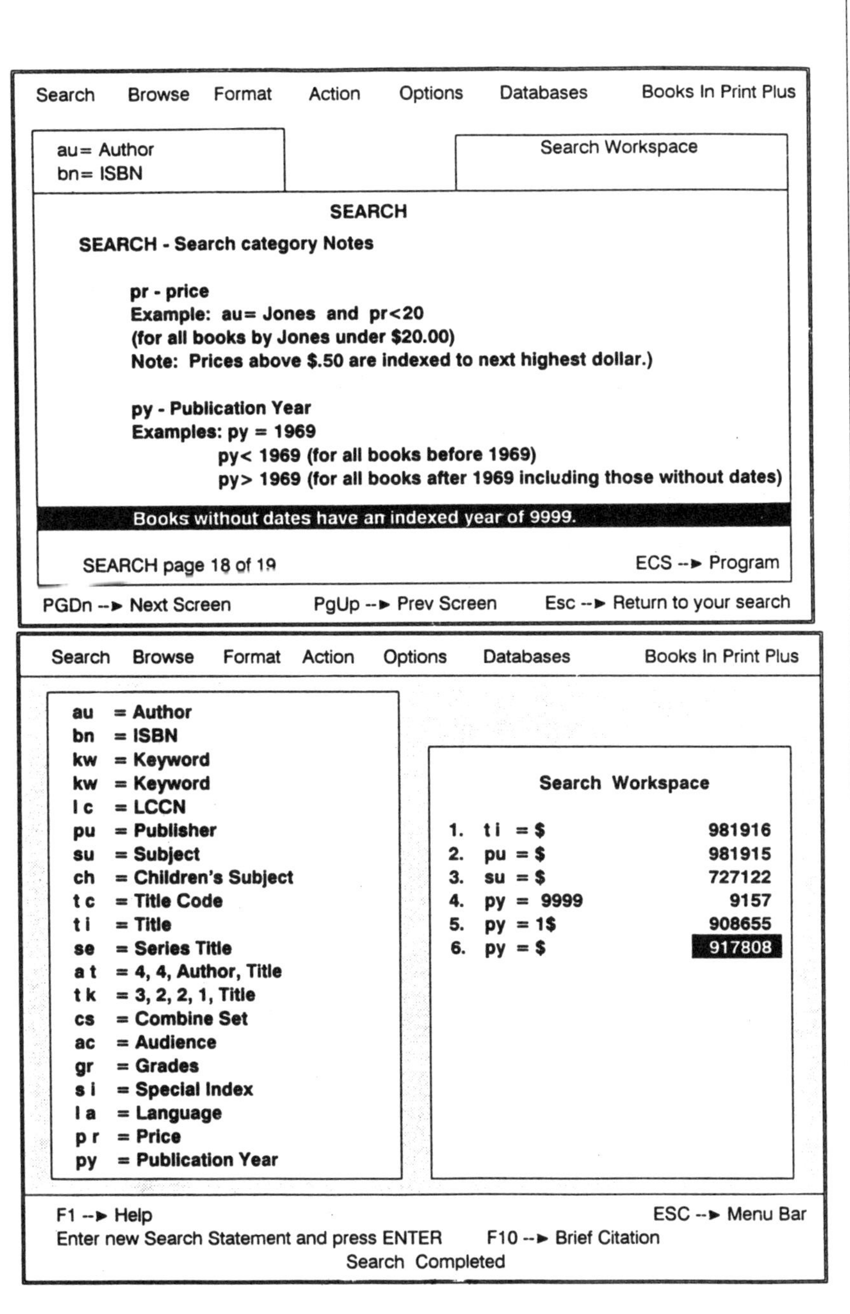

Figure 9.7

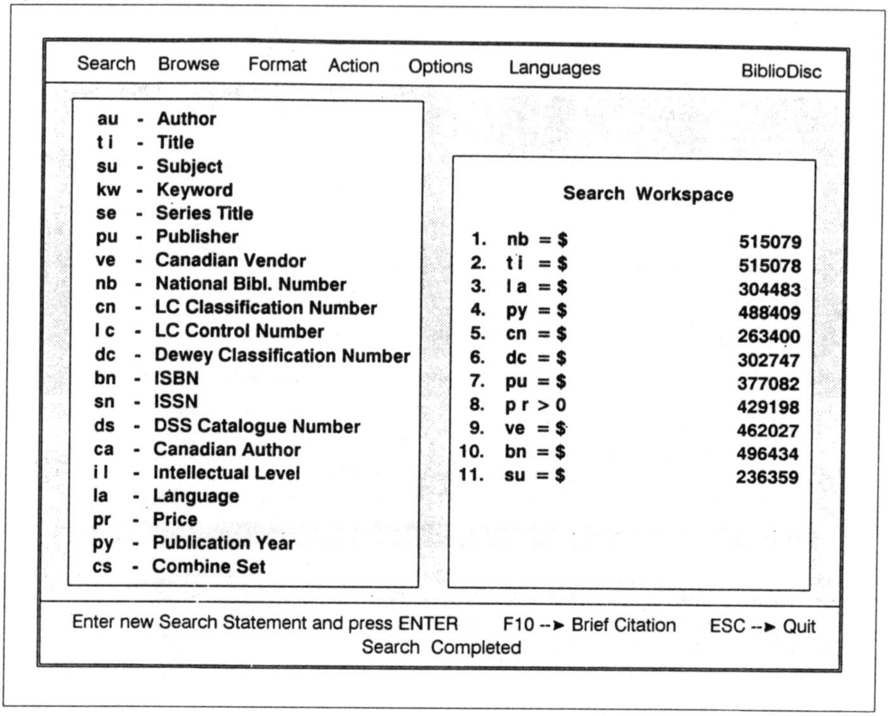

Search Browse Format Action Options Languages BiblioDisc

au	Author
ti	Title
su	Subject
kw	Keyword
se	Series Title
pu	Publisher
ve	Canadian Vendor
nb	National Bibl. Number
cn	LC Classification Number
lc	LC Control Number
dc	Dewey Classification Number
bn	ISBN
sn	ISSN
ds	DSS Catalogue Number
ca	Canadian Author
il	Intellectual Level
la	Language
pr	Price
py	Publication Year
cs	Combine Set

Search Workspace

1.	nb = $	515079
2.	ti = $	515078
3.	la = $	304483
4.	py = $	488409
5.	cn = $	263400
6.	dc = $	302747
7.	pu = $	377082
8.	pr > 0	429198
9.	ve = $	462027
10.	bn = $	496434
11.	su = $	236359

Enter new Search Statement and press ENTER F10 --► Brief Citation ESC --► Quit
Search Completed

Figure 9.8

the GPO database there are 503 records without a 'material type' (PT) code.

In some cases the normal search process reveals the incompleteness of the records in a very visible way. In the *PhoneDisc* database, after one types in a name, the system displays a short entry list of names, addresses and telephone numbers (Figure 9.11). The missing numbers are unmistakable. (Note: The latest edition of this product eliminates most of this incompleteness.)

Inaccuracies

Inaccuracy is a euphemism for erroneous, wrong data. Databases have plenty of them. Printed publications do, too, but what makes them particularly dangerous in databases is the fact that inaccurate terms show up in fields that are widely advertised as access points for searching, such as language, country, state, area and zip codes, and words from the abstract.

It is less of a problem if the same data also appears *correctly*, either in the same field or in some other field within the record. But when the incorrect data is the exclusive access point for a search, it will be missed. This is illustrated by three records from the otherwise impressively accurate *PsycLIT* database (Figure 9.12). In the first record, *Rorschach* is spelled both correctly and incorrectly within the

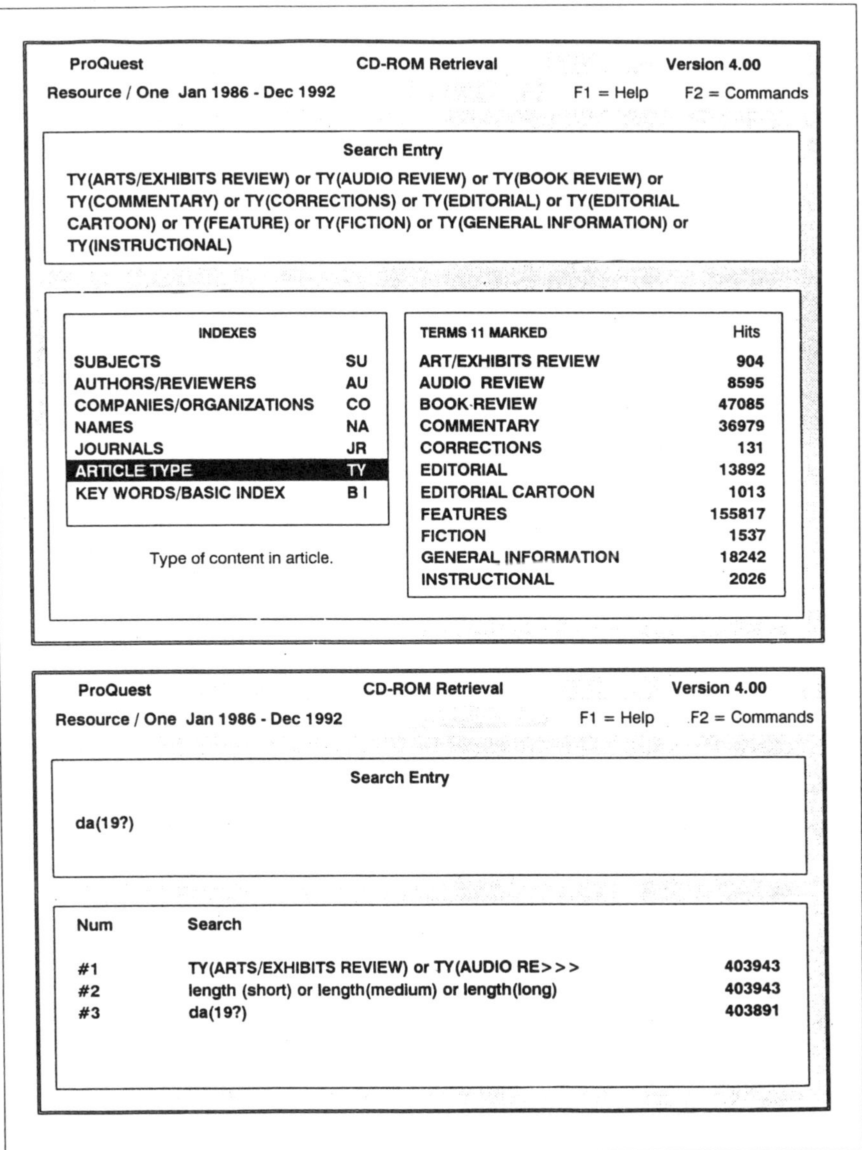

Figure 9.9

abstract, and thus causes no problem for retrieval of the record. In the second record, it is misspelled in the abstract but correct in the subject heading field. As long as one does not limit one's search to the abstract field, it will be retrieved. The third record will not be retrieved when searching for Rorschach, because the only time it occurs in the record it is misspelled.

Similarly, one may search one's heart out for Michael Koenig's thought-

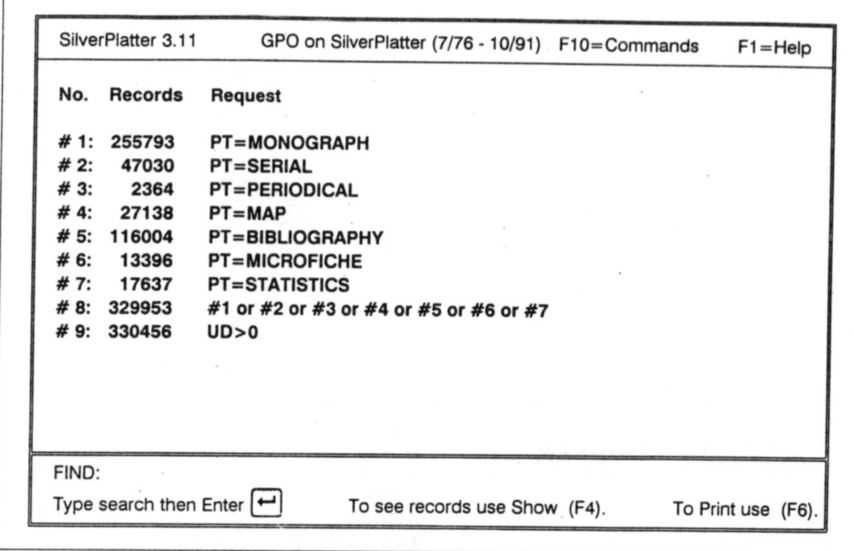

Figure 9.10

Enter Name:: **JACSO**

---------- (press Tab to limit) ------------------------------ PHONEDISC USA WESTERN EDITION -----

JACSKSON, LORA T 310 7TH ST #-303 ROCKFORD, IL 815-
JACSO, GIZELLA 1826 HANFORD AVE LINCOLN PARK, MI 313-383-6341
JACSO, ILONA M 1820 GUNDERSON AVE 708-
JACSO, LASZLO 662 S RAINBOW PL POMONA, CA 714-
JACSON, ADELINE F 327 CIMARRON LAKE ELMO, MN 612-
JACSON, D S 727 PEARL ST #-102 HAYDEN, CO 303-
JACSON, DEVIN 4100 NW 16TH ST OKLAHOMA CITY, OK 405-
JACSON, JAMES G 806 MACARTHUR BLVD OAKLAND, CA 415-
JACSON, S 4534 ELVIRA DR CORPUS CHRISTI, TX 512-
JACSTAS, CLINT BOX #-54 BROWNFIELD, TX 806-
JACTOUT, RUTH 3217 15TH ST PORT ARTHUR, TX 409-
JACTUES, SHEROLYN 669 1/2 CLOVER ST NEW ORLEANS, LA 504-
JACUART, WENDY B 2919 ROPNER CIR MAGN
JACUBEC, LAURA 801 NE MAPLE DR KANSAS
JACUBEC, MICHAEL S 7531 SUN GRACE DR
JACUBES, JO 5706 OVERBRIDGE DR ARLINGT
JACUBETZ, JOSEPH F 28 E DELRIO DR TEM
JACUBINAS, HENRY R 7668 CARDIGAN ST D
JACUBINAS, HENRY R 11 PIMENTEL CT NOV
JACUBIWAS, HENRY R 7668 CARDIGAN ST D
JACUBKE, EDNA M 1130 E 27TH #-85 SALT

JACSO, LASZLO
662 S RAINBOW PL
POMONA, CA 91765

714- *** Residence ***

F1-Help F5-Dial F6-Region F8-Print F9-Count ↑ ↓ Esc-Quit

Figure 9.11

```
Rorschach.doc

Compact Cambridge v4.1            Records                    CLP8092

  Record 1 of 4
SO : Revista de Psiquiatria y Psicologia Medica; 1981 Oct-Dec Vol 15(4) 227-235
LA : Spanish
SH : ALCOHOLISM; PERSONALITY TRAITS; EMOTIONAL STATES; SOCIAL BEHAVIOR
AB : 30 male chronic alcoholics (median age 44.9 yrs) and a matched group of
     nonalcoholics were administered the Rorschach and the TAT. The Rorshach
     test assessed Ss' affective stability and their social contact; ....

  Record 2 of 4
SO : Journal of Clinical Psychology; 1991 Jul Vol 47(4) 596-599
LA : English
SH : SCHIZOPHRENIA; MAJOR DEPRESSION; MENTAL DISORDERS/; TEST VALIDITY;
     RORSCHACH TEST; ADULTHOOD
AB : Data from J. E. Exner's (1985, 1989) normative samples on nonpatient adults
     and comparison samples of patients with schizophrenia, depression, and
     character problems were reanalyzed using a standard of clinical
     significance appropriate for N = 1.
     The Exner Rorshach seems to be a valid test for schizophrenia, but it
     demonstrated little differential utility for depression and character
     disorders. ................

  Record 3 of 4
SO : Journal of Clinical Psychology; 1981 Jul Vol 37(3) 555-563
LA : English
SH : SUICIDE; ATTEMPTED SUICIDE; MEASUREMENT/; PREDICTIVE VALIDITY; PSYCHIATRIC
     PATIENTS; HOSPITALIZED PATIENTS
AB : Examined the Wechsler-Bellevue Intelligence Scales, Rorshach, TAT, and Word
     Association Test scores of 40 patients for quantitative indications of
     suicide potential.............
                                                          More ↓
 Next (+)      preVious (-)   Up (PgUp)    Down (PgDn)   Clear-marks
 Print (F10)   Keep (F9)      Format       Goto
```

Figure 9.12

provoking article under his name, but one will not find it, because his name is misspelled twice in the record: once in the summary, and once as the subject heading in *Magazine Article Summaries* (Figure 9.13).

There are several ways to test systematically for the volume of inaccuracy in a database. The simplest is to browse around in a few indexes. Casually browsing in the place of publication index of the ISDS database shows some obvious misspellings of the city of Budapest (Figure 9.14).

Especially good fishing spots are the very beginning and very end of the indexes, where numeric data tends to collect in an alphabetic index, or alphabetic data in a numeric index. It is possible that the data is correct in itself, but is entered in the wrong field. The 'cuckoo's eggs' in the *Federal Register*'s agency (AG) index (Figure 9.15) are as erroneous from the searcher's point of view as genuinely incorrect data would be. A few such errors present no reason for concern, but a large number certainly should. Name indexes are also good browsing spots. The volume and variety of typos in the Bibliodisc publisher name index is unnerving (Figure 9.16), particularly because some of the entries are separated by several screens (as

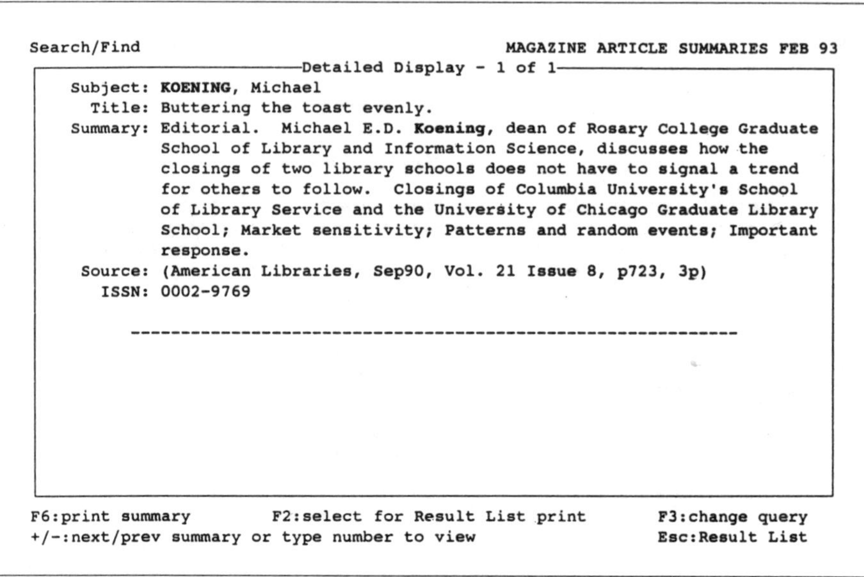

```
Search/Find                                    MAGAZINE ARTICLE SUMMARIES FEB 93
                        Detailed Display - 1 of 1
   Subject: KOENING, Michael
     Title: Buttering the toast evenly.
   Summary: Editorial.  Michael E.D. Koening, dean of Rosary College Graduate
            School of Library and Information Science, discusses how the
            closings of two library schools does not have to signal a trend
            for others to follow.  Closings of Columbia University's School
            of Library Service and the University of Chicago Graduate Library
            School; Market sensitivity; Patterns and random events; Important
            response.
    Source: (American Libraries, Sep90, Vol. 21 Issue 8, p723, 3p)
      ISSN: 0002-9769

      ------------------------------------------------------------

F6:print summary       F2:select for Result List print       F3:change query
+/-:next/prev summary or type number to view                 Esc:Result List
```

Figure 9.13

opposed to the misspellings of Budapest, which were, at least, conveniently congregated).

If an index is not browsable but *is* searchable, one may test for some types of inaccuracies by using comparative operators. For example, to find out how many records have non-alphabetic data in the Library of Congress classification code field, and non-numeric data in the Dewey classification field, use the **LC < A** and the **DC**

Search Browse Format Action Languages Tables Centres No Limits

Place of publication

Budaest	**2**
Budakalasz	**1**
Budakeszi	**1**
Budaors	**5**
Budapes	**21**
Budapest	**8943**
Budapeste	**1**
Budapestt	**1**
Budapet	**1**
Budapst	**3**

ENTER --► Select ESC --► Quit

Figure 9.14

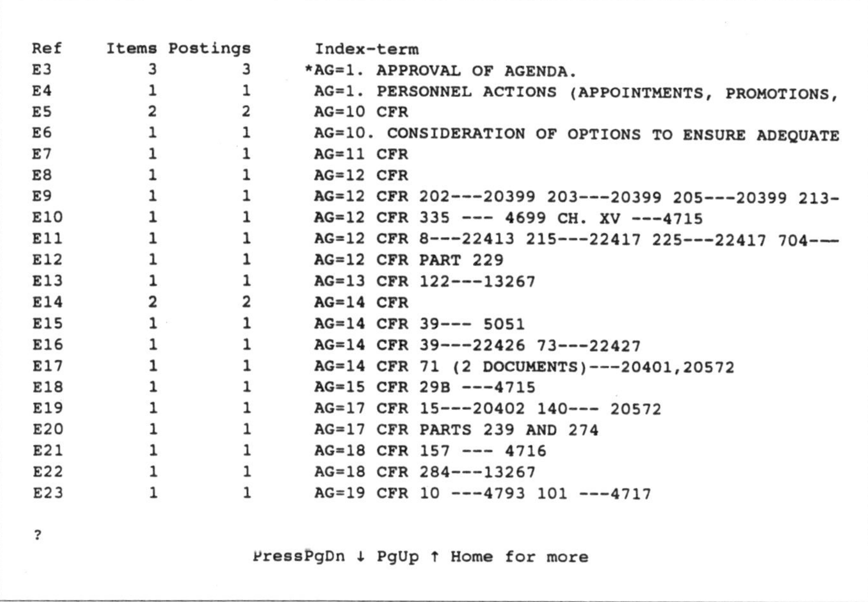

Ref	Items	Postings	Index-term
E3	3	3	*AG=1. APPROVAL OF AGENDA.
E4	1	1	AG=1. PERSONNEL ACTIONS (APPOINTMENTS, PROMOTIONS,
E5	2	2	AG=10 CFR
E6	1	1	AG=10. CONSIDERATION OF OPTIONS TO ENSURE ADEQUATE
E7	1	1	AG=11 CFR
E8	1	1	AG=12 CFR
E9	1	1	AG=12 CFR 202---20399 203---20399 205---20399 213-
E10	1	1	AG=12 CFR 335 --- 4699 CH. XV ---4715
E11	1	1	AG=12 CFR 8---22413 215---22417 225---22417 704---
E12	1	1	AG=12 CFR PART 229
E13	1	1	AG=13 CFR 122---13267
E14	2	2	AG=14 CFR
E15	1	1	AG=14 CFR 39--- 5051
E16	1	1	AG=14 CFR 39---22426 73---22427
E17	1	1	AG=14 CFR 71 (2 DOCUMENTS)---20401,20572
E18	1	1	AG=15 CFR 29B ---4715
E19	1	1	AG=17 CFR 15---20402 140--- 20572
E20	1	1	AG=17 CFR PARTS 239 AND 274
E21	1	1	AG=18 CFR 157 --- 4716
E22	1	1	AG=18 CFR 284---13267
E23	1	1	AG=19 CFR 10 ---4793 101 ---4717

?

PressPgDn ↓ PgUp ↑ Home for more

Figure 9.15

> 999999 command (Figure 9.17).

A variation of this technique is to search for data that begins with one or more character(s) that are invalid for that field, e.g. **ST=J$**, or **SC=18$** for a U.S. state code, or an SIC code. Alternatively, one might search for an anticipated or common typo. An excerpt from such searches in various databases sheds some light on the accuracy of data (Figure 9.18). This author's surname provides a good example for such searches (Figure 9.19). All-consonant Eastern European names, long Thai and Indian names are also good candidates for such a test.

Plausibility searching can come in handy with some fields whose value range is likely to be within certain logical limits. A publication year larger than the current year is likely to be an error, except for forthcoming books in *Books In Print*, or future events in a conference calendar database. Similarly, a birth year smaller than 1900 or larger than 1970 **(YR < 1900 OR > 1970)** in a who's-who directory of corporate executives is likely to be an error. In these types of searches, one would expect zero or very low postings.

For textual fields one might browse the field-specific index or search for the valid values, if the number of possible values is not too great. The type-of-document field, for example, may show a high amount of incorrect data as in the *Federal Register* example in Figure 9.20.

In some databases, certain data elements must be congruent to be valid. The same D-U-N-S code must always refer to the same company, the same ISSN must refer to the same journal name. Picking a few codes randomly and combining them with their textual 'mate' using the exclusion (NOT or AND NOT) operator will zero in

```
Search  Browse  Format  Action  Options  Languages                BiblioDisc

                          Publisher
      McGraw                                                            2
      MCGRAW HIL                                                     1800
      McGraw Hill                                                      29
      McGraw Hill Book Co                                               8
      McGraw Hill Ryerson                                               1
      McGraw Hill, Inc., Health Professions Division, PreTes            1
      McGraw Hill-Ryerson                                               1
      McGraw-Hall                                                       1
      McGraw-Hall Book Co. (U.K                                         1
      McGraw-Hall Ryerson                                               1
    ▸ McGraw-Hill                                                    3989

                                              ENTER ->Select  ESC ->Quit

Search  Browse  Format  Action  Options  Languages                BiblioDisc

                          Publisher
      McGraw-Hill                                                    3989
      McGraw-Hill (UK                                                   2
      McGraw-Hill [[distributor                                         1
      McGraw-Hill [Distributor                                          8
      McGraw-Hill B. Co                                                 1
      McGraw-Hill Bk. Co                                                6
      McGraw-Hill Bk. Co. (UK                                           3
      McGraw-Hill Book                                                  2
      McGraw-Hill Book Co                                             144
      McGraw-Hill Book Co. (U.K.) [distributor                          1
    ▸ McGraw-Hill Book Co. (UK                                         12

                                              ENTER ->Select  ESC ->Quit

Search  Browse  Format  Action  Options  Languages                BiblioDisc

                          Publisher
      Macdonald, Queen Anne Press                                       2
      Macdonald/Orbis                                                   2
      MacDonald/Queen Anne                                              3
      Macdonald/Queen Anne Press                                        1
      Macdonld                                                          1
      Macfarlane Walter & Ross                                         13
    ▸ MacGraw-Hill                                                      8
      Mackenzie Art Gallery                                             4
      Mackenzie Institute                                               1
      Mackenzie Institute for the Study of Terrorism, Revolu            4
      Maclean Hunter                                                    7

                                              ENTER ->Select  ESC ->Quit
```

Figure 9.16

on erroneous records, e.g. **du(08-146-6849)** and not **co(microsoft)**. Even if the postings are low, it is unnerving to see mismatches (Figure 9.21). In this example, the D-U-N-S number of MCI has been assigned to nine different companies, and that of Microsoft assigned to four different companies. The good news is that, in this case, the database producer promised to correct the errors, and indeed did so. The

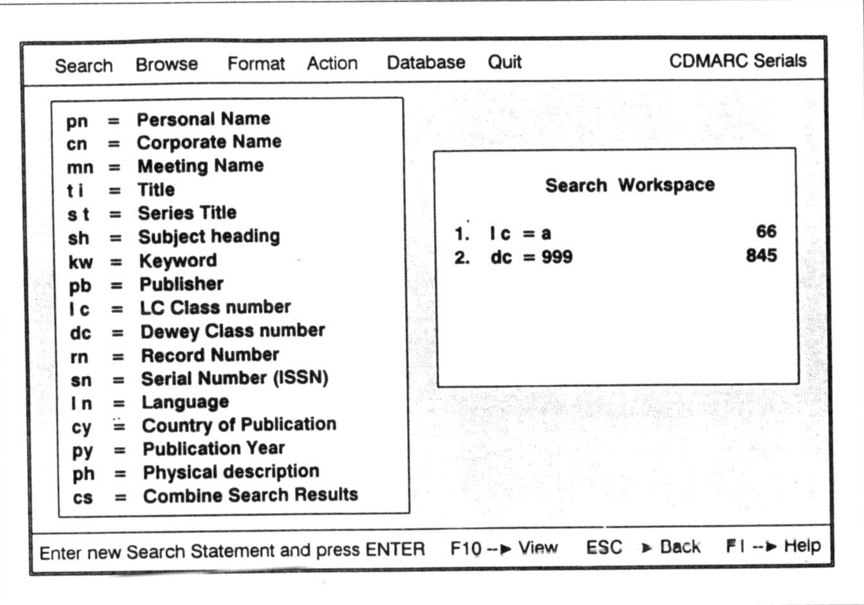

Figure 9.17

testing technique, however, remains valid for other databases.

Some errors are generated during the database creation process. PAIS cannot be blamed for the incorrect conversion, in its SilverPlatter version, of the diacritic characters (ö, ü) in thousands of German language corporate names, and journal titles such as *Eosterreichische Leanderbank*, *Meunchen Beorse*, or *Zeurcher Zeitung*

	Library Literature	ERIC	INSPEC	LISA	ISA
accommodat?	14	1979	9269	277	429
accomodat?	0	287	1	52	209
acquisition?	2210	13380	28676	3009	3362
aquisition?	0	9	1	21	23
government?	2091	33946	13670	6574	6412
goverment?	0	20	1	12	18
knowledge	467	36061	60894	3918	6645
knowlege	0	32	2	9	22

Figure 9.18

	JACSO	JASCO	OTHERS
ABI / INFORM	5	1	0
COMPENDEX	4	0	0
ERIC	4	1	0
INSPEC	23	0	1
ISA	11	7	0
LIBLIT	11	0	0
LISA	21	2	1

Figure 9.19

instead of *Oesterreichische Laenderbank*, *Muenchen Boerse*, *Zuercher Zeitung*, or the plain unaccented formats *Osterreichische Landerbank*, *Munchen Borse*, *Zurcher Zeitung*.

Similarly, the American Psychological Association cannot be blamed for the universal misspelling of *Portuguese* as *Portugese* in the language field in all records in the Compact Cambridge version of its database. Fortunately, the language index

```
Ref     Items Postings      Index-term
E4        398      398      DT=CORRECTIONS
E5          2        2      DT=DEPARTMENT OF AGRICULTURE
E6          5        5      DT=NOTICE
E7     11,143   11,143      DT=NOTICES
E8          3        3      DT=PRESIDENTAL DOCUMENTS
E9         75       75      DT=PRESIDENTIAL DOCUMENT
E10        33       33      DT=PRESIDENTIAL DOCUMENTS
E11         1        1      DT=PRESIDETIAL DOCUMENT
E12        17       17      DT=PROPOSED RULE
E13     1,335    1,335      DT=PROPOSED RULES
E14         1        1      DT=READER AIDS
E15         1        1      DT=RULE AND REGULATONS
E16         1        1      DT=RULES AMD REGULATIONS
E17         1        1      DT=RULES AND REGUALTIONS
E18         9        9      DT=RULES AND REGULATION
E19     1,718    1,718      DT=RULES AND REGULATIONS
E20         1        1      DT=RULES AND REGULATIONSI69
E21         1        1      DT=RULES AND REGULATIONSRULES AND REGULATIONS
E22        13       13      DT=RULES AND REGULTIONS
E23         9        9      DT=SUNSHINE MEETING
E24       577      577      DT=SUNSHINE MEETINGS

?
                  PressPgDn ↓ PgUp ↑ Home for more
```

Figure 9.20

90-34206
Title: West Germany to Sink $33 Billion into East's Public Net
Company: **Deutsche Post Telekom (DUNS: 04-476-0643)**

90-18818
Title: Every Market Needs a Different Message
Company: **Saatchi & Saatchi Advertising Worldwide (DUNS: 04-476-0643)**

90-12526
Title: Names in the News
Company: **Morimoto Manufacturing Co (DUNS: 04-476-0643)**

90-02615
Title: Growing Pains
Company: **Sierra Central Credit Union (DUNS: 04-476-0643)**

90-02139
Title: Trends in International Connectivity
Company: **Overseas Telecommunications Inc (DUNS: 04-476-0643)**

89-08479
Title: A Specialty Lines Underwriter Provides "Family Security"
Company: **WH Brownyard Corp (DUNS: 04-476-0643)**

87-13287
Title: Not-for-Profit Systems Centralize Financial Functions as They Grow
Company: **Catholic Healthcare West (DUNS: 04-476-0643)**

87-13280
Title: Some Troubled Hospitals Discover Creative Solutions to Avoid Closing
Company: **Beloit Memorial Hospital (DUNS: 04-476-0643)**

87-13248
Title: Choosing Sides in Twin Cities
Company: **LifeSpan Inc (DUNS: 04-476-0643)**

90-32775
Title: E-Mail for LANs: Redefinig Corporate Networking
Company: **Coca-Cola Foods Ins (DUNS: 08-146-6849)**

90-25815
Title: Bargain-Hunting
Company: **Zeos International Inc (DUNS: 08-146-6849)**

89-44416
Title: IMR Interview: James G. Kollegger
Company: **EIC Intelligence Inc (DUNS: 08-146-6849)**

Figure 9.21

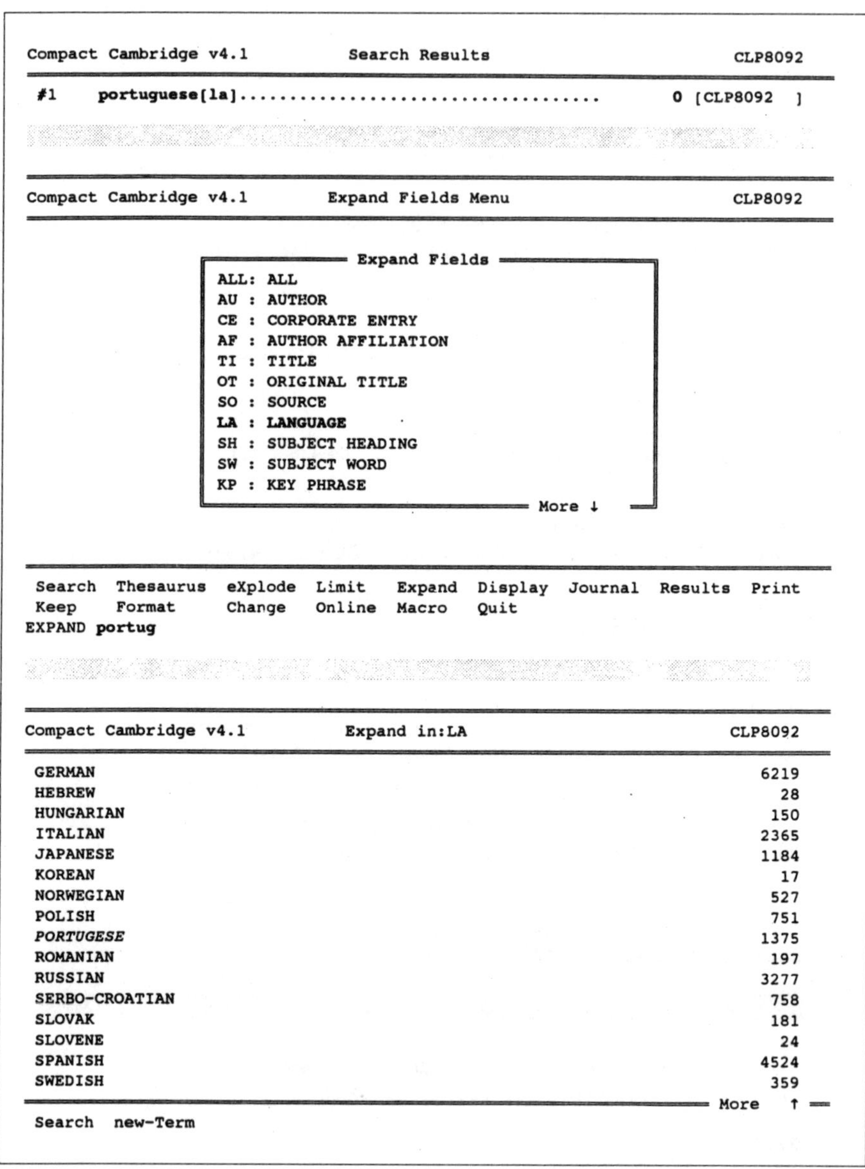

Figure 9.22

can be browsed, and after a surprising 0 hit search, a user has a chance of identifying the consistent misspelling (Figure 9.22). Consistency is appreciated, even if it is a consistent *inaccuracy*, because of the ease of adapting the search. Unfortunately, consistency in general is too often a problem.

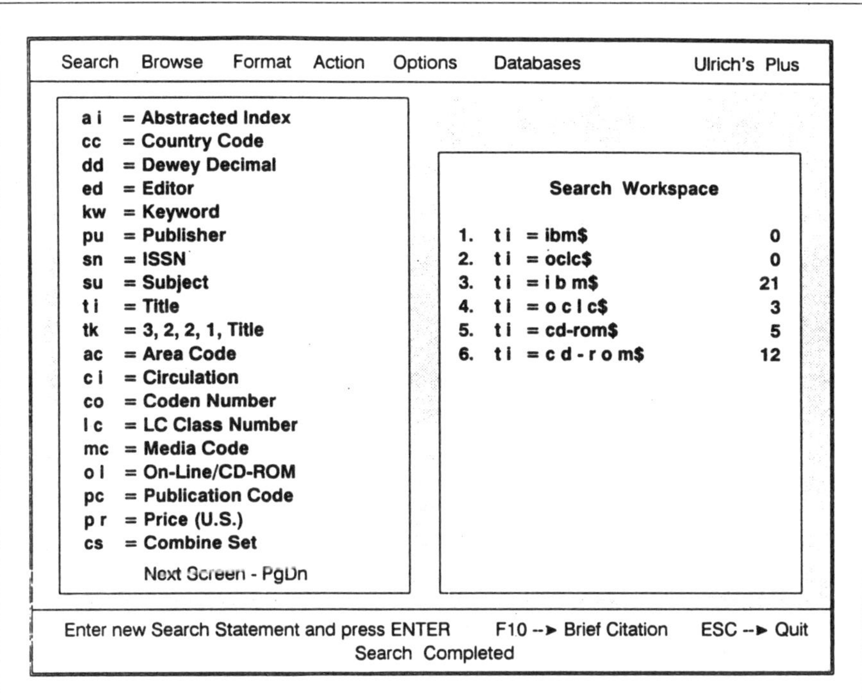

Figure 9.23

Inconsistency

Many database creation and search programs are prepared to handle 'natural' inconsistency; this 'comes with the territory' of processing disparate sources in compiling a database. Of course, it is up to the datafile producer to determine to what extent the software facilities are used to minimize the effects of inconsistency. The software in itself cannot help if the datafile producers do not do their part by creating correct and consistently-used cross references.

Source documents often use widely varying terminology, spelling and transliteration for the same concept, for names of persons or products, for titles of journals, and for geographic locations. Controlled vocabularies and authority files are often used to assign consistent access points to records about, e.g. CD-ROM, personal computers, Muammar Kadhaffi, AT&T Bell Laboratories, John Wiley and Sons, Beijing, the Journal of ASIS, and so on, so that the user can find all relevant records, irrespective of variations.

This, at least, is the theory. The question is whether the datafile producer is consistent in applying controlled vocabulary terms. Browsing and searching in the field-specific indexes (author, journal name, subject heading, document type, language, etc.) will tell a lot about consistency as well as accuracy. Sometimes it is

```
                 S&P Executive File

           Set   Items  Description
           ---   -----  -----------
      ?E BN=NETHERLANDS
      F1-Help  F2-Search

      Ref      Items Postings      Index-term
      E1          36        36      BN=MEXICO
      E2           6         6      BN=MOROCCO
      E3          68        68     *BN=NETHERLANDS
      E4          11        11      BN=NEW ZEALAND
      E5           2         2      BN=NIGERIA
      E6       5,421     5,421      BN=NONUS
      E7          15        15      BN=NORTHERN IRELAND
      E8          27        27      BN=NORWAY
      E9          25        25      BN=PAKISTAN
      E10          6         6      BN=PALESTINE
      E11         18        18      BN=PERU
      E12         44        44      BN=PHILIPPINES
      E13         86        86      BN=POLAND
      E14         15        15      BN=PORTUGAL
      E15          1         1      BN=PUERTO RICO
      E16         27        27      BN=ROMANIA
      E17         26        26      BN=RUSSIA
      E18          1         1      BN=SAN DOMINGO
      E19          2         2      BN=SAUDI ARABIA
      E20         86        86      BN=SCOTLAND
      E21          3         3      BN=SINGAPORE

      ?
                          PressPgDn   for more

      Ref      Items Postings      Index-term
      E22          2         2      BN=SLOVENIA
      E23         62        62      BN=SOUTH AFRICA
      E24          2         2      BN=SOUTH WALES
      E25         12        12      BN=SPAIN
      E26          4         4      BN=SRI LANKA
      E27          1         1      BN=SUDAN
      E28          1         1      BN=SURINAM
      E29         37        37      BN=SWEDEN
      E30         53        53      BN=SWITZERLAND
      E31          1         1      BN=SYRIA
      E32         13        13      BN=TAIWAN
      E33          4         4      BN=TANZANIA
      E34          3         3      BN=THAILAND
      E35         12        12      BN=THE NETHERLANDS
      E36          1         1      BN=TOBAGO, W.I.
      E37          3         3      BN=TRINIDAD
      E38          3         3      BN=TUNISIA
      E39         25        25      BN=TURKEY
      E40          4         4      BN=U. K.
      E41          1         1      BN=UGANDA
      E42          7         7      BN=UKRAINE
```

Figure 9.24

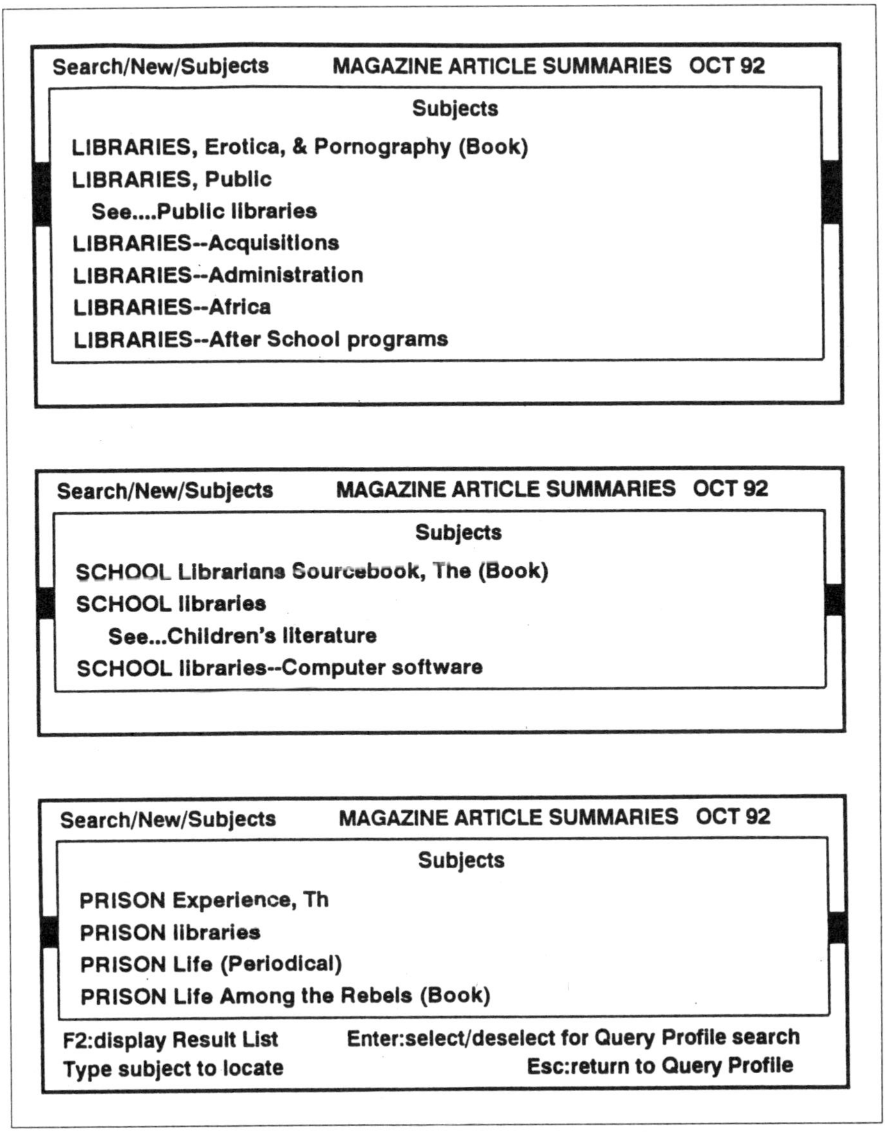

```
Search/New/Subjects        MAGAZINE ARTICLE SUMMARIES   OCT 92
                              Subjects
 LIBRARIES, Erotica, & Pornography (Book)
 LIBRARIES, Public
   See....Public libraries
 LIBRARIES--Acquisitions
 LIBRARIES--Administration
 LIBRARIES--Africa
 LIBRARIES--After School programs
```

```
Search/New/Subjects        MAGAZINE ARTICLE SUMMARIES   OCT 92
                              Subjects
 SCHOOL Librarians Sourcebook, The (Book)
 SCHOOL libraries
    See...Children's literature
 SCHOOL libraries--Computer software
```

```
Search/New/Subjects        MAGAZINE ARTICLE SUMMARIES   OCT 92
                              Subjects
 PRISON Experience, Th
 PRISON libraries
 PRISON Life (Periodical)
 PRISON Life Among the Rebels (Book)
F2:display Result List      Enter:select/deselect for Query Profile search
Type subject to locate                     Esc:return to Query Profile
```

Figure 9.25

arguable whether an entry is inaccurate or inconsistent. From the searcher's point of view, both types of quality problem may have the same effect: the non-retrieval of relevant records.

It is discouraging to see that Bowker does not consistently apply, for example, its own subject headings for the term *CD-ROM*. It is a disservice in itself that the subject heading is spelled with a space between the letters, since it is never spelled this way in the literature. But the real problem is that Bowker's own indexers seem

	RGA	MAS	RES-1
American Telephone & Telegraph Bell Laboratories	0	4	0
AT&T Bell laboratories	40	3	35
Bell Laboratories	see ref	0	39
Cambodia (and subdivisions)	270	25	349
Kampuchea (and subdivisions)	see ref	12	82
Burma (and subdi visions)	77	25	181
Myanmar	0	18	40

Figure 9.26

to ignore this spelling rule from time to time (Figure 9.23). The unwary user may miss 40 per cent of the relevant records when searching for serial publications with CD-ROM in their title, as it is spelled variably as *CD - ROM* and *CD-ROM*.

Similar inconsistencies are found in the publisher name, subject heading and country name indexes. These types of inconsistencies are particularly dangerous because the variants often occur several screens apart, and a user may not check beyond the current screen. In the Executives subset of *Standard & Poor's*, there are 68 entries in the country index for *Netherlands*. The user might easily overlook the 12 entries for *The Netherlands*, since these are not on the same screen (Figure 9.24). Because the field is phrase-indexed, the search command **S BN=NETHERLANDS** would not retrieve these 12 records either.

The problem is less dangerous if the inconsistent entries are adjacent to each other in the index, so that searchers are likely to spot them when browsing. When an index cannot be browsed, this type of problem is more difficult to identify. Spending a few minutes browsing the various indexes can certainly give an indication of the overall level of a database's quality.

Change over time in subject headings, corporate names and country codes are unavoidable, even in a database that uses controlled vocabulary. These unavoidable changes may become crippling inconsistencies unless cross references are unfailingly applied. Cross references (*see* and *see also* references) and thesauri were meant to handle such situations as the change of Burma to Myanmar, an author writing under a pseudonym, the spelling of gypsy moth versus gipsy moth, or the alternative use by indexers of the terms *euthanasia* and *right-to-die*.

It is usually a sign of poor quality when neither cross references nor a thesaurus is available in a database. It is alarming when the software does not allow one to browse field-specific indexes. The SPIRS software, for instance, has a combined index of terms created from the title, abstract, subject heading and a few other fields. This lumping together of terms makes it hard to check the quality of fields with controlled vocabulary. Even worse, some other fields (language, document type, publication year, country code, SIC code) that are indexed are not browsable at all. Apart from

```
                                                                     1 of 8
TI: The new concept of HYPERBASE and its experimentation on the 'First Emperor of
China' videodisc.
AU: Ching-chih-Chen; Miranda-S.; Seidel-S.; PROJECT-EMPEROR; EMPEROR-PROJECT;
SOPHIADOC
DE: Technical-processes-and-services; Information-storage-and-retrieval;
Information-retrieval; Subject-indexing; Computerised-information-storage-and-
retrieval; Computerised-subject-indexing; Subject-indexing; Hypertext; Hypermedia;
China; History; Interactive-videodiscs; Videodiscs

                                                                     2 of 8
TI: Hypermedia information delivery: the experience of the PROJECT EMPEROR-1.
AU: Chen-Ching-chih; Project-Emperor
DE: Technical-processes-and-services; Information-storage-and-retrieval;
Information-retrieval; Subject-indexing; Computerised-information-storage-and-
retrieval; Computerised-subject-indexing; Subject-indexing; Hypertext; China;
History; Interactive-videodiscs; Videodiscs

                                                                     3 of 8
TI: Potential of videodisc technology for international information transfer
AU: Chen,-Ching-chih; EMPEROR-project
DE: Interactive-videodiscs; Videodiscs-; History-; China-; Audio-visual-materials

                                                                     4 of 8
TI: The potential of the interactive videodisc for international cooperation as
documented by Project Emperor-1
AU: Ching-chih-Chen; Chen,-Ching-chih; Emperor-project
DE: Interactive-videodiscs; History-; China-; Audio-visual-materials

                                                                     5 of 8
TI: Wu Tung on Project Emperor-1: an interview
AU: Project-Emperor; Emperor-project
DE: China-; Computers-; Discs-; Optical-discs; Storage-media; Videodiscs-

                                                                     6 of 8
TI: Sample interactive courseware development on the use of PROJECT EMPEROR-I
videodiscs
AU: Chen,-Ching-chih; EMPEROR-I-Project
DE: Terra-cotta-army; Archaeology-; Videodiscs-; Audio-visual-materials

                                                                     7 of 8
TI: Interactive videodisc and 'The First Emperor of China'-online access to multi-
media information
AU: Chen,-Ching-chik; EMPEROR-project
DE: Interactive-videodiscs; Videodiscs-; Audio-visual-materials

                                                                     8 of 8
TI: Online information and interactive videodisc technology: case presentation about
PROJECT EMPEROR-1
AU: Chen,-C-C
DE: Interactive-videodiscs; Videodiscs-; Disc-storage; Storage-media; Technical-
processes-and-services; Information-storage-and-retrieval; Information-retrieval;
Subject-indexing; Computerised-information-storage-and-retrieval; Computerised-
subject-indexing; Subject-indexing
```

Figure 9.27

its use in quality checking, a field-specific index helps users learn and select the correct publication types, country names, language names, date format and so on.

Equally problematic can be the halfhearted use of cross references. Users tend to feel safe and let their guard down when they see cross references. They believe that they will always be reminded if an alternative term is used, but this is not so. EBSCO's *Magazine Article Summaries* provides a *see* reference from *Libraries, Public* to *Public Libraries*, but there is no cross reference from *Libraries, Prison* or

TI: Automatic merging of monographic data bases-use of fixed-length keys derived from title strings

DE: Computerised-detection; ***Duplicates-; Duplicates-***; Redundant-records; Bibliographic-records; Records-; ***Searching-***; Detection-; On-line-information-retrieval; Technical-processes-and-services; Information-storage-and-retrieval; Information-retrieval; ***Subject-indexing***; Computerised-information-retrieval; Computerised-information-storage-and-retrieval; ***Searching-; Searching-; Subject-indexing***; Computerised-subject-indexing; ***Subject-indexing***

Figure 9.28

Libraries, School to *Prison Libraries* or *School Libraries*, even though these subject headings have been assigned (Figure 9.25).

Checking a few notorious terms may give an overall feeling for consistency in cross referencing. Figure 9.26 shows the findings for a few terms from databases competing in the general interest periodicals market: *Magazine Article Summaries* (MAS), *Resource One* (RES-1) and *Readers' Guide Abstracts* (RGA).

Alternatively, searching for a specific subject can reveal how consistently the appropriate terms are assigned. Searching for articles about the videodisc product *Project Emperor* reveals a disappointing level of inconsistency in the *Library and Information Science Abstracts* (LISA) database (Figure 9.27). Considering the subject of this database and the fact that it was produced originally by the British Library Association (now maintained by G.K. Saur), the negligent treatment of descriptors throughout the database is particularly appalling.

Sometimes, even a casual look at records raises doubts about the quality of a database. Glancing through the subject headings of a few records in LISA shows that quantity does not make quality. The redundant assignment of the same subject headings two or three times within a record (Figure 9.28) shows up in tens of thousands of records and gives the impression that these apparently computer-generated subject heading assignments are not checked by human beings. The overall redundancy of the subject headings may have originated in the early 1960s, to provide cross references in the printed version of LISA.

Conclusion

Quality improvements can only be expected if users let datafile producers and database publishers know about the quality problems in their databases. Equally important is the need to systematically include the results of such tests as we have

Sample Database Label

Name: MYOB
Number of records (06/92) 251,523

Producer: CSUCSUSA
Quarterly increase : cca. 3,400 records

PERIOD COVERAGE	
From:	01/69
1969	4,470
1970	5,035
1971	4,935
1972	5,659
1973	5,932
1974	5,932
1975	5,980
1976	6,372
::::::	:::::::::
1990	13,040
1991	11,198

TIMELAG IN LAST UPDATE	
same quarter	7.2%
-1 quarter	9.4%
-2 quarters	6.2%
- 3 quarters	32.8%
- 4 quarters	17.9%
>1 year	26.5%

SOURCE COVERAGE	
Width and spread of coverage	
Active titles	87.2%
Concentration factor	90/56
Depth of coverage	
Cover-to-cover	70.0%
Selectively	25.0%
Occasionally	5.0%
Geographic source of publications	
USA	62.0%
Britain	11.0%
Netherland	7.0%
Italy	3.5%
Germany	3.4%

CONTENT	
Journal articles	71.9%
Conference papers	15.9%
Conference proceedings	7.1%
Books	3.0%
Dissertations	1.6%
English language documen	85.0%
Average length in characters	
Record w/o abstract	215
Abstract	305
Average descriptors/record	3

ACCESS POINTS	
Title	100.0%
Conference title	23.0%
Author	100.0%
Author affiliation	15.2%
Journal name	71.9%
ISBN	2.8%
Named Person	2.0%
Descriptor	99.2%
Publisher	27.5%
Editor	22.7%
Publication year	99.7%
Document type code	49.4%
Abstract	22.6%

- Abstracts are added to records from June, 1984
- Foreign language articles w/o English summary have no descriptors
- Some additional access points are available occasionally.

Figure 9.29

described in product reviews, in order to warn fellow users about problems so that they can search defensively.

There are other quality criteria that are worth closer scrutiny. These include the timeliness of databases, and their real scope and coverage. The techniques for discovering these quality problems are beyond the scope of this chapter but are discussed elsewhere by this author (see Notes).

In the ideal world, I would like to see an impartial advisory board label (Figure 9.29)[3] on each database package, in advertisements, documentation, and on introductory help screens.

The number of CD-ROM databases made for commercial distribution will dramatically increase as the cost of CD-ROM production continues to plummet. The jury is still out on whether these databases will bring along with them fewer or more quality problems. I hope for the former, of course, since many of these products are likely to be new and interesting sources of information not previously available in database form.

Notes

1. Basch, Reva (1991), 'The Secret World of SF=', *Database* **14** (February), 13–18.
2. Basch, Reva (1990), 'Database Reliability: The Black Box', in: *Proceedings of the 11th National Online Meeting*, 31–6.
3. Jacsó, Peter (1993), 'A Proposal for Database Nutrition and Ingredient Labeling', *Database* **16** (February), 7–9.
4. Jacsó, Peter (1993), 'Searching for Skeletons in the Database Cupboard. Part I: Errors of Omission', *Database* **16** (February), 38–49.
5. Jacsó, Peter (1993), 'Searching for Skeletons in the Database Cupboard. Part II: Errors of Commission', *Database* **16** (April), 30–6.
6. Jacsó, Peter (1992), 'Champagne Promises and Beer Realities – CD-ROM Users Beware', *Information Today* **9** (December), 25, 28.
7. Jacsó, Peter (1992), 'What is an Update? Currency Test Searching of Databases', *Database* **15** (June), 28–33.
8. Mintz, Anne P. (1990), 'Quality Control and the Zen of Database Production', *Online* **14** (November), 14–23.
9. Pagell, Ruth (1991), 'It's Greek to Me! Exchange Rate Translations and Company Comparisons', *Database* **14** (February), 21–7.
10. Quint, Barbara (1989), 'Caveat Searcher: Liars, Damned Liars, and Statisticians', *Database Searcher* **5** (October), 36–7.
11. Quint, Barbara (1989), 'Quality Control and Pricing Policies of Database Providers and Search Services', *Wilson Library Bulletin* **63** (March), 78–9.
12. Tenopir, Carol (1990), 'Database Quality Revisited', *Library Journal* **115** (October 1), 64–7.
13. Williams, Martha (1990), 'The Quality of Information'. Keynote speech at the National Online Meeting, May 1, 1990, New York.

Part IV

LIABILITY ISSUES

Chapter 10

SELECTED ASPECTS OF LEGAL LIABILITIES OF INDEPENDENT INFORMATION PROFESSIONALS*

T. R. Halvorson, Attorney at Law,
Sidney, Montana

Introduction

In this paper, I intend to:

- Review our fields of practice as independent information professionals (IIPs)
- Review ways in which an IIP might get into trouble
- Review types of lawsuits that might relate to our practices as IIPs
- Examine a series of conventional wisdoms about why such lawsuits would not be brought against us
- Consider forms of protection against liability.

Our fields of practice

The fields of practice represented by members of the Association of Independent

*Based on a paper delivered at the Seventh Annual Conference of the Association of Independent Information Professionals, San Diego, CA, 26 March 1993

Information Professionals (AIIP) are broad. Our members are engaged in:

- Document delivery (purchase, photocopy or loan)
- Preparation of bibliographies
- Literature searches, manual and computerized
- State-of-the-art reviews
- Handbook preparation
- Translations
- Library organization, development and collection maintenance
- Information systems development
- Technical writing
- Editing
- Data collection and interpretation
- Location and referral to experts
- Assistance in the selection and hiring of library and information personnel
- Speech writing
- Indexing
- Instruction and training.

Ways of getting into trouble

You can get into trouble if you:

- Deliver false data
- Deliver incomplete data
- Deliver out-of-date data
- Are late in fulfilling a search request
- Make an inaccurate report of the source information
- Fail to identify a source
- Fail to interpret the request accurately
- Fail to ascertain the purposes for which the information is requested
- Correctly answer the question, but do not answer the correct question
- Misguide the expectations of the client
- Commit parameter negligence; i.e. you neglected to consult the correct source
- Commit omission negligence; i.e. you consulted the correct source, but failed to locate the correct answer(s)
- Misrepresent yourself to obtain information which otherwise would be denied you
- Misrepresent the work you can perform
- Perform 'sloppy' searching
- Perform incomplete searching
- Engage in industrial espionage
- Present 'half-baked' research
- Do something illegal, e.g. copyright infringement

- Purposely give false information
- Breach client confidentiality
- Breach source confidentiality
- Accept vendor kickbacks
- Cross into another profession; practicing law or medicine at the reference desk in lieu of requiring the client to seek a lawyer or a doctor.

Causes of action

The law refers to different kinds of suits as *causes of action*. Some of the causes of action which could relate to independent information professionals are:

- Breach of contract
- Breach of warranty
- Breach of representation
- Malpractice (professional negligence)
- Negligent misrepresentation
- Fraud, deceit, intentional misrepresentation
- Product liability
- Breach of trust
- Deceptive business practices
- Misappropriation of proprietary information
- Copyright infringement
- Trademark infringement
- Theft
- Defamation (libel and slander)
- Breach of confidentiality.

We will devote our attention to breach of contract, breach of warranty and malpractice. In common speech we might use the term *malpractice* very generally to refer to any sort of wrong a professional might commit. In the law, however, it is a type of negligence, the negligence of a professional.

Conventional wisdom: it hasn't happened yet

The orthodoxy is, 'No one in this profession has been sued yet'. It is a theme you will find repeated throughout the literature. That is not a fact. It has happened.

An intermediary may be liable if, due to an inadequate search, his client suffers losses. In Germany, for instance, a court held a patent and engineering information service responsible for not having used updated materials. The court came to the conclusion that the information service had grossly infringed on its duties towards its clients.[1]

Conventional wisdom: elements of the claim and burden of proof

In the information context, the elements of a claim for professional negligence or malpractice can be stated more specifically as:

1. the information supplied was faulty in the sense of being either

    a. false
    b. inaccurate
    c. incomplete
    d. out of date
    e. imbalanced

    in some material way
2. reliance on the faulty information was a contributing factor to the economic loss suffered, in the sense that the information requested was material to the event or transactions that resulted in injury or damage
3. the reliance was reasonable and justified in the circumstances;
4. the faulty information was due to the intermediary's negligence, in

    a. failing to identify readily available, relevant, generally reliable sources of information, or
    b. failing to access the sources competently to identify and retrieve the information needed, or
    c. failing to communicate the results of the search in a timely or accurate way.[2]

There is a presumption of professionalism. The plaintiff in a civil suit has the burden of proving each element of the claim by a preponderance of the evidence. Conventional wisdom holds that a client would not sue in the face of these obstacles.

Jury instructions explain *preponderance* in varying language. Opinions differ, but I believe that when a damaged plaintiff is effectively displayed to the jury, the separate elements tend to blur into one general sense of whether the professional did something wrong.

The very term *professional* works against defendants in the minds of juries. Their majorities usually are not professionals. They expect plenty from anyone who so designates himself. Damages, plus a general sense of wrongdoing, are the paramount persuaders.

What we are betting on in this conventional wisdom is the advocacy theory of plaintiff's counsel. What does plaintiff's counsel believe about the way juries think? This conventional wisdom assumes counsel thinks juries truly separate the elements of the claim and require proof by a preponderance on each one.

Conventional wisdom: shared responsibility

Information flows downstream. At the headwaters is the information provider. As we follow the stream we encounter the service provider, the software developer, the network provider, the searcher and finally, the confluence with the river of end users. At every reach, persons have responsibilities. Any one might breach and their breaches might contribute to damage. This includes the end users themselves.[3]

When a client sues a searcher, the searcher might raise the defense of contributory or comparative negligence on the client's part, and might raise the negligence of those upstream. The searcher could join those upstream into the suit as third-party defendants.

A conventional wisdom holds that because of confusion created by this aura of shared responsibility, clients are unlikely to sue. That does not take account, however, of the behavior of plaintiffs' counsel in other areas.

In product liability cases, for example, there is a parallel stream from materials provider to manufacturer to wholesaler to distributor to retailer to user. Depending on a number of factors, plaintiffs' counsel in those cases might sue all of them, some combination of them or just the retailer, hoping the retailer will join some of the others as third-party defendants. Do not count on lawyers not acting habitually when bringing suit in the information industry.

Once in court before the jury, the shared responsibility defense can look like finger-pointing. It can look like a blame game that does not take the client's damages or the searcher's fault seriously. This can produce jury resentment and judgment. It was, after all, the searcher who directly raised expectations, took money and disappointed the client.

Conventional wisdom: time, trouble and expense of litigation

Litigation is 'A machine which you go into as a pig and come out as a sausage'.[4] According to conventional wisdom, the time, trouble and expense of litigation would dissuade a client from suing. It is true that litigation is protracted, troublesome and expensive. It is hard to anticipate, however, how this will affect the client's decision whether to sue.

The novelty of this kind of suit makes it difficult for plaintiffs' counsel to gauge time and expense at the initial stage. If they guess wrong, it might actually encourage suit by seeming more simple than it really would be.

Even assuming perfect guesses, the client's decision is not necessarily made with the lawyer's knowledge of the litigation process. A lawyer owes the client a duty to explain the litigation process before taking the client's decision. If you have had experience with litigation, you might know something about the surprises you learn along the way, surprises you wish you had known before deciding to litigate. If you were a plaintiff, you might have decided not to sue had you known what you learned later. That experience could be recapitulated in the experience of your client.

Time, trouble and expense are not stopping the large volume of litigation already under way in this country. There are various ways of accounting for this, but on one account or another, the suits go on.

Conventional wisdom: limitation of damages recoverable

A number of rules limit the damages recoverable in civil suits. In actions for breach of contract, the standard measure of damages is the difference between the value received and the value paid. In an information case, this is the difference between whatever value the faulty information might have and what the client paid for it.

In contract cases, there is a limitation against recovery of what the law calls *consequential damages.* Consequential damages are the economic damages the client suffered in the business transaction as a consequence of using the false or incomplete data.

Conventional wisdom holds that the limitation of damages in contract suits would dissuade a disgruntled client from suing. This view considers breach of contract claims in isolation, not in their context among alternative claims.

The rules of civil procedure allow for pleading different claims based on different theories of legal liability. The claims can be pleaded in the alternative and may be inconsistent.

These rules let a client sue a searcher not only for breach of contract, but for malpractice, breach of confidentiality and whatever else the client thinks the searcher did wrong, all in one lawsuit. Malpractice sounds in tort, not contract, where the limitation of damages in contract cases does not apply.

Another rule, in *Hadley* vs. *Baxendale (9 Ex. 341 (1854))*, allows a plaintiff to recover consequential damages only if the defendant knew or should have known of them at the time of the formation of the agreement between the parties. Conventional wisdom holds that this would insulate the information professional from exposure to consequential damages. That rule might be fine as an insulator for other kinds of defendants, but for information professionals I believe it would not be so fine.

Information professionals have an obligation to assist clients in determining their true information needs. This is achieved in part by the reference interview. A properly conducted interview often will put the information professional on notice of consequential damages that could be incurred as a result of a negligent search. To plead the *Hadley* v. *Baxendale* rule could amount to a confession of negligence and leave the information professional in a 'should-have-known' position.

On another level, leaving aside the damages a client might be awarded, people sometimes sue for other reasons. Plaintiffs commonly account for their decisions to sue with statements like 'It's the principle of the thing', or 'The guy was such a jerk when I told him I wasn't happy', or 'I wanted to stop this from happening to the next person'. We have to recognize these motivations and qualify our sense of security based solely on the pecuniary motive for suit.

Conventional wisdom: the poverty defense

Dr Marilyn Levine enunciated what John H. Everett called 'the poverty defense':

> The only people who sue are those who stand to gain something, and so far they have nobody so big to sue that they can gain more than their lawyer costs.[5]

Everett wisely qualifies this notion and warns his readers, but you still find it repeated in the literature.

Lawyers are taught to sue the 'deep pockets' and courts tend to hold those pockets liable. That much is true. The addition of just one firmly-established legal principle to the deep pockets theory of liability can get our shallow ones picked in someone's lawsuit. This principle is known as *vicarious liability*, the law that one can be liable for the faults of another.

Let us use the example of medical literature searching. In *Harbeson* vs. *Parke Davis, Inc. (746 F.2d 517 (9th Cir. 1984))*, the US Court of Appeals for the Ninth Circuit held that the doctrine of informed consent requires a physician to furnish a patient with sufficient information to make an informed decision about his care. This included a duty to provide the patient with current information reasonably available in the medical literature. The physicians were not aware of the threat Dilantin posed to the unborn. Studies linking the drug to birth defects were reported in the medical literature, however, at the time of the patient's decision. The court held that physicians have a duty to acquaint themselves and their patients with this information.

With the explosion of medical information and medical literature, a physician can hardly keep abreast of it. Physicians must rely on medical librarians. As leaders of health care teams, physicians are liable for the negligence of nurses, therapists, and other attendants working under their supervision.[6] This can extend to the medical librarian.

> If a medical librarian becomes associated with a professional liability action, it will probably be as part of a case against a physician through the legal doctrine of vicarious liability. This is where one party (the physician) who may be entirely innocent of any personal fault, is considered responsible for the negligent actions of another (the librarian). If a physician engages a librarian to perform a literature search, it is the physician who is held responsible if a patient suffers because the search was deficient.[7]

At the least, this will get the medical literature searcher involved as a witness in depositions and trial testimony. Conceivably it could involve the searcher as a party, because of independence.

Vicarious liability rests on the power of supervision and control. It is thought right to hold liable one who could have prevented the harm by supervision and control of the person who actually was negligent. This power usually exists between employer and employee. The medical librarian employed by a hospital, clinic or other institution probably is subject to sufficient supervision and control to apply the principle of vicarious liability.

Does the basis for vicarious liability apply with equal force to the independent medical information specialist? This specialist is not an employee but an independent contractor. Might doctors attempt to show that the independent information professional is sufficiently independent to render vicarious liability inapplicable?

Here's a scenario. Because of deep pockets and vicarious liability, the patient sues the doctor for the librarian's malpractice. Not to get into our pockets, but to protect his, the doctor sues the librarian to show the librarian's fault and sufficient independence to avoid vicarious liability.

This is only a scenario. Perhaps it is improbable. But it is reason enough to reconsider the poverty defense. The poverty defense is not airtight. And, as observed above, a plaintiff might sue because 'I wanted to stop this from happening to the next person', or other reasons not answered by our poverty.

Conventional wisdom: the helpful librarian

A number of authors have pointed to the image of the helpful librarian as a barrier to being sued. The patron's concept of the librarian impedes the thought of suing.

That is affected somewhat by the fact that reference services used to be performed without fees. The Restatement of Torts says where only economic loss is suffered, the gratuitous character of the provision of false information precludes liability for negligence.[8]

In the traditional library setting, the image of the helpful librarian might have some efficacy. But America didn't used to sue Marcus Welby, M.D. Now we sue him every day. As independents, we never were Marcus Welby.

Our image is no defense.

Conventional wisdom: incorporation

Businesses incorporate for a number of reasons, not the least of which is limited liability. The liability of investors is generally limited to what they pay for stock.

Legal opinions differ on whether incorporation provides limited liability for professional malpractice of information professionals. It does not do so for the malpractice of doctors, lawyers, accountants, architects, engineers and other professionals. If ours is to be treated as a true profession, it won't for us.

I *would* incorporate because it might help. Judges come from the ranks of lawyers and may be as divided in their opinions as lawyers are. You might get lucky and have a judge who thinks it provides limited liability, or be sued before the courts universally recognize us as professionals.

Conventional wisdom: insurance

Insurance often does not cover breach of contract, dishonesty, fraud, crimes, malicious acts, property damage and personal injury. You should not need to worry so much about dishonesty, fraud, crimes and malice. You should be able to avoid them. Lack of coverage for breach of contract, property damage and personal injury are serious concerns, however.

You need to know that professional insurance might not be available to cover what we do. I have looked at the policy language of a few policies currently held by information professionals, and while it will help with problems that can occur in what some of us do, I am not satisfied that the coverage they provide is broad enough for us to rest easy.

Even if you do find a policy with adequate coverages, you need to know that policies are of different types. *Occurrence* policies protect against covered claims that occur when the policy is in force regardless when claims are made. *Claims-made* policies require that the claims be made within the policy term. *Risk tail* insurance provides retroactive coverage for claims made after you leave the profession.

Conventional wisdom: disclaimers

Generally speaking:

1. a disclaimer which is delivered only simultaneously with or after delivery of search results probably is not part of the contract and probably is ineffective
2. disclaimers can be rendered ineffective by express contract terms, express warranties, express representations, brochures, letters, advertising and verbal puffery
3. agreements are not effective against negligence founded on breach of statutory duty
4. agreements are not effective against negligence where a particular statute renders them invalid
5. agreements excluding liability or limiting remedies for future negligence are strictly construed
6. there is not much you can do with a disclaimer to avoid liability for fraud, deceit, intentional misrepresentation, product liability, breach of trust, deceptive business practices, misappropriation of proprietary information, copyright infringement, trademark infringement, theft, defamation or breach of confidentiality
7. the more our profession is treated like doctors, accountants, architects, engineers and other professions, the less disclaimers will be effective against negligence.

Some poor disclaimers

A number of disclaimers in use by independent information professionals have been reported in the literature. Most of them include language that might cause more trouble than the balance of them are worth. Consider these words:

> Our staff uses the most appropriate, most current sources available
>
> Our staff makes every effort to verify facts and check on the accuracy of the information provided
>
> Every effort is made to ensure the accuracy of information provided.[9]

Do we really want to take on responsibility for checking the accuracy of information retrieved from an online database and call that a disclaimer? Do we truly make 'every effort'? What is the inventory of efforts that 'every' would include? Scrutinize the language and try to view it from a damaged client's perspective. Then edit it.

Drafting considerations

The best disclaimer I have seen thus far is one reportedly used by Susan Feldman at Datasearch:

> The Datasearch contract includes the following under 'Limitations of Liability': Datasearch makes reasonable and diligent efforts to obtain accurate information for clients and uses authoritative sources of information, including online databases, such as DIALOG, and respected reference works. However, Datasearch does not warrant that it will find all possibly relevant articles on the named topic. In addition, Datasearch makes no warranty as to the accuracy of the information in the databases, reference works, and other materials gathered, and disclaims any liability for errors in the information, data, and other materials provided to clients under this agreement. Unless explicitly stated in writing, Datasearch provides information but does not analyze it. Evaluation of the value and accuracy of the information, data, and other materials provided is the responsibility of the client, and any reliance upon these sources is at the client's own risk. Datasearch explicitly disclaims any liability for any incidental or consequential damages resulting from such client reliance.[10]

To that I would add:

1. We provide the service of retrieving information and acting as a conduit to deliver to you the information as supplied by sources 'as is' and 'with all faults', within the budget and time constraints, query and source parameters, and other limitations specified by the client and relying upon information supplied by the client

2. We have never said the data would be error-free or without defects, or if we did, we are now correcting, retracting and withdrawing that statement and warn you that, although we have relied on sources commonly used in the market, it might have errors or defects
3. No warranty, either expressed or implied, including but not limited to those of merchantability, fitness for a particular purpose, arising from a course of dealing or arising from usages of trade are made
4. You have not informed us of any fact indicating that or putting us on notice to inquire whether the information will be used by any third persons.

Be aware that disclaimers must be conspicuous.

The true defense: competence

Your best defense is competence. 'Even if effective, no clause could protect an information provider who is grossly negligent'.[7]

Let us consider the standard of care and the sources of the standard of care in negligence cases. Then we will look at ways to avoid trouble.

Standard of care

Section 299A of the *Restatement of Torts, Second* sets forth the undertaking of persons in a profession or trade as:

> Unless he represents that he has greater or less skill or knowledge, one who undertakes to render services in the practice of a profession or trade is required to exercise the skill and knowledge normally possessed by members of that profession or trade in good standing in similar communities.

Section 552(1) of the same source, captioned 'Information Negligently Supplied for the Guidance of Others' says:

> One who, in the course of his business, profession or employment, or in any other transaction in which he has a pecuniary interest, supplies false information for the guidance of others in their business transactions, is subject to liability for pecuniary loss caused to them by their justifiable reliance upon the information, if he fails to exercise reasonable care or competence in obtaining or communicating the information.

The specific applicable standard and whether the defendant conformed to the specific standard are questions of fact to be determined by the jury. The plaintiff will be required to introduce evidence of what the specific standard involved in the case is. There are a number of possible sources for specific standards which a plaintiff might use. These sources could include:

- how the searcher represented himself or his service
- testimony of other professionals who state the standard that they consider applicable to the circumstances of the case
- ethical codes of professional organizations
- standards presented in the professional literature.

Self-presentation

'[V]erbal representations could also make such a [disclaimer] clause ineffective'.[12] The description of our services and promises we make in brochures often will form part of our contracts and will affect the standard of care for negligence claims.

> It should be noted that it is possible to raise the required standard of care by representations in advertising brochures, letters of introduction, or through verbal puffery. Any statement which could raise expectations relating to your ability could also raise your potential liability. Such expectations become the standard upon which the buyer can reasonably rely.[13]

Here are some clauses from brochures of independent information professionals:

> collect comprehensive company information
>
> a comprehensive computer and manual search of ...
>
> comprehensive database search to identify all publications and research reports authored by the individual

Is the information we collect about companies comprehensive? Does *any* set of databases allow a searcher to identify *all* publications and research reports authored by an individual?

These are express contract terms and unless a written contract is made before the search, or a disclaimer is delivered before the search, a post-search disclaimer probably will not help much against claims of breach of these terms.

Expert witnesses

While a profession is young like ours, plaintiffs might have difficulty finding witnesses they can qualify in court as experts to establish the standard of care applicable to particular cases. We have to anticipate, though, that some independent information professionals would be approached. If we do not agree to testify, members of other professional groups whose work overlaps with ours would be approached. We may find ourselves in court opposite special librarians, corporate librarians, reference librarians or others.

Ethical codes

We need to consider

> whether our professional association with each other constitutes an assumed knowledge base and behavioral code, by which a judge or jury could determine whether a defendant's behavior was indeed professional. Thus, codes of ethics and their ultimate purpose.[14]

The ethical codes of a number of library and information associations might be applied to the question of standard of care. The selection in a particular case probably would be based on membership of the defendant in one or more such associations.

The Code of Ethical Business Practice of the Association of Independent Information Professionals states, among other things, that members are expected:

- to give clients the most current and accurate information possible
- to help a client understand the sources of information used, and the degree of reliability which can be expected of them.

This language does not sanction simply dumping whatever some database says on the client's desk. We are to assess the comparative accuracy of sources, choose the most accurate, and explain the degree of reliability of competing sources.

How might this translate into particular circumstances? We all know, or should know, for example, about the several suits against Dun & Bradstreet and what has been publicly revealed about their information-gathering practices. Under the AIIP Code, are we not to explain this kind of thing to clients whom we know will rely on information from this source? The preamble of that Code says we are 'objective intermediaries between the client and the information world'. To me that implies an obligation to inform our clients.

Use of the AIIP Code to set the standard of care in malpractice cases might not be welcome. Perhaps we would want to follow what the legal profession has included in its Rules of Professional Conduct:

> The Rules presuppose a larger legal context shaping the lawyer's role. That context includes court rules and statutes relating to matters of licensure, laws defining specific obligations of lawyers and substantive and procedural law in general.
>
> Violation of a Rule should not give rise to a cause of action nor should it create any presumption that a legal duty has been breached. The Rules are designed to provide guidance to lawyers and to provide a structure for regulating conduct through disciplinary agencies. They are not designed to be a basis for civil liability.

That works for lawyers because they do have active disciplinary agencies. Since independent information professionals do not, incorporating a similar provision into the AIIP Code might not be useful. It would not hurt to insert an adaptation, however, remaining mindful that its effectiveness could depend on instituting disciplinary agencies.

Professional literature

The following 'Suggested Guidelines for the Ethical Behavior of Online Intermediaries' was published in *Special Libraries:*

1. The online searcher has an obligation to his/her institution and client to maintain awareness of the range of information resources available in order fairly and impartially to advise the client
2. The online searcher must strive to maintain a reasonable skill level in the systems available to him/her for searching
3. The online searcher must eschew bias in the selection of appropriate databases and systems in order to meet the needs of the client
4. The online searcher must make the client aware of the searcher's level of expertise in searching a given database or system if that may affect the search results
5. The online searcher should be aware of the level of confidentiality required by both the setting and the request, and respect those boundaries
6. The online searcher must make clear the appropriateness of the online search in meeting the client's needs, and the limitations of the search process for the client's intentions
7. The online searcher must guard against tendencies to fill the client's needs as the searcher sees them or as the client initially states them, but rather must utilize appropriate interview techniques to ascertain the client's needs
8. The online searcher must, if appropriate, apprise the client of major errors in previous searches, both in strategy formulation and database selection
9. The online searcher must resist attempts by the client to select inappropriate databases and/or systems.[15]

Clients would find the professional literature rich in material which could be used in court to set the standard of care in malpractice cases.

How to avoid suit

Avoiding parameter negligence

Parameter negligence can be overcome to a valuable extent by use of records. The court in *Fidelity Leasing*[16] looked at D&B's operating procedures and its adherence to them in the particular instance to determine liability for providing false information. Deviation from one's own procedures can be the definition of fault.

Records should include:

1. checklists of sources
2. the search strategies used for each source
3. the results obtained
4. the parameters of each source

    a. time period covered
    b. format (index, abstracts, full-text, etc.)
    c. from what sources it draws its data
    d. breadth of its subject coverage
    e. frequency of updating[17].

Avoiding omission negligence

Avoiding omission negligence is more difficult. Some efforts you can make are:

1. learn from experience to anticipate unexpected elements that may appear in a database and how such elements may elude your search
2. anticipate mistakes like these and attempt to compensate for them:

    a. misspellings
    b. inaccurate information
    c. typographical errors
    d. misclassifications;

3. try to verify the information you find by finding another source that substantiates it, and if you do not find one, caution your client
4. warn your client about possible inaccuracies in the database
5. pass through to the client copies of the database provider's disclaimer
6. keep up on issues involving fallibility of the data you are searching and the evolving nature of the information industry
7. acquaint yourself with the reputations of the databases for accuracy.

General avoidance of suit

Here are some guidelines for the general avoidance of suit:

1. be modest in your claims
2. be careful what you and employees say in brochures, sales talk and publicity
3. use good manners
4. practice competence
5. keep up on literature

6. attend conferences
7. invest in training and education
8. provide client education
9. make effective use of the reference interview
10. discuss how sources work, indexing, limitations, coverage, etc.
11. explain what you are going to do and what else might be done; ask how much of it the client wants done
12. explain what you have done
13. refuse work you can not handle well
14. refer, subcontract and network to deal with work overload and jobs beyond your expertise
15. keep records
16. establish, follow and refine complaint procedures
17. use written contracts
18. use disclaimers
19. report 'dirty' data
20. consider special disclaimers for D&B searches, because of, e.g. the *Greenmoss Builders* case.

Besides competence, the two keys are:

- Be careful what expectations you raise. To a large extent you form your client's impression of what to expect and whether you've performed well.
- Be careful how you treat clients who complain. Suits often are filed because of how you make a person feel after a problem arises.

Conclusion

Conventional wisdom about why independent information professionals would not be sued does not comfort me. After study of this topic, the best advice I can give is:

1. be careful how you present yourself and what you promise
2. use protections like disclaimers, corporations and insurance, but don't rely on them
3. apply your best efforts to perform your contract and comply with the standard of care
4. be decent and helpful when clients complain.

Notes

1. Sabine, Denis and Poullet, Yves (1990), 'Questions of Liability in the Provision of Information Services', *Online Review* **14** (1), p. 21 at 23–4, n. 4 (citing 'Doppelparker-case' (OLG Karlsruhe GRUR 1979 p. 267)).

2. Gray, J. A. (1988), 'Personal Malpractice Liability of Reference Librarians and Information Brokers', *Journal of Library Administration*, **9** (2), p. 78 (supplemented slightly).
3. Tarter, Blodwen (1986), 'Information Liability: New Interpretations for Electronic Publishing', *Online* **10**, 61–7, September.
4. Bierce, Ambrose (1906), *The Devil's Dictionary*, Mt. Vernon, NY: Peter Pauper Press, 1970.
5. Everett, John H. (1989), 'Independent Information Professionals and the Question of Malpractice Liability', *Online* **13** (3), p. 65 (6), May.
6. King, J. H., 'Vicarious Responsibility', in *The Law of Medical Malpractice in a Nutshell*, pp. 225-49, West Publishing Co., St Paul, MN, 1977.
7. Hafner, Arthur W. (1990), 'Medical Information, Health Sciences Librarians, and Professional Liability', *Special Libraries*, **81** (4), p. 306 (Fall).
8. Restatement of the Law of Torts, Second, Sec. 552, Official Comment. American Law Institute, Washington, DC (1965).
9. Everett, op. cit.
10. Ibid.
11. Pritchard, Teresa and Quigley, Michell (1989), 'The Information Specialist: A Malpractice Risk Analysis', *Online*, May 1, p. 57 (citing *Fidelity Leasing Corp.* vs. *Dun & Bradstreet, Inc.*, 494 F.Supp. 786 (E.D.Pa. 1980); *Kleartone Transparent Products Co.* vs. *Dun & Bradstreet*, 453 N.Y.S.2d 433 (1982).
12. Sack, Steven Michael (1986), 'Legal Puffery: Truth or Consequences; Even Casual Misstatements by Salespeople can put your company on the Wrong Side of the Law', *Sale & Marketing Management* **137**, October p. 59(2).
13. Pritchard, op. cit.
14. Mintz, Anne P. (1991), 'Ethics and the News Librarian', *Special Libraries*, January 1, p. 7, discussing Robert Hauptman, 'Professing Professionalism', in *Ethical Challenges in Librarianship* (Phoenix, AZ: Oryx Press 1988).
15. Shaver, Donna B., Hewson, Nancy S. and Wykoff, Leslie W (1985), 'Ethics for Online Intermediaries', *Special Libraries* **76** (4), 238–45 (Fall).
16. *Fidelity Leasing Corp.* vs. *Dun & Bradstreet, Inc.*, 494 F.Supp. 786 (E.D.Pa. 1980).
17. Pritchard, op. cit.

Chapter 11

DATABASE QUALITY AND LIABILITY: THE UK CAMPAIGN

Sandy Norman, Acting Assistant Director (Information Technology), The Library Association, London England

Introduction

Problems with the evaluation of databases, and with quality assurance as applicable to electronically-stored information, are not new. They have been aired many times since the advent of online databases. Over the last few years, however, the need to address these problems has become more acute with the increase in use of large databases, both online and CD-ROM, and with the rising expectations of users who have come to expect high quality products and recognized standards of control. Information professionals on both sides of the Atlantic have been addressing the problems of database quality. In the USA in August 1990, SCOUG (the Southern California Online Users Group) held a weekend retreat to formulate an action plan to devise a rating scheme for evaluating bibliographic, full-text and directory databases.[1] In the UK in 1991, The Library Association, in cooperation with UKOLUG, began their campaign with a one-day workshop to discuss the problems, suggest improvements and work out a strategy for encouraging database providers to adopt standards of quality.

This chapter is divided more or less into two parts. The first part gives a UK/European perspective on the need for quality assurance, concentrating mainly on the liability aspect, which affects everyone in the information chain from database providers to end-users. Database quality and liability have become inextricably linked. The second part outlines the activities of The Library Association and UKOLUG in the campaign for quality.

Database quality

Why do we need to encourage database quality?

- Because we, as information professionals, are concerned with giving the best and most accurate service to our clients or users
- We have certain professional standards to live up to
- We expect the services we buy to be of a reasonable quality. We do not want to spend time 'cleaning up' information before passing it on
- Last but not least, because we may be liable for providing a service which causes damage to a third party.[2]

Database evaluation

It is relatively easy to evaluate a book or a journal prior to purchase. The evaluation of print-based reference materials is well documented. Information professionals would refuse to accept a print-based work which contained numerous spelling or typographical errors, where the index contained non-existent words, had pages missing, or held duplicate records. We can see at a glance whether a book is out of date; we can browse the index and contents page and judge it accordingly. Print publishers have routine editorial controls to help eliminate errors.

There is a tendency to judge an electronic information service as something new and, therefore, an attitude that users need to be patient while this young industry sorts out its problems. But reading information from a computer screen is not much different from reading it from a book. Someone writes, someone else publishes it, and the user expects that, like a book, someone has made sure that the information is correct. Many books start life, before being printed, in electronic form.

What is different is the format, which, although it brings with it the possibility of opening up new avenues to information, is in practice very restricting. Evaluation, although possible, is not as straightforward. Databases, unlike books or journals, cannot be browsed; the indexes cannot be examined in detail by the typical user. The need for editorial controls in an electronic information service is even more necessary when words are used as search terms. One spelling mistake or typographical error in a person's name and the person becomes invisible. Entry is by specific search terms using command languages which change from system to system, and which range from relatively simple to extremely complex. Then there are the added restrictions of online time and cost.

Purchasing or leasing a CD-ROM product or subscribing to an online database involves considerable financial outlay. Choosing a suitable database service can be very hit-or-miss, and could prove to be an expensive mistake. Librarians report that since the proliferation of databases it has become more difficult to choose which product is most appropriate for their library. Reviews are valuable but tend to be general and not application-specific. Once a system has been chosen and is in place, it is difficult to withdraw, despite the fact that it may be mediocre, without upsetting users.[3]

Error detection

Most information professsionals are aware that mistakes occur in electronic information and that not all of them, e.g. real word errors like *form* and *from*, *nuclear* and *unclear*, can be easily identified and corrected. This can obviously be dangerous in certain situations. With tables and financial statements, evaluation of accuracy becomes even more difficult. Data can also be corrupted by file transfer. Who knows how much data may be lost in the process? Producers have admitted that whole files sometimes fail to be loaded.

With the increase in end-user searching, search results may not always be questioned as to their relevance, value for money or precision. End-users are not as skilled as information professionals in evaluating the data, and many believe that what comes out of a computer must be accurate. This is what Hepworth calls 'acts of faith at the keyboard.'[4] Blind faith in the system may not matter too much to an individual doing some private research for a leisure pursuit, but to a company wanting credit ratings for a client, or a health professional looking up drug effects, accurate, current and complete information is essential. The success of CD-ROM, its enthusiastic adoption by end-users, has implications for librarians who have to spend far more time training on search strategy and educating users about the limitations in content, and the lack of reliability and accuracy of data.[4]

Many database providers do their best to correct errors; sophisticated error detection and correction mechanisms do exist.[5] Many spelling checkers can correct all types of spelling errors regardless of their source. Users have been asking for some time which suppliers use them, to what extent they are used, and to be given assurance that they work. Checking for duplicates should also be an integral part of search software.

It is possible to alert users to errors. User pressure has succeeded in pushing one company, NewsNet, to provide an error-logging mechanism – the FIXIT command – whereby the user becomes involved in error detection and reporting. User pressure has achieved other notable successes as well.[6] It was revealed at a EUSIDIC Conference in 1992 that DataStream International UK, in order to show confidence in their quality management, actually gave £10.00 to any subscriber who spotted an error in their databases.

Cleaning up information costs money; having to check increasing quantities of information before passing it on costs money, too. Information professionals are becoming more vocal about the quality of the products they use. They are under pressure to provide a quality service in order to prove their worth in today's troubled times. In the UK, the cutbacks in the public service sector are forcing libraries to provide the best customer care in order to stay in existence. In the private sector, librarians have always been accountable, but the situation is now even more acute. In the UK, unfortunately, unemployment among special librarians has grown considerably over the last few years. To independent consultants, a quality service is their life's blood.

Liability

Users of information expect their information to be reliable and accurate. If it isn't, then someone, perhaps the one who passed the information on, is at fault and could be blamed. This brings us to the question of liability. The author would like to emphasize that she is not a lawyer but an informed information professional only, and is addressing liability issues from this perspective.

Who takes the blame for providing misleading, inaccurate or incomplete information from an online or CD-ROM database which could lead to damage, either economic or personal? Mistakes and problems can occur at every stage of the search process: the original author who may have some facts wrong; the publisher who fails to spot errors; the database producer who misses a file; the indexer who misspells a vital entry term; the abstractor who overlooks an important concept; the online vendor/service provider who fails to update regularly; the software developer who has not adequately debugged the system; the telecommunications network provider who loses data in transmission; the searcher/intermediary who does not search thoroughly; the end-user who believes that that is all there is on a subject; or even the client who does not brief the intermediary adequately. One cannot always be sure whose fault it is. But the real question is: Who is *liable*?

Law of contract

To begin with, we must look at the law of contract for a partial answer. If we have a complaint about the quality of a product or service – be it a can of peas, an item of dry-cleaning, or a faulty car battery – we approach the store which sold it to us or provided the service. Between the supplier and the purchaser there is a tacit agreement or contract to sell and to buy certain goods or services. If the goods or service are not fit for the purpose for which they were intended, or are not of the quality that was expected, then the purchaser expects redress in some way. If we buy a faulty car, we take it back to the vendor to be fixed or replaced or have our money refunded. We are protected by consumer law.

It is not quite the same in the information world. At each stage of the construction of a database service there is some form of contract between two parties – author/publisher, publisher/database producer, database producer/host and so on. The question of quality of the product or service should be a matter between sets of parties. Our contract is usually with the end link of the chain – the online vendor or CD-ROM supplier – those to whom we pay our bills. If we have a contract with a client to provide specific information and the client is not satisfied, any complaint would be directed to us. Similarly, if we have problems with any part of the online or CD-ROM service, then it makes sense to direct our complaints to that service. However, this is not always as easy as it sounds, especially when it comes to the more serious charge of contractual liability. Online hosts and CD-ROM suppliers usually disclaim any responsibility for serious database problems. This will be discussed later.

In the UK, simple contracts of sale are covered by the *Sale of Goods Act 1973*, whereas contracts which involve a service are covered by the *Supply of Goods and Services Act 1982*. Anyone who supplies a product or service in the course of business is subject to this Act. Broadly speaking, this means that any person who supplies a commercial service is subject to its implications of undertaking to use reasonable care and skill in carrying out that service.[7]

Under the *Supply of Goods and Services Act*, 'business' is defined to include professions and the activities of any government department or local authority. So, not only is the online host/database provider/CD-ROM supplier subject to this law, but so are information professionals who provide a service for a fee. We could also be sued for failing to recognise that information provided to a client was liable to damage the client's interests.

But how valid is our concern? Is there a cause to worry? Although there has not been a case in the UK for information negligence or malpractice, this does not mean that there never will be. Litigation will not necessarily bypass information professionals. There are increasing warning signals in the professional journals about 'information liability' which should put us on our guard.[8]

Information is no longer considered free; information costs money and therefore has a value. Although the concept of 'information' has been defined by the courts as not being a form of property capable of being stolen, information is a tangible product and should be subject to quality control just like any other product.[9] Therefore, if the information is faulty in some way – in the manner of a defective motor vehicle which could result in an accident causing physical or economic damage – then someone is liable and must pay.[8] Quality assurance is therefore essential not just to maintain standards of information provision but also to avoid litigation and consequent bad publicity.

Law of tort

Even if you provide a free service you could well be accused of negligence under tort. What exactly is tort? In simple terms, tort rests upon the assumption that you have a duty of care to those around you and that, if you are negligent in some way, the injured party can take legal action. If, for example, you leave a skateboard in the middle of your garden path and the postman trips over it and injures himself, you could be accused of not taking reasonable care. What constitutes reasonable care would have to be decided by a court of law.

An example which has a bearing in the information provision area is the famous *Dun & Bradstreet* vs. *Greenmoss Builders* case, where Dun & Bradstreet, the credit reporting agency that provides financial information about businesses, erroneously reported to a client that Greenmoss had filed for bankruptcy. Dun & Bradstreet were sued, found liable and had to pay extensive compensatory and punitive damages.[10] There have been other cases of negligent mis-statements, but nothing specifically pertaining to our profession.

Another concern is what is called vicarious liability. The person who commits a tort is always liable for its consequences. In addition, if anyone has authorized the commission of a tort then that person is liable. A person can also be indirectly responsible for another's torts. So, one party who may be entirely innocent of any personal fault is considered responsible for the negligent actions of another. To give an example: in a medical library, a doctor could be sued for malpractice because of a deficient search by a librarian. Doctors have frequently been found liable for the negligence of nurses and other health workers under their supervision. Cases of vicarious liability are not new in the medical profession.[11]

However, there would be a greater risk if, because of this threat, we withdrew our professional help and left doctors to fend for themselves. Doctors have little time to keep up to date with new medical information; they rely on the expertise of information professionals. Without adequate training on search strategy techniques, doctors who attempted to search themselves could be subject to even more litigation. The 'satisfied but inept' end-user in the medical field may fail to realize that the search was not as thorough as it could be; it could lead to the wrong treatment for a patient and, at worst, death.[4] We are the information professionals; as such, we must act professionally and endeavour to supply a service using reasonable care and skill in order to avoid liability of any sort.

Liability exclusion clauses

Liability exclusion clauses are almost always part of the contracts between subscribers and online vendors or CD-ROM suppliers. An example of a typical small-print clause is as follows:

> While XYZ will seek to ensure that the information provided is accurate and up to date, XYZ makes no warranties or representations express or implied that the information is accurate and up to date or that it is suitable for any purpose, and will not be responsible for any errors or omissions in the information nor for any consequences of any errors or omissions.[9]

Whether this is enough to protect themselves is again a matter for testing in court, but who will do this? The UK *Law of Unfair Contract Terms 1977* states that exclusion clauses are subject to a test of reasonableness.[7] Is the above clause reasonable? It is a classic case of *caveat emptor*. The company cannot guarantee that the information is accurate, nor can it guarantee that it is of any use to anyone. Any user reading a clause like this would believe that there must be something wrong with the service if the information provider appears to be refusing to bear any responsibility. One reason given for the widespread use of such disclaimers is that there is no clear identification of the risks that may occur when disseminating information in this way.[10] One database provider, Brian Earle of ICC, stated publicly at the 1991 UKOLUG lecture at the International Online Information Meeting that contract liability disclaimers exist only in order to qualify for professional indemnity insurance coverage. This, too, indicates the lack of confidence in service responsibility, and the fear of litigation.

To be fair, it is difficult for any information provider to guarantee that all the information is accurate and up to date, and that it is suitable for any purpose. We know that hosts and CD-ROM suppliers are responsible for thousands of databases, some of which are of dubious quality. One host representative has admitted that they would be very willing to withdraw some of the poorer databases if enough pressure were put on them. Anyone who wishes to offer a quality service must take customer service into account. We are *their* customers, and we cannot make allowances if the service to *our* customers suffers as a result.

EC Draft Directive

Another issue for those of us in the UK is a proposed EC Directive on Service Liability.[12] The main feature of this directive is that it reverses the burden of proof. Under English law, it is up to the individual who has suffered damage to prove that negligence existed; under the EC proposal it would be up to the service provider to prove that they were not being negligent. Even if the service provider can prove that damage was caused jointly by a third party, the service provider will still be liable. Therefore if we, as suppliers of information, passed on to a client information gleaned from an online search which resulted in damage to the client, we could still be liable, even if we are not entirely to blame.

The EC Draft Directive is not as alarming as it sounds, however, since the definition of damage means (a) death or any other direct damage to the health or physical integrity of persons; or (b) any direct damage to the physical integrity of movable or immovable property (i.e. private property); and (c) any financial damage resulting directly from (a) and (b). So, although possible, given the preceding example from the medical sector, it is unlikely that we as information professionals would be too adversely affected by this directive.

It is our responsibility, however, to provide service that meets the normal standard expected from a member of our profession. We still have a responsibility to ensure that any information we disseminate comes from a reputable source, and that we have exercised our professional skills and judgement to ascertain that the information is reliable. Although this is not an unreasonable expectation, it could impose an unrealistic burden: Of course, we should check data before passing it on to a third party, but we can only verify so much. It is up to the database providers to give us assurance that their products are of good quality, or at least to indicate the limits of their reliability. Remarkably, liability exclusion clauses will not be permitted under the proposed EC directive.

To sum up the discussion of liability, we are caught in the middle of the information chain: We expect commercial database providers with whom we have a contract to supply a service using reasonable care and skill. When we pass on any information to a client, whether for payment or not, we have to exercise the same reasonable care and skill; we must make sure that the information is fit for the purpose for which it is required, and that our efforts will not result in a charge of negligence or vicarious liability. This begs the question: What is 'reasonable care and skill'? How is this defined, and how do we cover ourselves when providing information, the quality of which is out of our direct control? What do we do if we think our database producers have not exercised reasonable skill and care? How do we protect ourselves?

What to do to avoid liability

No-one is perfect; we all make mistakes. It is worth carrying out a risk analysis of your own service to see where you might be liable, and to take positive steps to avoid it.

We must be professional and be seen as professional. This is not an idle statement, since courts of law judge whether a professional acted with 'reasonable care and skill' according to the standards of that profession. To be a 'professional' is to be in possession of 'a standard minimum of professional knowledge and ability which is not shared by the general public'.[13]

Information professionals should look to their professional association for standards and guidance. The Library Association's Professional Code of Conduct states that: 'members must be competent in their professional activities including the requirement to keep abreast of developments in librarianship in those branches of professional practice in which qualifications and experience entitle them to engage'.[14] In other words, read the professional literature and keep up to date on developments which may affect your service.

Also, we should seriously consider having professional indemnity insurance for our services. Information professionals working for themselves might seek legal advice on this. Those working in an organization should consult their organization's legal advisers to see exactly who would be on the line in any liability case. The Library Association, among its benefits to members, has an arrangement with an insurance company to provide professional indemnity insurance.

Although it may not be seen as 'professional' to include liability exclusion clauses in contracts or service descriptions, clients should always be made aware of the exact limitations of the service being offered. A good information professional will be able to strike a balance between promising a wonderful service and scaring the client into thinking there is something wrong with it.[15]

The quality of our service rests partly on the quality of *their* service. We could be liable for their mistakes. We should not be afraid of complaining to the database hosts or CD-ROM suppliers when we feel that we are not getting full value from their service, e.g. too many duplicate records, incomplete records, and so on. We must not feel intimidated by disclaimers from vendors which state that they are not responsible for the quality of the databases, the information, the indexing, and so on, down the line. Our contracts are with those to whom we write the cheques. It is up to the hosts and CD-ROM suppliers to complain in turn to the next link in the chain. Along with quality comes liability. We can attempt to apply quality assurance to most of our own service, but not to a service which we cannot control.

The UK database quality initiative

The work on quality has been driven by the enthusiasm of a few committed professionals and the push and shove of a mass of disillusioned online/CD-ROM searchers from all library sectors. Enthusiasm has waxed and waned. Feelings of frustration and powerlessness have been common. At times, the work has taken an entirely different direction. Nevertheless, the message is getting through and progress, although slow, is being made. The example given to us by our colleagues in the US is acknowledged.

Background

The Library Association, on behalf of its members, has long been committed to improving the quality of information resources of all kinds, and to encouraging the development of standards. In 1989, a working party was set up by its Information Technology Committee specifically to look into database evaluation and database quality. The impetus for the project arose out of Jean Plaister's Library Association presidential address in October 1988, where she stressed that the proliferation of electronic databases, and the tendency for users to accept computer-derived information unquestioningly, meant that there was a demand for more and improved evaluation of online and CD-ROM databases.[16]

The working party included Jean Plaister herself, as well as an information consultant, the head of a business information service, the head of a city-based industrial library, and a school librarian, and was supported by the Library Association Information Technology staff. Although preliminary findings revealed that much had already been researched and published in this area, the working party identified two areas where work was needed which they felt would be of potential benefit to the information profession:

1. There was a need to promote awareness among the profession of the existence of published reviews and evaluations of databases. (Note: The aim was to produce a published listing of all user reviews. Despite many attempts to persuade various groups to undertake this effort, it has not yet been achieved. However, a database of such reviews, along with a clearing-house for problems, is underway, and is reported on elsewhere in this volume.)
2. There was a need for improvement in the quality of online databases. It was recommended that a workshop be organized to bring together an invited group of about 20 online practitioners, who could identify quality indicators and suggest areas for improvement in all aspects of database quality, with a view to influencing online database producers.

LA/UKOLUG workshop

The Library Association, along with UKOLUG (the UK Online Users Group), held a workshop on database evaluation in May 1991 to ascertain the problems and the interest and enthusiasm of the delegates in mounting a campaign to encourage database quality. Not for us the idyllic surroundings of a SCOUG retreat in sunny California. We had to put up with a room in LA headquarters in Ridgmount Street in London!

In order to concentrate solely on issues of concern to users, the invitations to attend the workshop were directed mainly at online practitioners and CD-ROM searchers, from all sectors of the profession, who had considerable experience of the problems. Once we had formulated some idea of what the users wanted, we felt we could then approach the database service providers with feedback and the offer of our own help. We felt also that it was crucial to invite those whose voices would be listened to – users who had spending power within their organizations, or who were recognized as an important voice by the industry.

The aim and objectives of the workshop were as follows:

Aim: To improve the quality of online and CD-ROM databases (information, access, retrieval and manipulation facilities)

Objectives: To define areas where quality assurance was essential.
To draw up a charter representing a minimum standard of quality that should be offered by providers of database services.
To seek ways of ensuring that the charter would be adopted by database providers.

Workshop leaders were given the charge to identify quality indicators and to suggest areas for improvement in all aspects of database quality. Workshop participants appreciated that database providers were working in a commercial environment, and that unreasonable demands for improvement which failed to recognize this would achieve nothing.

The idea of a 'charter' was nominal only. It could have been called a Bill of Rights, statement of principles, code(s) of practice, or model conditions of contract. As it happens, 'charter' was the right word, although at the time it was not seen as such, for the climate that followed. Customer charters have since become the 'flavour of the month' in the UK. There are charters for hospital patient care, rail travel and power services, as well as for some public library services. Every day a new charter appears. Our notion of a charter was just before its time!

It was hoped that the scope of 'the charter' might be a minimum standard for providers, or a list of recommended practices. There had to be a clear set of stated objectives. Rather than setting an absolute quality standard, it was felt that perhaps quality indicator thresholds should be defined. There could then be thresholds to reach, or exceed, which would give a competitive advantage. For example, database service A might provide the minimum standard of quality as defined in the charter, whereas database service B offers 'added extras' in terms of quality assurance. There would obviously be a price difference, but the consumer would be able to make a considered choice.

We thought, also, that the charter should focus on principles and on the end result, and not become an enumerative list of 'do's' and 'don'ts'.

There was a general opinion that efforts were being made by the larger 'supermarket' database providers to give good service, but that the main problems lay in individual databases, especially those produced on CD-ROM.

Workshop delegates realized that it was essential to recognize the work already begun by other groups and organizations and to draw upon it. For instance: EUSIDIC (the European Association of Information Services), which is active in the area of updating and correcting electronic databases; the CD-ROM Standards and Practice Action Group, which exists to promote the development of common standards and codes of practice throughout the UK CD-ROM industry; and of course SCOUG, the Southern California Online Users Group, which we discovered already had a well thought out comprehensive list of quality indicators.[1]

The group decided in the end that it was best to aim for a formal statement on quality assurance and to bring it to the attention of other interested organizations. It was suggested that we organize a forum in order to obtain an overview of the present initiatives in the area of standards, codes of practice and quality systems, and to identify any gaps.

It was also important to highlight the campaign, and a decision was made that the 1991 UKOLUG annual lecture at IOLIM (the International Online Information Meeting) in London would be on the subject of quality management in the online industry.

The workshop organizers were never sure that, by the end of the day, they would have any results to show for their efforts. It all depended on participants agreeing to the need for quality assurance, the idea of a charter, what to put in the charter, and how to proceed with the end product. Finally, a list of quality indicators and areas for improvement, if not an actual charter, was produced. This would be used as the basis for a core statement. A way forward had been identified.

Database quality forum

The subsequent forum was held in September 1991. It consisted of information consultants, representatives from database providers, the European Information Industry Association, EUSIDIC, CD-ROM SPAG, the British Library, the Office of Arts and Libraries (at the time, the Government ministry which looked after the public library sector; it is now called the Department of National Heritage), UKOLUG and the Library Association.

The discussion was interesting and constructive; it sent us off on an entirely new track which, for a time, left us without a coherent action plan. The main point to arise was that everyone in the information chain was responsible for providing quality service. The quality of the whole was dependent upon the quality of its parts.

The forum delegates also felt that some investigation was needed to set up a body which would work toward the development and accreditation of standards of database quality. It was envisaged that this would take up to five years to achieve.

Since that meeting, an informal LA/UKOLUG Task Force on Database Quality was set up on behalf of the consumer. This was mainly to keep the pot boiling, review progress and investigate the formation of an accreditation body. We prepared the following statement about the benefits of quality assurance to the supplier:

1. To identify the company as the supplier of a high quality service or product
2. To gain access to new markets (e.g. end-users)
3. To ensure that the service is right the first time, every time, within budget and timescale
4. To ensure that the quality of the system can be assessed by a prospective client
5. To ensure that the company is in a position to demand that its subcontractors meet its own in-house standards (e.g. a host in relation to a database producer).

What progress?

After the workshop and the forum, progress was slow. The knowledge that SCOUG had a thorough set of quality indicators gave us no incentive to develop ours further. There seemed to be no point in reinventing the wheel. Other organizations in Europe were keen for us to broaden our campaign to include quality management as a whole. 'Quality' has been adopted as a goal by many companies in the UK (though not necessarily by information companies!). Many are seeking accreditation under BS5750, and others are going for complete quality, or TQM.

The main progress has been in alerting information professionals to the problems. The Library Association produced information leaflets on the campaign and alerted users to the liability aspect. The LA has also produced a general Quality Information File to provide introductory information to members who are investigating quality.[17] At the 1991 UKOLUG IOLIM lecture on database quality management, it was evident that online hosts, at least, had been listening to the user community and were making a commitment to the concept of quality: 'The 1990s will be the decade of quality', said Richard Ream, a Vice-President of Dialog; Brian Earle, Managing Director of ICC, admitted that quality would be a key development not just for profit, but for survival.

The topic was also included in several professional conferences in 1992, including Database 2000 – the UKOLUG State of the Art Conference; the Library Association Industrial Group's 25th anniversary celebration; and the EUSIDIC Spring Meeting in Rotterdam, where David Minkoff of DataStream International UK was evangelic in his conviction that Total Quality Management was the answer.

And what next?

A database monitoring exercise is being planned, along the lines of the EUSIDIC telecommunications monitoring project, whereby all the users' problems could be discovered over a one-week period.

Also, arising from a discussion at the 1992 UKOLUG Conference in Guildford, Surrey, there is movement under way to set up a clearing-house centre, possibly funded in part by the online/CD-ROM industry itself, to which users could report all quality problems. The centre would forward each problem to the responsible party, and a response would be sent back to the user. This would not replace host help desks, but would remain an independent centre. It is hoped that both parties would benefit: the user would be able to identify problems, and the information providers would be helped to improve the quality of their service. A database of problems could then be developed. The centre would also maintain a database of published reviews. This was one of the important areas of work identified by the original Library Association Database Evaluation working party back in 1989. (See Chapter 13 for current developments in this area.) Both of these ideas can be put into practice. The will is there for them to happen. What is lacking at present are financial resources.

The database quality work just described has been successful in concentrating the minds of information professionals on the importance of quality in the products they use. However, there is still much to do.

Notes

1. Basch, R. (1990), 'Measuring the Quality of the Data: Report of the Fourth Annual SCOUG Retreat', *Database Searcher*, October, pp. 18–23.
2. Norman, S. (1992), 'Database Quality and Public Liability', In Armstrong, C. J. and Hartley, R. J., *Database 2000: UKOLUG State-of-the-Art Conference 1992*. Oxford: Learned Information, pp. 107–12
3. Nissley, M. and Nelson, N. M. (eds) (1990), 'CD-ROM Licensing and Copyright Issues for Libraries', Westport, CT: Meckler.
4. Hepworth, J. B. (1992), 'Developing Information Handling Courses for End Users', in Armstrong, C. J. and Hartley, R. J., *Database 2000: UKOLUG State-of-the-Art Conference 1992*. Oxford: Learned Information, pp. 67–75.
5. O'Neill, E. T. and Vizine-Goetz, D. (1988), 'Quality Control in Online Databases', in *Annual Review of Information Science and Technology (ARIST)*, **23**, p. 125–56.
6. Basch, R. (1992), 'An Overview of Quality Assurance Issues', in Armstrong, C. J. and Hartley, R. J. *Database 2000: UKOLUG State-of-the-Art Conference*, Oxford: Learned Information, pp. 85–91.
7. Sykes, Phil and Abell, Angela (1989), 'Liability for Information Provision: The Public Sector Experience', *Proceedings of the annual conference of the Institute of Information Scientists*, pp. 71–9.
8. Gray, J. A. (1980), 'Strict Liability for the Dissemination of Dangerous Information', *Law Library Journal* **82** (3) Summer, pp. 497–517.
9. Jones, D. (1990), 'Liability of Information Service Providers', *Library and Information Briefings*, **25**, 11/90.
10. Denis, S. and Poullet, Y. (1990), 'Questions of Liability in the Provision of

Information Services', Paper presented to the EUSIDIC Conference 1989. *Online Review* **14** (1), Feb, pp. 21–32.

11. Hafner, A. W. (1990), 'Medical Information, Health Sciences Librarians, and Professional Liability', *Special Libraries* **81** (4), Fall, pp. 305–7.
12. 'Service liability to fall upon libraries', *Library Association Record*, **94** (2) February 1992, p. 88.
13. Dragich, M. J. (1989), 'Information Malpractice: Some Thoughts on the Potential Liability of Information Professionals', *Information Technology and Libraries*, Sept, p. 265–72.
14. The LA Code of Professional Conduct. In *The Library Association Yearbook 1992*. London: LA Publishing Ltd, 1992. p. 150 para.2c.
15. Everett, J. H. (1989), 'Independent Information Professionals and the Question of Malpractice Liability', *Online* **13** (3) May, pp. 65–70.
16. Plaiste, J. (1988), 'Professionals Make Things Happen: Presidential Address, 11 October 1988', *Library Association Record* **90** (11), 11/88, pp. 637–41.
17. Quality Information File. The Library Association 1993.

Part V

THE ROLE OF USER GROUPS

Chapter 12

EVALUATING THE QUALITY OF FINNISH DATABASES

Ritva Juntunen, Elisabet Mickos and Tuulikki Jalkanen, VTT, the Technical Research Center of Finland, Espoo

Introduction

Online searches can falter on the strangest of obstacles: the connection breaks, the login procedure is changed, the password is not valid, the search statement is too long, the retrieved data is out of date, the manual does not give the help you need, you cannot search on essential fields, the invoice does not show how the sum was calculated. When one is using several online systems, the problems accumulate: the search languages and commands are different, the structure of the databases varies, every service has its own login procedure, charging and invoicing follow their own rules, the user contracts show great variety, and so on.

Besides these defects familiar to all experienced online users, the heterogeneity of databases and search programs forms an obstacle to their wider use. One of the obvious problems is the lack of – or indifference to – standards. In addition, there have been few appropriate channels for making claims or suggestions for improvement. The division of responsibilities among hosts, producers and coordinating bodies has not been explicitly defined. When the information is false or inadequate, the end-user tends to blame the one who retrieved the information. Who should pay for wrong decisions or lost opportunities?

During the past few years problems of this kind have been discussed in the professional press. It is interesting to notice that discussions and new projects have begun at much the same time in various parts of the world. Many of these projects have already been acknowledged by the hosts and producers of big international databanks, and some improvements are underway.

However, there are hundreds of local and national databases that cannot be reached by an international consumer movement of online users. In Finland we have had good experiences with a joint effort to evaluate Finnish databases and thus improve their quality. As this project has proved to be unique, we feel that online users in other countries might benefit from our experiences and perhaps start similar evaluation projects.

The Finnish database environment

Remoteness from the mainstream of information flow has forced Finland to be very active in the use of foreign databases and in the development of our own. Online services and usage in Finland are very strong; the Finnish online age started in 1974 with the use of international databases, and the first Finnish online databases appeared in 1975. The total user population (organizations and information service units) in Finland was estimated in 1989 to have been almost 3 000. A comparison with the USA and Sweden reveals that per capita hourly usage of online services in Finland is on the same level as in the USA and somewhat higher than in Sweden. Of this online usage, 78 per cent was of domestic and 22 per cent of foreign services.

A possible reason for the high usage of modern information retrieval methods is the high quality of information professionals and information services in Finland. One strong factor in that regard is the Finnish Society for Information Services, which has made great effort, for almost 45 years, to develop professional skills and information services. Another factor is the high production of domestic databases.

Small countries cannot, however, afford to use established international information retrieval software. They have to develop their own systems. Accordingly, we have in Finland several 'homemade' retrieval systems that do not strictly follow recognized standards or guidelines. They are not as sophisticated as the major international retrieval systems, yet they are continuously being improved. These developments and changes, as necessary as they are, are one reason for the consumer movement among database users in Finland.

Another reason is that the production of Finnish online databases is going through a dynamic stage. About forty new databases were made public in 1992; the total number of publicly available online databases in 1993 was well over 200. On the other hand, Finnish databases are normally specialized and small, typically containing from 1 000 to 10,000 references. The Finnish databases are produced by more than 100 different organizations, and made accessible by about 60 organizations using ten different command languages and various sorts of menus. In order to retrieve domestic information, the Finnish online user has to know several different login procedures and search languages, and a variety of database structures. Fortunately, the largest host offers access to more than 80 databases with the same login procedure and command language.

There have been various domestic and Scandinavian efforts to coordinate and simplify the online situation, but the lack of standardization in the Finnish online industry is still indisputable. Accordingly, it is not surprising that the practical database consumer movement started in Finland as early as 1988. In addition to the jungle of search and login/logout procedures, there was inconsistency in the retrieved information. Intermediaries realized that passing along incorrect information would be an economic catastrophe. All of these factors led to the start of a spontaneous online consumer movement to improve databases and online systems by testing and informing producers and hosts.

It is probably easier to influence the quality of domestic than international databases. The Finnish movement started with domestic databases, but the same methods and criteria can be used in every country by everyone.

Viewpoints and methods

The general and final aim of the evaluation project has been to improve the quality of Finnish databases. This can only be achieved if all parties involved in the database business are made aware of the inadequacies encountered by online searchers. Therefore, the purpose of the project was originally to collect, analyze and distribute information about the quality of databases.

The entire idea arose from the frustration of information retrieval professionals, who decided to form a working group for the evaluation of Finnish databases within the Finnish Society for Information Services. The group intended to maintain the practical viewpoint of the user. This initial position strongly affected the realization of the project, and determined the group's definition of the phrase 'database quality.[2]' This phrase would, no doubt, be defined quite differently by an online host representative, a producer, an amateur searcher, a scientist, a systems analyst or, indeed, a philosopher.

'Quality' is here understood to mean how the database serves a professional information retrieval specialist. The determinants of quality in this sense are validity, reliability and usability with respect to content, technical functioning and general ease of use.

A wide online search of literature and projects dealing with database quality was made in 1989. To the surprise of the working team, this search did not yield any guidelines or tools for the actual evaluation project. Therefore, the first part of the project was aimed at defining the concept of database quality, creating the criteria for measuring it, and making plans for the actual evaluation. This work, originally planned as a brief preparatory step, took over one year. Once the group had developed the tools, the actual evaluation process was fairly quick: it took seven months to evaluate eight databases and draw up a report.

The list of criteria for measuring database quality was gathered from several specific studies, and from the experiences of the team members, who were all experienced in online retrieval. To test the applicability of the criteria, a few sample searches were carried out. The list was then edited according to the searchers' comments on the relevance of the criteria. Internationally, such lists are often called 'wish lists', but the Finnish criteria list was, in fact, used for the evaluation of databases. As far as we know, a real evaluation of databases based on a set of specific criteria or a wish list has not been practised anywhere else.

The list of criteria drawn up by the Finnish group can be used as a tool for evaluating an existing database or as a checklist in the design of a new one. The criteria list given in the Appendix is more accurate and more complete than the one the evaluation panelists received. Their comments during the evaluation process were incorporated into the final list. Just like the databases themselves, this list has to be updated and 'quality controlled'. As there are different types of databases, it is obvious that not every criterion can be applied to every database.

The group carried out the initial evaluation phase as a peer review. Each database was scrutinized by a panel of two to four professional users, who made their comments on the basis of the criteria list. The voluntary panelists were experienced users of the database to be evaluated. The working group decided on a peer review method, i.e. panels of experts using a common list of criteria, for the following reasons:

- The panelists are themselves retrieval professionals and thus represent the user's view;
- Having several reviewers for each database reduces the danger of subjectively distorted views;
- The criteria list ensures that the same points are considered by each panelist.

The panelists' reports and comments were collected and analysed by a coordinator who, in collaboration with the working group members, then combined them into a final report.

Realization of the evaluation project

Following is a short summary of what the Finnish group did in order to improve the quality of Finnish databases:

- Formed a working group with seven information professionals as members;
- Made a preliminary plan;
- Arranged financial support from TINFO, a section of Finland's Ministry of Education;
- Made online searches of literature and projects dealing with database quality;
- Created the criteria for assessment;
- Tested the criteria;
- Chose eight different (reference, factual and full text) Finnish databases from four different online systems;
- Evaluated these databases with the help of 30 volunteers experienced in using the databases they evaluated;
- Drew up a 70-page report and made it public;
- Arranged a meeting of online hosts, producers and users;

- Decided to continue the evaluation of databases, if possible even to influence the quality of international databases.

Only a fraction of Finnish databases were reviewed in 1990. The working group realized that a one-time study would soon become obsolete. Therefore, they are now concentrating on planning a continuous monitoring system of Finnish databases, including systematic, regular reports to all parties involved. In this connection, international contacts and cooperation have been of great value.

Results of the Finnish project

The team's main discovery did not surprise anybody. The heterogeneity of, and defects in, today's databases forms an obstacle to their wider dissemination. This was established even more distinctly in another Finnish study where a couple of laymen tested Finnish databases and found them almost impossible to use.

The final report includes altogether over 50 pages on the quality of Finnish databases. This was actually the first time the contents and usability of these databases were objectively reported. Before, new users had only the hosts' brochures, which of course have a marketing purpose, to rely on. Without going into details about individual databases, some of the major problems will be presented here. These include insufficient information, poor user guidance, limitations in the search program, spelling mistakes and factual errors.

Informing users

In all the databases considered, the evaluators pointed out the need for increased and/or improved information about, for example, opening hours of databases, automatic disconnections, changes in the search programs, contents of databases, principles of content analysis and updating. They agreed that more detailed information on the costs of database use should be given both during retrieval and on the invoice. Information from database hosts or producers should, in the future, be more available in online form. Easier and faster delivery of original documents, by online ordering for example, should be emphasized.

Characteristics of search programs

The use of Boolean operators (AND, OR, NOT) was found unnecessarily difficult, rather limited or even impossible in some of the databases evaluated. Search programs would be more versatile if, in addition to the use of Boolean operators, it were possible to use left-hand truncation, character-masking in the middle of the search term, and proximity operators. Sorting the results of the search, saving the search strategy and having access to automatic selective delivery of information also contribute to search program versatility. (These limitations concern, in general, only the smaller online systems.)

Contents of and errors in databases

Users should be informed about the criteria used to select documents for the database. Up-to-date source lists should indicate, at least roughly, how thoroughly each publication is reviewed.

The lexicon and classification directories should be readily available and up to date. They should reflect new concepts and terminology. The use of lexicons and classification systems in information retrieval could be improved, for example, by enabling the online browsing of the thesaurus and the direct use of selected words in the search command.

In general, not many spelling or factual mistakes were discovered in the databases evaluated. This may be due in part to the fact that faulty documents are often not retrieved in searches. One database, however, abounded in typing mistakes, which indicates the necessity of using a spell-checking program at data entry. In another database, the panelists found a lot of incorrect or obsolete information, which was mainly due to ineffective updating.

Credit information

The evaluation program included four Finnish credit information databases. In this case, reliability of the data is essential. The evaluation was carried out as a joint venture between information specialists and end-users of credit information, e.g. heads of credit control departments. Online hosts and producers of credit information attended the panelists' meetings. Credit databases differ very much from 'traditional' reference databases. The criteria lists were therefore tailored especially; in particular, the criteria for quality of contents had to be reviewed. The views of information and credit professionals complemented each other. When users already know a database thoroughly, the effort to make a formal evaluation is not too tedious. In this case, however, the help of end users of credit information was invaluable. The database hosts and producers acted as a listening post, answering questions and giving further information when needed. Some faults were detected and these errors were immediately corrected by the producers.

Effects of the evaluation

The working group followed up later to see whether the quality of the databases and systems they had evaluated had changed at all. The group was happy to learn that some of the errors had been corrected. However, database producers reacted differently, even within the same host system: producers of commercial databases were more apt to correct the defects pointed out. The producers of legal databases proved to be the most resistant to change. It seems more difficult to influence general policy; it is easy to blame lack of money. However, we have been told that our report has speeded up the future action plan of one of the biggest hosts in Finland. We were left with the impression that database users are being taken much more seriously now, as a group of consumers, than before.

Guidelines for database evaluation

On the basis of the Finnish experiences, the following 12 guidelines were developed for online searchers wishing to evaluate and improve their databases.

1. Establish an evaluation group

According to our experiences a successful group contains the following elements:

- The group is formed within an established organization or society in the information service field;
- The members of the group are experienced online searchers with different backgrounds;
- The members have experience with different kinds of databases and online systems;
- The members are volunteers with a personal interest in the databases.

2. Organize the funding of the evaluation project

The economics of the project depend on different factors and have to be planned. Pay attention, for example, to the following possibilities:

- Arrange grants for the evaluation work;
- Use volunteers as much as possible;
- Ask for free passwords during the evaluation period.

3. Develop criteria or a wish list

For the evaluation, a list of significant quality measures must be made:

- Study documented criteria or wish lists;
- Make your own choice concerning criteria to be examined;
- Test the criteria in some databases;
- Adjust the criteria according to different databases and online systems.

4. Find a coordinator

The choice of a suitable coordinator for the work is very important. He/she should:

- Be online experienced;
- Be paid for the work;
- Participate in the group's meetings;
- Guide the panel groups;
- Summon the conclusions from the panel;
- Write the report with the assistance of the working group.

5. Choose the databases

In the choice of databases to be evaluated, pay attention to the following aspects:

- Start with popular databases;
- The databases should be of interest to the members of the group;
- The number of databases should be in proportion to the size of the group; do not choose too many.

6. Establish panel groups

Two to four professional searchers are needed for the testing of each database:

- At least one should be an expert in the content of the database;
- The panelists should be voluntary;
- A panelist should have a professional interest in improvements in the database.

7. Inform producers and hosts

All the concerned database producers and hosts should be informed about the testing of their databases:

- Ask for updated manuals and other information;
- Ask for free passwords for the evaluation period.

8. Test the databases

The panelists test the databases in cooperation with the coordinator:

- By following the criteria lists;
- By making necessary corrections/additions to the lists;
- By recording comments for the coordinator to collect for the report.

9. Present the results

Presentation of the results to the producers and the hosts is an important part of the evaluation. The coordinator:

- Compiles the report;
- Prints the report and makes it public;
- Informs producers and hosts;
- Arranges user and producer/host meetings;
- Informs the press.

10. Check for improvements and corrections

It is very important to check that desired improvements and corrections are made:

- Assign the panelists to check specific databases;
- Inform producers/hosts about the results.

11. Monitor databases

A single evaluation is not sufficient; continuous monitoring is preferable:

- Arrange financial support;
- Establish guidelines for monitoring.

12. Cooperate internationally

Join other evaluating groups and exchange experiences; cooperation will strengthen your efforts:

- Write articles about the evaluation process;
- Participate in online conferences;
- Participate in searcher discussions on computer bulletin boards;
- Cooperate with other national and international groups.

Conclusions and future aspects

An evaluation of database quality from just the user's viewpoint may seem somewhat narrow. However, the evaluation of Finnish databases from the professional searcher's perspective produced definite concrete results and initiatives for other investigations.

Continuous quality control of databases

Databases are dynamic products. Their content and structure undergo continuous development. Database development involves renewing existing databases or creating new ones. A single written report on the quality of a database becomes outdated and useless before long. Therefore, the aim of the Finnish database evaluation project has been to create a continuous quality control system that should include the most frequently used Finnish databases. Nevertheless, this project has only evaluated, to date, eight of the more than 200 databases that exist.

Development of the criteria

As there are different types of databases, it is obvious that not every criterion can be applied to every database. The subject focus may have more significance in respect to some quality requirements (e.g. medical information/verity of data contents). For example, during the evaluation it turned out that the emphasis in the criteria list is on bibliographic databases. The reviewers of factual databases remarked that several criteria were not applicable, and that for some aspects there were no criteria at all.

The use of factual databases is, however, so interesting these days that some Finnish university students are now studying various aspects of their quality and quality measurement. Full-text database search software and techniques are under development too. The efficiency of different full-text techniques is being investigated in Finland.

In the future, more attention should also be paid to international developments in database quality and its evaluation. Such cooperation will enable the further development of the list of criteria and other methods of database evaluation. These could later be developed into international standards.

Cooperation among database users, hosts and producers

Database development and the correction of defects call for more active cooperation among database users, hosts and producers.

Database hosts in many countries cooperate successfully with users via user groups. Several foreign database hosts have a contact person in Finland, or a national centre. Both give advice to users in addition to receiving feedback from users and transmitting it to the hosts and producers. The Finnish group wants to create a similar system for the users of Finnish databases.

Even during the first phase, the working group became fairly well known among Finnish database hosts and producers. When the evaluation report came out in March 1991, some hosts interpreted it as a set of hostile accusations against themselves. However, in a meeting arranged in the spring of 1991 for members of the group, hosts and producers, mutual understanding was reached, and an assurance of cooperation in the future. The meeting concluded by establishing user groups for all the evaluated databases. Some of these groups have already started working. The working group will actively follow and monitor the efforts of these individual groups.

The project and the final report have so far led to better communications among users, hosts and producers in Finland, which indeed was one of the original aims.

Future projects

The range of database characteristics to be evaluated is very wide. During this evaluation project, the group identified some additional issues that should, in the future, be examined as independent projects. Examples of such issues are:

- Contracts with database hosts: their coverage, details, guarantees, etc.;
- Brochures and manuals: their coverage, details, promises, etc.;
- Accuracy of factual databases;
- Separate evaluations of databases for experts (e.g. statistical, medical, legal);
- Ultimate responsibility for the quality of information.

It is of great importance that the quality of databases be studied continuously. Databases are not stationary either technically or in terms of content. New databases are born, some databases change, other ones disappear; the database situation is continuously changing.

Appendix

Criteria list

The criteria for quality assessment are divided into five categories: telecommunications, retrieval software, data contents, search aids and costs. The criteria list drawn up by the Finnish working group can be used as a tool for the practical evaluation of databases, as well as for designing a new database.

As noted earlier, the criteria list given below is more accurate and more complete than the one the evaluation panelists received. Their comments during the evaluation process have complemented the list.

1. Connecting to system and communications

- Are hours of availability given in manual/brochure/online?
- Are these hours suitable/adequate for users?
- Are terminal requirements mentioned in manual/brochure?
- Are alternative connection options mentioned in manual/brochure?
- Can database be accessed through 'kiosk' service or is user contract always needed?

- Are there frequent disturbances in lines (engaged, bad, dropping-off, etc.)
- Are lines crowded?
- Is number of access gates sufficient?
- Are there many steps in accessing?
- Does the system give explicit prompts and messages?
- Are upcoming changes announced in advance?
- Can user change his password by himself?

2. Search language and other technical aspects of the search

- Is search menu-driven or based on commands; is it possible to choose one or the other?
- Is search language very 'original'?
- Does search language resemble Common Command Language (CCL)?
- Can search commands be given in Finnish/English?
- Can commands be abbreviated (e.g. FIND or F)?
- Can one command sentence include several commands?
- Are upcoming changes announced in advance?
- Are error messages and prompts explicit?
- Does manual describe how incorrect key-ins can be corrected?
- Is an online help-desk available during search hours?
- Are response times reasonable?
- Is there a system message if response time will be slower?
- Can search processing be interrupted?
- Can search output (displaying/printing) be interrupted?
- Is there a time-out, i.e. no keystrokes for certain time breaks connection?
- How long is time-out?
- Does system remind user before breaking off connection?
- In such break-off, will search history be saved in memory?
- In involuntary break-offs, will search history be saved in memory?
- Is user ID then automatically freed?

3. Effectiveness of search program

Are the following features available/explained in manual:

- Logical operator;
- Positional operators;
- Truncation (right/left);
- Combining sets;
- Multi-file searches;
- Thesaurus;
- Free-text search;
- Search by fields;
- Temporary/permanent saving of search profiles;

- Selective Dissemination of Information (SDI);
- Scandinavian letters;
- Other special characters;
- Response time/intermediate messages from the system;
- Printing:
  Various print formats
  Online/offline prints
  Sorting results;
- Original sources:
  Full-text format/print
  Ordering online;
- Instruction messages from system in failure situation;
- Help online;
- Automatic disconnection;
- Deletion of duplicate hits in multi-file searches.

4. Content quality

- What is update frequency?
- Is it mentioned in manual/brochure?
- How current is material entered in each update?
- How often are corrections made?
- Are database contents explained thoroughly in manual/brochure?
- Is time span of material documented in manual/brochure?
- Is regional coverage of material documented in manual/brochure?
- Are source materials and choice criteria explained in manual/brochure?
- Is current source list available online/in print?
- Does source list mention which sources are included fully, which partially?
- If certain sources are included partially, does manual explain criteria for selection?
- Are selection criteria followed consistently?
- Are changes in selection criteria announced?
- Are there any fundamental publications that should be included in sources but are not? Are any irrelevant publications included?
- Do references contain abstracts?
- Can original publication be located by reference?
- Are abbreviations in references spelled out in manual?
- Are indexing principles given in manual?
- Are indexing principles followed consistently?
- Is indexing relevant and sufficiently accurate?
- Are upcoming changes in indexing announced in advance?
- Is indexing based on general classifications (e.g. UDC) or own system?
- Are classification directories, lexicons, etc. easily available/affordable? Or are they included in manual?

- Are classification directories and lexicons available online?
- Are there duplicate occurrences of same document in database?
- Is there consistency in spelling and indexing (e.g. American/British English)?
- Is there consistency in transliteration of foreign names?
- How are transliteration principles expressed?
- Are there spelling mistakes?
- Is information accurate and factual? (Are there, e.g. false references to sources or facts?)
- Are abbreviations standard?
- Are abbreviations automatically linked to thesaurus?

5. Practical aids to information retrieval

- Are the following guides available and readable:
  User's guide
  Software guide
  Quick reference card?
- Are guides/manuals in Finnish?
- Are guides/manuals available in other languages?
- Is manual sufficiently thorough and accurate?
- Do various guides/manuals refer to each other?
- Are basic instructions for using system available online?
- Is manual readable and easy to use?
- Does manual mention other ways to obtain the information covered in database (e.g. CD-ROM, other databases)?
- Does manual explain correspondence of such parallel products?
- How is manual/guide updating organized?
- Are upcoming changes announced in advance?
- Is news delivered by mail/online?
- Does manual accurately reflect practical use of the system and database?
- Are new users given cheap or free practice time?
- Are there training diskettes or cheap practice time for new databases?
- Is there an online or telephone-based help desk?
- How is user training organized: where, how often, what level, what price?
- How is information about training/courses distributed?

6. Costs

- What are the pricing principles (connect time/number of commands/online prints/formats, etc.)?
- What are the fees?
- Do the fees vary by time of day?
- Do the fees include documentation?
- Is it possible to estimate costs in advance?

- Is online cost information available automatically at end of session/on request?
- How are invoices made up (detailed by database/session/search)?
- What is the invoicing period?

Chapter 13

THE EYE OF THE BEHOLDER

C. J. Armstrong, Information Automation Limited, Penbryn, Bronant, Aberystwyth, Wales and the Centre for Information Quality Management

Defining quality

Definitions of quality – as of any abstract ideal – are always difficult. They tend to the unhelpfully philosophical, if not to the outright resigned, as voiced in the idea that both managers and customers will 'know it when they see it'! The one universal truism with respect to quality is that it means all things to all men: one person's quality criteria will not match those of another. Further, quality in one industry will mean very different things to its customers than quality in another. The steel industry might regard quality as demonstrable in strength, rigidity and hardness, while the woollens industry looks for strength, suppleness and softness. The nearest that anyone has ever come to defining quality in a universal sense is that it is 'fitness for purpose,' the appropriateness of the product to the customer's requirement. Fitness for purpose also means that the product lives up to the customer's expectations. A company which produces a spherical rubber artifact can justifiably be said to be producing something fit for the purpose of throwing or kicking around; but if the bounce goes out of it when it is wet, or it punctures very easily, it will not live up to anything but the most cynical customer's expectations.

In an industry that is essentially a service, and whose primary currency is intangible information, quality is not only difficult to define, it is difficult to quantify. It has been suggested that quality can be measured by inference from the quantity of various attributes of the product or service; a kind of vertical dimension reflected in the number of items in a collection or the number of journal subscriptions.[1] The validity of such measurements is questionable, although there is no doubt that each attribute can play a very real part in the overall quality of a service. The majority of this chapter will deal with defining what we mean by quality and what we expect in terms of quality in one particular area of the information delivery chain: databases.

As with other industries, quite a lot of work is currently underway with respect to accreditation and formulation of standards. The current interest in Total Quality Management (TQM) also affects the information industry. While this is important for particular institutions (and therefore for the information industry *per se*), I believe that before such important work as accreditation or the formulation of standards can take place, it is crucially necessary to understand the nature of quality within the information industry and to define those areas in which quality is central to functionality. I also believe that, in this case, it is necessary to move from the specific to the general: Total Quality Management is about an overall philosophy of quality within an organization which will unarguably and logically lead to quality in products or services. Before TQM can be implemented, it is necessary to understand what specifics of the business are the outward manifestations of quality. As W. Edwards Deming said, 'The first step in transformation is to learn how to change'.[2]

In the final analysis, quality is about people – the users who require those products or services which are fit for the purpose for which they are intended. Obviously, information in its many guises is seen as our central product.

It is interesting that only now, in the 1990s, are we suggesting that users of information services and libraries begin to question the validity of the product with which they walk away. Is it because the immediacy of electronic data leads us to have higher expectations, because the printed word could not be changed and was therefore not to be doubted? Or is it simply a sign of the times? In fact, I suspect that it is a curious reversal of the first two points: with the so-called information explosion (more accurately, the proliferation of microcomputer technology on everyone's desk), non-librarians and non-information specialists – naïve users – have suddenly acquired ready access to information which was previously in the control of the librarian. The very wonder of such immediate and simple access imbued the information with a kind of gospel-veracity which could not be questioned. Because it came from a computer database, it could not be wrong. While information seeking was inescapably linked to the printed page, the information specialist controlled the quality by selecting the volumes to be purchased by the library, and the users could take what they received at face value. Now, as control passes from the library or information unit, users tend to transfer this same faith to the database. This chapter will seek to discover whether such faith is misplaced.

What is quality data?

For the remainder of this chapter, our discussions will centre on data as manifested by databases and databanks, whether delivered to the user on diskette, CD-ROM, tape or online. Quality data is information culled from these databases which is complete, timely, accurate, consistent with other material in the file and easily located. Users might also expect the database to have a coverage and scope commensurate with that described by the producer, good documentation and online help, good training and customer support, and a cost which matches in some clear way the value of the information.

Although covered elsewhere in this volume, it may be useful to expand on these quality criteria here. The Southern California Online User Group (SCOUG) originated ten broad database quality categories which subsequent discussions expanded into an almost endless list of areas in which database producers and information suppliers should individually or jointly seek to satisfy their users. To complicate further an already complex area, some of these criteria have to be applied differently to different types of database (bibliographic, textual, etc.) and some seem to have an unclear area of responsibility (host/publisher/information provider/etc.). Two further points complicate the list: first, any third-party assessment would have to take into account the perspective of the end-user as well as that of the expert user; secondly, because a database is often implemented very differently on different systems, it is necessary to consider each version of each database that is up on more than one online system or available in more than one medium – online, CD-ROM or diskette.

It is probably fair to suggest that not all of the SCOUG criteria are equally important – although the external, user-oriented aspects make this a subjective view. Some criteria – probably those which relate to the actual data – have a more immediate relevance to the user, while other, more service-oriented criteria are simply aspects of a service which users might like to see improved or which they consider inadequate in general terms. Figure 13.1 represents the SCOUG criteria in a relevance-matrix.

At this stage, Figure 13.1 represents a preliminary view which is very much open for debate; however, the essential division between hard and soft criteria is important, since users are only likely to report voluntarily on the former – the visible, noticeable errors on the print-out or the readily apparent problems of timeliness or coverage. In Europe, some preliminary work has already been undertaken which attempts to quantify or prioritize these quality criteria from the user's point of view.

What constitutes a database in this context is also difficult to decide. During 1991 and 1992, *multimedia* was the word of the year, and CD-ROM publishers produced myriad offerings, including encyclopaedias, textbooks, interactive children's stories, 'expanded' books and reference works, as well as the more mundane bibliographic databases. While, in a perfect world, all of these should be infallibly accurate and perfectly matched to the user's needs, we are here more concerned with hard-core databases as used in the workplace – the factual and bibliographic databases that are consulted professionally.

However it is delivered, a database package includes more than just the data. Without the software and manuals which give access to that data, the database is virtually useless. In fact, we are so dependent on the software that we must believe whatever it tells us about the database. Even in-house and personal databases can only be used by means of database management software or text-retrieval software. Without it, it is virtually impossible even to discover how many records exist in the database, let alone how many and which records correspond to certain criteria. It is

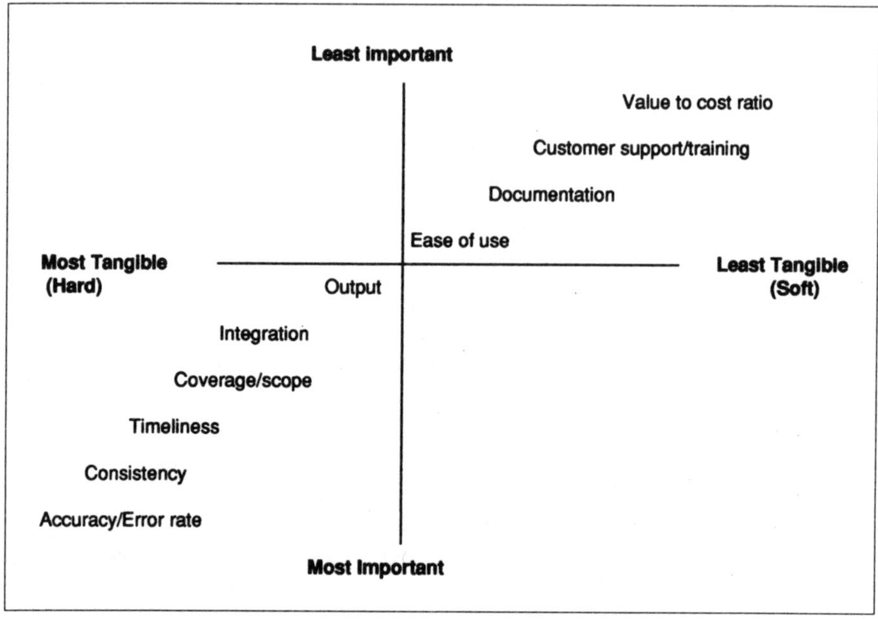

Figure 13.1 *Relevance matrix for SCOUG quality criteria*

the software that users query, and it is the software that displays an answer; even if by some quirk of programming the software locates the wrong fact or displays only a part of the answer, not only can users do nothing about it, but in all probability they will never know. The bottom line is, what the user sees on the screen may not represent exactly what is in the database.

In effect, when users license a database from an online host or a CD-ROM publisher, they are paying for access to data. Locating data requires of the user certain skills and abilities which cannot be assumed by the vendor; unlike the book or the encyclopaedia, which is sold on the assumption that its purchaser can read and will be able to navigate its pages by means of an index or implicit alphabetic order, the database cannot be sold on the assumption that its users will be able to locate items within it. Clearly too, it cannot be sold on the assumption that it will be browsed or read end-to-end. The difference lies in the fact that databases are sold with so many different types of access mechanisms, and despite what the vendors – and some database reviewers – say, not one single interface is really intuitive. Necessarily, a part of the database package is the interface; equally, if vendors are realistic about it, training and documentation as well as day-to-day help have to form a part of the deal. Without these, the database is simply like a coverless collection of unsorted pages.

Clearly then, a 'database' has to be defined as a package including both data and access mechanisms, and when discussing the quality of data we have to include the quality of the software, the manuals which instruct us in its use, any training we receive, online help, and so on.

Data quality

Having established that quality embraces all aspects of the database as delivered to the user, it is necessary to discover from what points quality problems may stem. The most obvious problems arise from errors in the data itself; they may result from the way in which it was loaded onto the database, or from the raw material itself. Since the indexing which provides the access is a semi-automatic and direct product of the record content, it is crucial to ensure that the content is correct in every aspect. Spelling checkers should be applied so that no aberrant forms of words appear in the index, standard forms of authors or company names should be used, chemical names should be checked and/or linked with synonyms and Chemical Abstracts Registry Numbers, dates should be checked for logic, and so on. If this is not done, the record may be indexed by an incorrect term and may not subsequently be locatable. If, for instance, the publisher *R. R. Bowker* appears in the index variously under 'R' and 'B', some references will be missed. In one particular instance cited by Jacsó, the country *Österreiche* was transliterated into both *Oesterreiche* and, quite incorrectly, many more times into *Eosterreiche*, while *München* appeared only in its incorrect form as *Meunchen*. Again, many references would be lost to users despite their presence in the database.[3]

Two recent reviews pointed out similar problems. The *British Newspaper Index* on CD-ROM uses both abbreviations and full-terms such as *govt/government*, *parlt/parliament* and *min/minister*; in order to search comprehensively, both forms must be discovered and used. The reviewer suggested that both indexing and entry practice need to be reviewed.[4] Similarly, in the *Oxford English Dictionary* (second edition) on CD-ROM, author searching for quotations (admittedly, the producer advises use of the author list) must be handled with care, as *Coleridge* and *S. T. Coleridge* (sufficiently far apart to cause browsing problems), *Wordsworth* and *Wordsw; Shak* and *Shakes* (although not Shakespeare, in full) all figure.[5]

Another quality issue highlighted by Jacsó is the question of access points. A database may be described as having 20 access points – author name, title, publication date, journal name, CODEN, document type, etc. – although some percentage of the records, in fact, lack one or more of these fields. Searches employing one of these field specifics, e.g. all documents classified as *reports* or all publications from 1990, will not retrieve those records in which the field is missing – and this might be quite a high percentage – even though they do in fact match the search criteria. Access points should be universal, but if they are not, the documentation should say so. Not all users who retrieve an unexpectedly small result will try an alternative strategy.

In some cases material is taken from one database to form a part of another, while, in others, market forces may mean that a database is taken over by a new host or publisher. In either case, new software will require particular attention to the content of fields. It may not be simply a case of ensuring that there is an equivalent field; in one case where SilverPlatter took over the *Education Library* database from OCLC, the date field proved resistant to the charms of their software. The problem turned out to be the *c* (for copyright) placed in front of the year by cataloguers; while the OCLC software dealt with this problem, SPIRS was unable to, and thus rendered about two-thirds of the database inaccessible by normal date searching techniques.

Where the database is being created from raw material in some other format, it is necessary for field content to be validated. A number of standpoints are adopted on this issue; one producer offers individual information providers (colleges, in this case) the chance to validate their records, but does not expect a high take-up; another, the UK advertising media database *BRADbase*, uses monthly questionnaires to update the database. Reed Information Service and Datastream, among others, have stated policies and verify every item prior to release, while Jordans are in print as saying '... the primary source for our data is Companies House, although many data providers, including ourselves, make use of information supplied by the companies themselves. We accept this information at face value and make use of it in good faith ... if errors are found, there are limits to the extent to which we can make amendments, since we must basically accept the public record as correct.'[6] Thus, if the material is received from the source replete with errors, there is little that can be done, as any attempt to verify it will probably result in confirmation of the error.

Undoubtedly, some of the quality problems stem from the database production process. As evidenced by the doubt frequently expressed by users about where to direct their complaints, there are quite a few bodies involved in that process. Who these bodies are and what their particular roles may be varies, unfortunately, with both the delivery medium and the type of database involved. As portable databases gain in both importance and share of the marketplace, distribution channels proliferate. They may be sold bundled with hardware, from computer stores, or through affiliate-labelling agreements; in any case, the end user is further distanced from the actual producer. The participants in the generation of a marketable database package may include some or all of the following: the data owner or information provider, one or more database producers, the software producer, a publisher, and a host or vendor. For example, the mythical newspaper, *The Bronant Gazette*, is published in print form by Bronant Newspapers, Ltd., who own the original copyright; a database producer called News Data takes the print copy and produces a database which contains all the editorial sections (not advertising, weather, sports results and radio and television listings); this database is then sold or licensed to four bodies: an online host who starts a new database called BRONT; a second database producer who adds the content to a cumulated database called MINORITY NEWS SERVICE; an online service containing the full text of hundreds of newspapers worldwide which can be searched individually, grouped by country or grouped by subject; and a CD-ROM publisher who adds it as a discrete database on a disc called SMALL PAPERS '93. There are now a minimum of four databases which can describe their contents as *The Bronant Gazette*, four search softwares which can be used to access the same database – more if BRONT is hosted by several online services – and the text will have fallen under the eye of a series of different editorial teams, keyboarders, scanners, indexers and abstracters. At each stage, different processes, such as formatters, spell-checkers, duplicate record identifiers, automated indexers, and so on will have contributed something to the particular database being developed.

In each case, documentation will be developed which describes the database/newspaper from the point of view of that particular retailer or host, and in terms best suited to their particular market. If one host concentrates on databases in the biomedical sector, the newspaper may be described in such a way as to emphasize its medical content, or it may be described in such a way that it sounds like a subset of a larger database rather than a file in its own right. Each seller will probably identify the database slightly differently – BRONT, *The Bronant Gazette*, *Bronant Gazette on Disc*, etc. – and may, in its database documentation, identify only the immediately previous player in the development chain as the publisher. Looked at in this light, it is easy to understand how minor errors and inconsistencies slip into databases and their documentation.

The 'slip' may well become a landslide once the necessary access mechanism is brought into the picture. Software is rarely tailor-made, and only somctimes is it customized to the requirements of a particular database. Either the original database or the platform onto which it is being transported may have insufficient fields, or the wrong type of fields; the use of indexing vocabularies or thesauri may vary between the host and the information provider. *British Newspaper Index*, running under a standard version of Data Technologies' CD-Answer software, is a case in point. One reviewer pointed out that the software treats numerals in the page numbers field as characters, 'so that, for example, searching on *1* ... yields entries on page 1, 11 through 19, 21, 31, and so forth'.[4]

Another possibility for the introduction of errors exists in the editorial process itself. Some databases originate, not from an information producer with a responsibility for the data, but from the publishers themselves. In this case a text or series of texts which are out of copyright and/or in the public domain, such as Shakespeare or the Bible, are simply placed on a CD-ROM with some general purpose text-retrieval software and re-sold. The editor may load the text as images, as an unformatted ASCII file or as a formatted file. Only in the first case can the intentions of the original author be fairly represented; if the original layout is either lost or changed, the value of the text to its users may well be lost. In one edition of Shakespeare on CD-ROM which I reviewed, the editor had replaced archaic spellings with a more easily understood form, stating that the text had been reformatted in order to take advantage of the computer screen. Such cavalier treatment surely meant that the use of the disc in schools was severely curtailed, while its use for serious study was reduced to the level of answering crossword puzzle clues.[7]

It is also necessary to note that while attention is normally focused on the data as it arrives on the user's desk, there is a further stage which is almost equally important. When records or excerpts are extracted from the database and downloaded onto a user's microcomputer, there is considerable scope for casual quality degradation. If the records are loaded onto a local database, it is the user's responsibility to ensure that they remain faithful to their original form and content, while if they are being used to generate a printed report, care must be taken to ensure that they are neither misquoted nor misrepresented. Mistakes can creep in at any level and if the database searcher is not the actual final user of the data, he too has a responsibility – a liability – in the information chain.

It is not the intention of this chapter to suggest that every database suffers from poor handling, bad editing and careless manufacture; rather, I believe that we have to understand the process by which the information reaches the user. A great deal of care has to be exercised with a product that has no physical presence and that, as a result, can so easily be changed. Most responsible database producers, online hosts and CD-ROM publishers are very aware of the problems which surround data handling and many of them have inaugurated quality control mechanisms.

The data owner or information provider

In conventional representations of the information chain, the author figures at the top of the list as the originator of the material; it is his or her intellectual effort which has gone into the creation of the text. For our purposes, the top position is held by the publisher of the original text-based document. Only if the database is bibliographic or has no print equivalent does the highest level become the compiler of the database itself. (Care must be exercised in the use of terms such as 'print equivalent' – while, historically speaking, abstracting and indexing journals may have given rise to the online database, in these high-tech days it is more likely to be the other way around; the print product is frequently a spin-off from the database. The term 'print equivalent' in this context refers to a printed work which exists in its own right prior to the generation of the database; examples might include the *Oxford English Dictionary*, *The Collected Works of Shakespeare*, *The Oxford Textbook of Medicine* or *Bretherick's Reactive Chemical Hazards Database* by Butterworth–Heinemann.) What is perhaps most surprising is that, in most discussions relating to the quality of information, little or no mention is made of the source. An encyclopaedia or handbook on CD-ROM may be criticized for the quality of the data but rarely is mention made of the hardcopy volume and the printing errors that it contains.

The database producer

Distinct – at least in many cases – from the owner of the information is the database producer. This is not always true, of course; the Royal Society of Chemistry and the Institute of Electrical Engineers, for instance, both maintain their own databases. In other instances a company such as Information Access Company (IAC) may develop a database on behalf of a third party. A data owner may develop a database from their own data as well as from that of a brother organization – such is the case with *Engineered Materials Abstracts*, jointly produced by ASM International in the United States and the Institute of Metals in the UK – or from data supplied by a number of sources. Examples here might be the *CAB Abstracts* or *Energy Science and Technology* databases.

The publisher

In some ways, the publisher of a portable database occupies the same position as the host/vendor of an online database in bringing together the software and the database in a discrete package. Where optical publishing is used, the publisher is also responsible for the mastering and reproduction of each disc. Most publishers have their own software, which is supplied with each database licensed. Few publishers have more than one software package available, although in most cases they tailor their software to the database being used.

The host or vendor

Maintaining a number of databases on a mainframe computer and providing access to them by means of a search software, online hosts or vendors bear ultimate responsibility for what their clients can locate. Their databases must be updated, reloaded, indexed and maintained, and at the same time made available for remote-access searching. Their responsibility should, and frequently does, extend to some level of quality monitoring on the databases they mount. This begins when the database is first acquired, with a series of test files used to design display screens and check the access offered by the software. It continues throughout the database's life with random checks of records, cognisance of customer complaints and comments (duplicate records, dirty data, etc.) and monitoring of such things as the timeliness of update arrivals at their offices. Data-Star adds a banner to the existing database if an update has not been received, for instance, and in at least two cases has removed a database which they have considered below standard.

The host does not have the right to correct or change data in a database produced by another company; errors and duplicates have to be reported back to the source, usually for correction in the next update. If the information provider has an 'edit/delete-allowed' password, they might be dealt with immediately.

To some extent the validity and quality of the data has to be taken on trust by the host; it is not unreasonable for this to be so, once they have assured themselves of the worth of the database. It is, however, not reasonable for databases to be mounted, updated and maintained with no quality checks at the host's institution.

The publisher as information provider

The final possibility stems from the case in portable databases where the producer or publisher is also the information provider, perhaps creating a database from public domain texts or material which is out of copyright. Examples are *Speaker's Lifetime Treasury* (aids for the professional speaker from NISC); *Darwin Multimedia CD-*

ROM (all of Darwin's writings, sketches and maps, from Lightbinders); *Cyclopedia of Toasts and Speeches* (Sony Discman product from Shufunotomo); *Desktop Bookshelf* (2 000 classic works from Aristotle to Aesop, from Chaucer to Conan Doyle, etc. from UNICA); and the Ex Libris series from Nimbus, each of which contains all the writings of a particular author. A frequent problem with this type of database is that they are produced by a team with no subject expertise, using a general purpose software and public domain materials. Often, insufficient market research has taken place, so that the product is badly targeted – too dense for school use, but not learned enough for higher education and scholarly study; an archive of material may have been created, but who will use it? One review of the 1989 *Electromap World Atlas* found that the textual material had been drawn from out-of-date print sources: the population, inflation rates and export data had been taken from sources dated between 1986 and 1988, certainly justifying the warning about the time-sensitive nature of the data given at the end of each report.[8]

The *Butterworth–Heinemann Bretherick's Reactive Chemical Hazards Database* mentioned earlier is an example of good practice, where a publisher has taken their own material – a print directory or handbook of acknowledged quality – and turned it into a CD-ROM using appropriate software.

The software producer

Not a direct link in the information chain, the software producer nevertheless impacts considerably on the database as received by users. It is probably simpler to consider individually the four possible positions that software can occupy in the process. These are: the mainframe software on a host computer, which allows remote users to access one or more databases stored on that mainframe; the software supplied on disc or diskette with a portable database; the front-end software which mediates between the user and the mainframe host software; and the database management system (DBMS) or text retrieval package used with a local or in-house database. Users who access online, portable and in-house databases could find themselves working with three, four or more different software packages. Within any of these categories, the software may be command-driven or menu-driven. Windows-based software (a variation of menu-driven) and other variations which rely on screen handling are possible in all except the first category.

Linked firmly with the software is the database structure. In some cases, where many years of investment have gone into a mainframe/host software which supports tens or hundreds of databases, change is expensive in terms of both development and existing database upgrading. In such situations, the software dictates the possible options to database producers and information providers. Sometimes, software may be developed or tailored especially for a single database application so that it can access the particular fields or record structure required; in other cases, existing software is used irrespective of data structure, or with unstructured data.

It is certainly true to say that a software package – with retrieval capabilities, limiting possibilities and display formats – that is ideal for bibliographic data will not be perfect for textual material, and may not be able to handle images at all. Clearly, some choices have to be made; equally clearly, every database is matched to a software at some level. If this were not the case, no search or display function would work at all. What is less certain is the degree to which quality enters these discussions.

Two examples will serve to clarify the discussion. Software designed to work with bibliographic data may offer field searching and Boolean logic, but no way in which terms can be related to each other positionally. Used with a full-text database, this would allow a successful hit to be reported when in fact the two words sought are pages apart, at opposite ends of the document, and have little or no logical connection. Similarly, a limit capability which works with the publication year field, PY, will not work on a database where YR is used to code that field.

Host mainframe software

Most of the major host softwares have a history stretching back 20 or more years. During this period, they have all been upgraded, but in no instance has one been changed so radically as to leave Boolean logic behind in favour of term weighting with its concomitant database restructuring. These search tools are probably the simplest in terms of search capabilities, but because they are initially command-driven, they require the most of the user, who has to learn statement syntax such as: *SELECT term1 AND term2* or *PRINT/DISPLAY/TYPE set-n in format-x*. Many of these softwares have, additionally, a menu-driven interface (sometimes not available for all the host's databases) which ride on their back and, in return for a little unwieldiness, loss of speed and inflexibility, obviate the need to learn the command syntax. Essentially they translate the menu responses to a pseudo-command which then functions in the same way as the original command-driven interface.

Traditionally, it is possible to select which fields are to be searched, how search terms are to be linked (Boolean or contextual/positional logic), how the results are to be limited and how displayed. This demands a database record structured in fields which may be indexed by phrase or term. Not all fields will be searchable and not all fields will be displayable.

Portable database software

Most portable database software can be described as having similar capabilities but quite considerably different communication with the user. As the range of databases and database types made available on CD-ROM has increased, so too, to some extent, have the softwares.

Portable software – that is, software shipped with the database to be run on the user's microcomputer, has two major advantages: it can be upgraded or changed at will because the new version can be distributed with the next database update; it can take advantage of local processing power and even of existing local software (for example, Windows) in order to provide an interface which matches user expectations. It can, far more easily than remote mainframe software, take advantage of colour, screen handling and windows, and user-customization, as well as provide context-sensitive help and directed searching.

No matter how it is disguised, most of the currently available search softwares still depend on Boolean logic, contextual logic and traditional searching patterns. Thus they still are inexorably linked to the database structure. The one variation in this pattern is the hypertext-type of database, where links are forged between one part of the database and another.

Front-end software

In order to ameliorate the shortcomings of mainframe/host software – failings even more marked in comparison with microcomputer-based software – a number of packages are now available which are loaded on the searcher's microcomputer and which stand between the searcher and the host software. By providing a friendlier, more accepted style of interface, they attempt to make the operation of the host's software simpler. Some have come into being in order to provide graphic structure searching of chemical databases; others are an attempt to woo end-users in various subject areas. Some are provided by the host systems themselves (for instance, FT Profile's Freeway or CompuServe's WINCim), while others are provided by third-party organizations. Almost all hide the true structure of the database, and even the true structure of the search, from the user, and can therefore distort the results. Although they cannot really be called a part of the database package in the same way as the first-level access software, it is important to realize the effect they can have on searching. Where they are supplied by the host or publisher, they do form a part of the overall database package.

Text-retrieval software

With the increasing amount of downloading from databases and the proliferation of softwares such as Pro-Cite and EndNote that are specifically designed to take downloaded records and manage them in a local database environment, it is important to understand that they too have a part to play in the chain by which information is moved from source to user. Perhaps a particular library or information center undertakes an SDI search of a particular database once each month and downloads the results into files marked 'pharmacology patents', 'medical ethics citations', 'hospital management references', etc., which are then added to their own in-house database(s). When their users come into the library and request citations on medical ethics or hospital management, that software should be capable of retrieving all those appropriate records and no more. If, because of poor data translation and loading, or unmatched search software, this is not the case, then the information center, the final link in the chain, has failed.

The software responsibility

Jointly or individually, the search software is the only means by which users can discover the contents of the database. It therefore occupies a position in no way less important than the data itself. By failing to display one field in any of the possible formats, that information is forever withheld; if the index is constructed in such a way as to ignore a field or to use its contents wrongly, no amount of searching will retrieve the right records. Instances of this might be the indexing of the year as a term rather than as a number, thus preventing limit options such as *earlier than 1990* or *later than 1980*; author names not inverted; or indexing of descriptors as terms only rather than as phrases.

The user

As was stated at the beginning of this chapter, the only effective measure of quality is its fitness for purpose, and the only appropriate person to judge this is the user.

User confusion

While it is certainly not the database industry's intention to confuse, much of its marketing and packaging activity does just this. In the portable sector of the industry, databases are not synonymous with products. Yet, it is frequently the product, the disc, that is described in catalogues, directories and publicity material. It is very common for a CD-ROM to contain several databases; these may be marketed either under the name of the most prominent database or under a collective name. Very frequently, the marketing material will talk in general terms about the product without making any distinction between it and the databases it contains. From the user's point of view, it may not even be apparent that more than a single database is concerned. Can they be searched jointly? Can they be searched individually? Do they have the same database structure and field labels?

While it may seem irrelevant for users to worry about how their new products have been created, if they do not know what they are being sold, they have no way of judging it for its adequacy or facility.

To confuse this situation further, some companies add another tier to the complexity by marketing a series of databases as a group or a library, although on separate discs. Here, the intention is to develop a series of products for the same vertical segment of the market. Ideally, they should all have the same database structure, data formats and software. They can usually be searched sequentially using saved search strategies. Normally, subscribing to the entire group will allow a considerable cost advantage to the user.

Clearly, no-one can complain about such user-oriented thinking. However, a problem arises if the nomenclature in the hierarchy is not clear (what is a *library*, a *disc*, a *database*?) and if the individual databases on their individual or joint discs are not clearly distinguished. Users have to know if it is the entire library (say, the *Biomedicine Library*) that covers their interest in bioengineering or simply the disc entitled *Bioengineering Abstracts*. Which should they buy? Sometimes, both the library and one of its component databases have the same name. The point, again, is that documentation and marketing material fall within the concerns of the quality controller; what each level of the product contains must be made quite clear.

The final and most recent confusion for the purchasing public are the 'affiliate label' marketing drives. Once upon a time, when most products were intended for library customers, it was fairly straightforward to contact and sell to potential customers. As the number of CD-ROM titles increases exponentially each year, this is no longer the case. In an attempt to reach larger numbers of prospective buyers, several organizations have joined forces with producers in order to establish a viable marketing network. As a part of this scheme, at least three – Multimedia Publisher's Group (MPG), Sony and Compton's NewMedia – have developed distinctive packaging and logos, with the result that products such as the *Macmillan Dictionary for Children* or Quanta's *USA Wars: Civil War* appear under the Sony or Compton NewMedia label. In itself, this is not a matter for particular concern, since the real producer is never completely hidden, but as new titles are taken on by the affiliate label, additional press releases and advertisements are generated. In these, a slight change in title emphasizing an aspect the affiliate labeler considers important to his or her market segment – say, *World Factbook* to *Multimedia World Fact Book* – combined with a newly written description which emphasizes different aspects of the product, can make an old product sound, quite legitimately, like a database new to the marketplace. It is very easy for the publishers of product directories to exacerbate the problem by taking these new press releases at face value and adding items to their directories which are, in fact, already listed.

Another area which provides scope for confusion is geographic licensing. A portable database publisher may only license the text content for sales within the UK, while another publisher has the US or rest-of-world rights. This is the case with *Hutchinson's Encyclopedia*, developed in the UK by Attica Cybernetics, who added considerable multimedia content to make a very presentable package. Because of the licence agreement, they may only market in the UK and, as a result of the smaller user-base, they have not deemed it worthwhile to produce a Macintosh version. Another example is *Harrap's Multilingual Dictionary*, variously marketed around the world as *Languages of the World, CD-ROM Multilingual Dictionary Database, CD Word 12+1* (Japan), *CD-ROM Multilingue*, or *Elektronisk Ordbok pa CD-ROM* (Sweden). This may only be a problem for industry watchers and directory producers, since the actual purchaser/user only has access to the version available in their own country, but it does mean that a variety of versions of some databases are available on disc, just as different online hosts carry different versions of certain databases.

As the range of material on CD-ROMs increases, so too does the population interested in their use and acquisition. When libraries were the major target, relatively few distributors, other than the producers themselves, existed. Now, hand-in-hand with the affiliate-label drive – indeed as a part of it in some instances – the number of retail outlets is increasing. CD-ROMs can be purchased in general computer stores, in Macintosh, IBM and Atari dealerships, and through both platform-specific and general hardware/software mail-order suppliers. These suppliers do not concentrate on library-oriented, information-based products, although in many cases these are available on special request. In less peripheral cases such as encyclopaedias, desk-top reference discs, dictionaries, discs of textual works, etc. it is quite likely that they can be supplied off the shelves. As the number of outlets increases, it is unfortunately true that the level of expertise and customer support falls; the *new* suppliers do not have an information-based pedigree and in some cases do not have the ability to do more than shift goods.

However, whatever their justification for selling CD-ROMs and portable databases, it is undeniable that they all are liable for the shortcomings of their goods. Just as any electrical wholesaler is responsible for the good working order of the refrigerator or washing machine purchased, the software houses, mail-order suppliers and retail stores must ensure that what they sell is fit for the purpose it was supplied to meet. Perhaps a more appropriate comparison can be made with the bookshops which sold copies of *Lady Chatterley's Lover* at a time when its content was thought liable to deprave. They were effectively held liable for the content of a book on their shelves. It will be interesting to see the first legal case brought against a high-street vendor for 'dirty data' on a CD-ROM!

Responsibilities and expectations

While I do not propose to deal with the legal aspects of liability in this chapter, it is interesting to speculate on where the responsibility for quality might fall. Slightly mischievously, I have suggested that it may involve retail stores; to a degree, that seems right. It is, however, more reasonable to presume that responsibility ultimately devolves upon those institutions higher up the chain – the parties responsible for producing the disc, the database or the original work. I should also like to suggest that some degree of responsibility falls on the shoulders of users (see Chapter 7). *Caveat emptor* is always true, no matter what is being purchased, but this is not only the users' responsibility. Users fall more-or-less neatly into two sets: the information professionals who normally search databases on behalf of some third party, and the so-called naïve or end-user who searches on his or her own behalf for data relevant to his or her own work. This latter group is threatened by quality issues to a greater or lesser extent depending on their cosmic information consciousness and aptitude. Plutchak described the balance between end-user satisfaction and end-user competence by the matrix shown on the rear face of Figure 13.2 (although with the word 'Safe' left out).[9] If we add an external influence – a third dimension, data quality – to the original *dissatisfied/satisfied* and *ept/inept*, we have a picture which represents the effects of poor databases on end-users: the left-right horizontal scale is satisfaction, the vertical scale equates to the degree of skill or efficiency with which the end user manipulates the database system, and the depth of the figure shows data reliability. In the cube, it is those at the right-hand side for whom I am

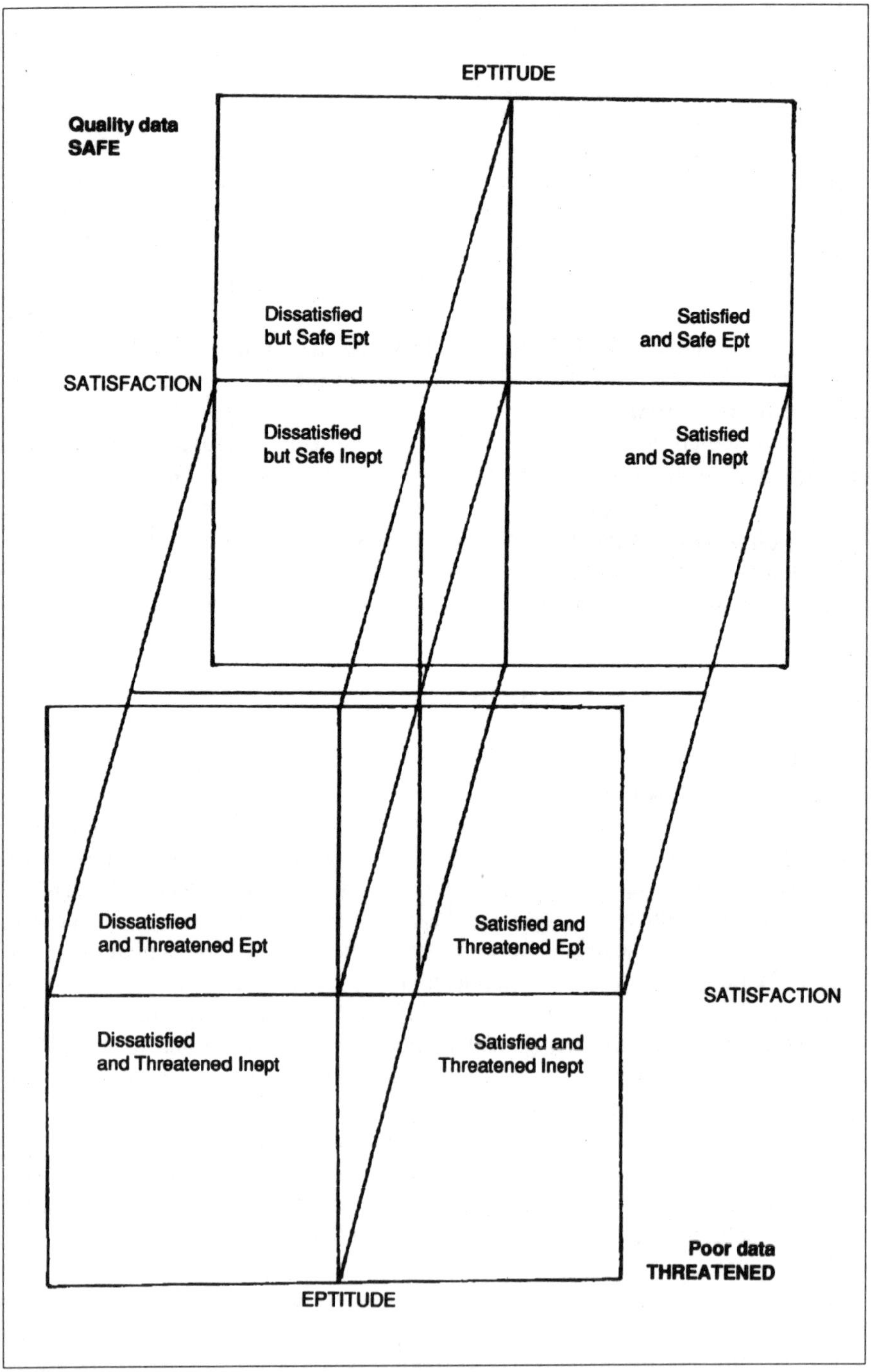

Figure 13.2 *Extended version of Plutchak's matrix*

suggesting we must care; more especially (but not exclusively, as 'safe' is only 'relatively safe') those nearer the front of that face.

One difficulty for the end-user group is the devolution of the purchasing power away from the library/information unit. As long as an information specialist controls use, as was the case with conventional printed reference works and online systems – guides users to the correct source, only purchases reputable reference works, studies and uses the most effective ways of locating correct, best or most information – it is less important if one particular work is flawed because of its coverage or data quality. Information specialists know the limitations and can select or suggest alternative sources; they act as 'quality filters,' to use Carol Tenopir's phrase.[10] Now that raw information can be placed directly in and used by 'untutored' hands, a quality guarantee is even more important. Thus, to the information-professional user falls a responsibility for quality control – a responsibility, which although principally that of the provider community, has to be theirs to control.

The user's responsibility

User responsibility, by which we largely mean information professional user responsibility, falls into two categories: education of the naïve end-users (NAIVE was once light-heartedly cited as New And Infrequently Venturing End users) so that they become aware of the issues; and a watch-dog or 'consumer association' role. While, as John Hepworth said, end users have been liberated by the easy-to-use CD-ROM search software – liberated, that is, from the safeguard of a second opinion on their search needs and results – the professional can hold a watching brief to look after their best interests.[11]

It is all too common to see end-users accept what they find at the terminal as 'the truth, the whole truth and nothing but the truth'; in fact, this is rarely the case, and end-users have to be persuaded of this. In his paper on courses for end-users, John Hepworth emphasizes the need for both evaluation of search performance and evaluation of system and database understanding. 'If search skills are as conceptual as I have suggested, the role which end-user training assumes will often be one of damage limitation.'

While not all of us are in a position either to train or influence end-users, all who search databases, whether online or disc-based, can contribute to the gradual heightening of quality. Already, in the two or three years since quality issues surfaced, database producers and database hosts are beginning to respond to user needs. It is not simply that the user force exerts pressure on the suppliers, but rather that suppliers are only too ready and willing to respond to user needs. This has been frequently stated, several times at the UK Online User Group Conference at which John Hepworth's paper was presented. Until quality concerns are brought onto the agenda, the responsible parties cannot respond. In order to bring all major databases up to an acceptable standard over a period of time, all users must take a proactive role and actually judge databases, reporting on problems as they occur.

The producer's responsibility

It is easy at this point to talk about the relative value of various forms of information – say, bibliographic as opposed to textual/factual – and the corresponding relative 'care' which suppliers can commit to their product. In fact, although it is certainly true that an error in a factual database on drug usage is potentially more disastrous than an error in company turnover, which in turn is more problematic than the wrong pagination in a bibliographic citation, such distinctions are specious and should be ignored. No supplier can prejudge the uses to which his or her data may be put. Consequently all data and all databases have to be equally carefully prepared and presented.

As this chapter has made clear, while both beauty and quality may be in the eye of the beholder, the producers are ultimately the responsible parties. While users may have a responsibility to report on or draw attention to quality issues that come their way, the various parties detailed earlier in this chapter are liable for actually maintaining quality in their databases. Many, as has been shown, already have policies which can be cited to demonstrate their good intentions and practice; others are not so forthcoming.

What still lies open to question is, what aspects of the databases are controlled by the quality imperative? This chapter has been at pains to argue the need to include everything from the raw data all the way through to the documentation, training and help desk. But few online hosts, and a still smaller percentage of CD-ROM publishers, are so generous in their definition. Indeed, a very small percentage shows any inclination to treat quality as a serious issue at all. While the major players – those who have grown with the industry over many years – undoubtedly acknowledge and treat quality seriously, many small database producers are far less concerned.

Total Quality Management implies quality in all aspects of a business or institution, emanating from senior management and reaching to all levels and products; quality is defined variously as 'zero defects', 'conformance to requirements' or 'customer-optimized products'. More importantly, current thinking suggests that quality is 'getting it right the first time,' rather than correcting problems as they occur – a state of being only possible if the entire organization is commited to the pursuit of excellence.

Before Total Quality Management and zero defects can be achieved, there has to be a state of discovery in which existing practice and existing products are examined to discover their 'distress potential,' their ability to upset the new nirvana. For the most part, the database industry has now reached this state of discovery. This is not to say that many individual producers or hosts have not gone beyond this and begun to rectify errors and the processes that allowed them to occur. But, in general terms, the database industry has not achieved a plateau of universal (or near-universal) good quality.

It is at this point that the two halves of the information industry can unite in working towards quality. The users – who, after all, are the best-placed to judge such things – can discover, quantify and prioritize quality issues; and the suppliers can work towards rendering such efforts superfluous! Of course, it must be clear to users that when a data fault is discovered, they are not simply seeking its correction in isolation, but rather highlighting a loophole in the supplier's process which allowed such a fault to occur.

How to measure quality?

Ultimately, quality is recognized by standards or accreditation, but the information industry has a long way to go before such standards can effectively be applied to certify high-quality databases. It is arguable that such products should be readily identifiable without the need for such artificial flags; the sign-on screen with details of database scope, timeliness, coverage, updating, etc. would provide a hint, while the documentation, and the data itself, would demonstrate quality beyond any doubt. In reality, standards serve the useful purpose of identifying a database as one that any user can search without concerns about either the efficacy of the search process or the value of the results.

This is not to imply that standards can be applied blindly and relied upon implicitly. An article on British Standard BS5750 in the UK newspaper *The Guardian* noted:

> Application of the standard does not assure quality, only consistency. If the design or manufacturing process is bad and results in an article of poor quality, BS5750 will help to ensure that further articles are made to a consistently poor standard.

But how to measure a database for quality commendation in the first place? Given that quality is defined by user criteria, such awards should be the gift of the user-base as a whole. In reality, this is impracticable; a fixed set of criteria will have to be designed and met.

Before the mechanics of accreditation can even be designed, much work has to be undertaken. Beginning with the SCOUG criteria, it will be necessary to:

- Discover user quality concerns
- Test databases to discover 'weaknesses'
- Isolate valid criteria
- Measure user perceptions
- Test the criteria
- Design criteria tests.

Once accreditation has begun, measures will be required to keep the accreditation both current and valid. Databases which have achieved accreditation must not be allowed to slip below certain minimum standards. Those minimum standards will have to be constantly reviewed in order to ensure that they continue to make sense in terms of the types of databases, the technology and the access mechanisms which come into being. Peter Jacsó made exactly this point with respect to the MPC logo and standard.[12] The minimum specifications necessary to qualify for its use were set in 1991, but by the end of 1992 these were so outmoded that almost any microcomputer on the market could qualify, even those that were only able to reproduce jerky video and poor sound. Multimedia today demands a much higher specification.

The mechanics of database evaluation

Much has been written about how databases can and should be evaluated. It is not the purpose of this chapter to discuss such techniques. Unfortunately, it is still the case that many people regularly review databases at a superficial level, paying scant heed to their actual content. Discussions frequently centre on the mechanics of the software and the perceived value of the content – as in reviews which begin with statements such as '[database] is the leading English-language abstracting and indexing service in [subject] and covers n-thousand periodicals retrospectively to 1978; updating is quarterly and there are half-a-million records at this time', and go on to detail hardware requirements, how the software works and the documentation. These are all valid and valuable concerns for the reviewer, but what of the nub of the system – the data? Unless reviewers cover, and cover in some depth, the contents of the database, looking at all the quality issues which have been discussed above, the review is scarcely worth the paper on which it is printed.

In terms of database reviews for certification, evaluation will have to be based in some way on a series of standard tests – tests which will have to vary according to the kind of database (statistical, bibliographic, factual, textual, image, etc.) and to some extent, according to the medium on which it is delivered (online, disc, diskette, tape, etc.). For databases which are available on several different media, on several hosts or through several publishers, it will also be necessary to look at all the variations and discern whether all, or only some, are quality products.

To complicate the procedures further, it is arguable that the only person qualified to evaluate a database is a regular and skilled user and a subject specialist. Conversely, the case could be made that naïve users should be used in order to obviate skills acquired by the experienced searcher which neatly navigate around database or software shortcomings. Deciding how such evaluation teams can be contrived seems likely to tax the upcoming certification authorities to a point of distraction!

Some European/British initiatives of the early 1990s

Already, in the early 1990s, a number of initiatives – pre-accreditation process initiatives – have begun in Europe. EUSIDIC, the European Association of Information Services, has begun a programme of work looking at quality in the information industry as a whole, and through EUROLUG (the European Online User Group) and in conjunction with the Library Association and the UK Online

User Group (UKOLUG), some initial questionnaires have been distributed.

A Library Association/UKOLUG Task Force on quality management has been in place for over two years (as of this writing) and it is anticipated that much initial work on database quality will be undertaken under its auspices. Working from the premise that the route to database certification/accreditation lies through much territory in need of mapping, it is intended that they shall be responsible for evaluating and prioritizing the various user quality concerns. A five-year programme is to be set up which will enable users considerable opportunity to voice their quality concerns.

A body with the working title of the Centre for Information Quality Management (CIQM) has recently been set up so that both industry and users have common ground on which to air their quality problems. CIQM is to have two main remits: to provide users with an immediately identifiable, single access point and a simplified mechanism by which errors can be reported and forwarded to the appropriate body, be it information provider, host, CD-ROM publisher, or whatever; and to set up a series of monitoring exercises to determine the extent to which particular quality criteria actually present a problem to users.

Its role with respect to data problems discovered by users in the process of their work would be four-fold. Clearing-house activities would centre around the provision of an impartial service to users which would allow a single European address, telephone, e-mail, bulletin board and fax point to which any problems relating to quality in databases could be reported. On receipt, the clearing house would:

- Categorize and log the data problem in order to provide statistics
- Identify the source of the problem
- Forward details to the correct responsible body
- Receive replies (host/information provider to user) to forward to the user.

The second area of work centres on a series of monitoring weeks, each concentrating on one or two aspects of quality. While this will produce less information than a full-scale, across-the-board exercise, it makes the projects manageable from the point of view of the user. It is relatively straightforward to assess each search undertaken for one or two success factors – perhaps consistency and accuracy in the first instance – and to do so fairly quickly. By reducing the number of quality factors to be monitored, a simplified report form can be designed so that users can categorize the problem without the need to describe it at length.

The recording system developed by the clearing house will make due allowance for database types (bibliographic, directory, full-text, numeric, image, graphic, etc.), database medium (online, CD-ROM, diskette, etc.), database content (factual to bibliographic), database subject (business to humanities), and user level (naïve, expert, regular, infrequent), as well as language and geographical constraints.

Over and above these central tasks will be an educational and profile-raising exercise designed to reach the end-users referred to above. Possibly one of the most important aspects of the centre's work will lie in the education of users of database information – both end-users and intermediaries – in the need to view data with a degree of circumspection. The natural corollary to a quality supplier is a critical user.

While all of the activities detailed here will serve to heighten user awareness to some degree, a programme of lectures and talks will be necessary in order to make all users of databases aware of quality issues. Particularly important are those users who have no formal information background and who come to online or CD-ROM as an accident of their work. In all centre activities it will be important to remember that the so-called end-user is more vulnerable to data problems than are information intermediaries, who have been trained in reference work and who should have some understanding of the need to evaluate reference tools.

Discussions about the centre have been continuing for some time. The initial idea was mooted at the UKOLUG State-of-the-Art conference previously referred to, and some suggestions for funding the centre were made at that time, too.

It has already been stated that database hosts and information providers would welcome such positive action with respect to database quality. The centre proposes to persuade industry that financial support of the clearing house represents a positive and necessary quality indicator on their part. In return, the clearing house could authorize the use of a log-on flag such as:

> This host [and/or information provider] supports active quality control through CIQM.
> If you discover a data problem please contact ...
> or
> This host [and/or information provider] is a member of the CIQM scheme.
> If you discover a data problem please contact ....

This is much in the spirit of the 'quality business card' suggested by TQM guru Claus Møller: a technique to raise personal quality in which a business card is devised which incorporates a personal guarantee of quality of work. This is quite distinct from accreditation or certification; it is simply a means of indicating to users that some hosts or information providers are committed to the idea of quality data.

Industry funding for the centre was initially suggested by Earl Beutler, the President of Research Information Systems (and a contributor to this volume) at the same time that the clearing house concept was first raised and discussed.[13]

Conclusions and the information provider's charter

We all have a responsibility to quality; this much is without question – the joint responsibilities, actually, of discovery and remedy. Our immediate concern is to discover a methodology by which the information industry can and will produce only quality products. It should be possible to see the day when information possesses an implicit charter – not along the lines of the current UK 'citizen's charters' in which public bodies set their own easily-attainable targets and thus achieve credibility from the credulous, but rather a charter by which users will know that the current premise upon which many end users operate is fact rather than fiction; that is, that if they locate some data, they can rely on it, and if they fail to locate data, there is none to be had.

In the meantime – in the period leading up to certification, accreditation, standards, and a charter – we are all charged with the duty of catching the tiger by the tail! Quality may mean many things to many people, but with a little diligence it should be possible to determine those quality issues which are most important to users of information. Organized activities such as those undertaken by the Centre for Information Quality Management will play a large part in discovering where problems lie. If the initial effect is simply to have a particular record corrected or a certain software glitch eradicated, then so be it. The long-term goal is to make such errors and glitches impossible. To quote another TQM guru, Philip Crosby, 'Quality is conformance to the requirements which a company itself has established for its products based directly on its customers' needs. Traditional quality control ... represents failure rather than assurance of success'.[14]

In the end – when databases either have or do not have a quality certificate – will users vote with their purses, or will the free market continue to encourage the proliferation of random databases purchased on the basis of their publicity material? We shall see. It would be nice to think that, at least where it matters, quality-accredited databases will become the accepted, the standard, and perhaps even the *only* sources of information.

Notes

1. Garvin, D. A. (1988), *Managing Quality: The Strategic and Competitive Edge*, New York: The Free Press, p. 40.
2. Deming, W. E. (1988), *Out of the Crisis*, Cambridge: Cambridge University Press.
3. Jacsó, P. (1992), *CD-ROM Software, Dataware and Hardware: Evaluation, Selection and Installation*, Englewood, Colorado: Libraries Unlimited.
4. Terbille, C. (1993), BNI: British Newspaper Index [review]. *CD-ROM World* **8** (1) (January).
5. Lepkowski, F. J. (1993), 'The Discreet Charm of the OED: The Oxford English Dictionary, Second Edition, on CD-ROM. *CD-ROM World* **8** (1) (January), 84–90.
6. Tagg, L. (1992), 'Initiatives: Data Accuracy', *Business Information Review* **9** (2) (October), 60–7.
7. Williams, I. and Armstrong, C. J. (1991), Shakespeare on Disc, in *CD-ROM Information Products: The Evaluative Guide* ,Volume 2, (eds C. J. Armstrong and J. A. Large), Aldershot: Gower, pp. 367–85
8. Armstrong, C. J. (1991), World Atlas (Electromap), in *CD-ROM Information Products: The Evaluative Guide*, Volume 2 (eds C. J. Armstrong and J. A. Large), Aldershot: Gower, pp. 387–404.
9. Plutchak, T. S. (1989), 'On the Satisfied and Inept End User', *Medical*

Reference Services Quarterly **8** (1) (Spring), pp. 45–8.

10. Tenopir, C. (1993), Guest Editorial, *Database Searcher* **9** (1) (January), pp. 3–5.
11. Hepworth, J. (1992), 'Developing Information Handling Courses for End Users, in *Database 2000: UKOLUG State-of-the-Art Conference 1992* (eds C. J. Armstrong and R. J. Hartley), Oxford: Learned Information and UKOLUG, pp. 67–75.
12. Jacsó, P. (1992), 'MPC: Is This Fools' Gold?', in *Online 92 Information: Proceedings of the 16th International Online Information Meeting*, London, 8–10 December 1992, Oxford: Learned Information, pp. 159–62.
13. Beutler, E. (1992), 'Ensuring Integrity of Data', in *Database 2000: UKOLUG State-of-the-Art Conference* (eds C. J. Armstrong and R. J. Hartley), Oxford: Learned Information and UKOLUG, pp. 97–100.
14. Crosby, P. B. *Quality is Free*, New York: McGraw-Hill, 1979 and *Quality Without Tears*, New York: McGraw-Hill, 1984.

Chapter 14

QUALITY ISSUES IN THE INFORMATION SECTOR: AN INTERNATIONAL PERSPECTIVE WITH PARTICULAR REFERENCE TO THE EUROPEAN SCENE

Alan Gilchrist, principal in GAVEL, a consortium of European information consultants, and the Cura Consortium

Introduction

It is generally accepted that the quality management movement originated in Japan after World War II, though under the leadership of the American physicist W. Edwards Deming. It was another 30 years until Deming's ideas were taken up seriously in the West, particularly in his native USA, and more slowly in Europe and the other industrial countries. On the other hand, the British can take some credit for being an early publisher of an important standard in the area of quality management, viz BSI 5750[1], which was first published in 1979 following the production of a government White Paper. This standard was entirely revised and republished in 1987, and is now identical with its International and European equivalents, ISO 9000 and EN 29000 respectively. Another radical version of these standards (actually a series of standards) is planned for 1996; it is likely that one important area of change will reflect, to a far greater degree than presently obtains, the particular needs of the service sector. Consequently, it must be admitted that the take-up of quality management principles in the service sector is both more recent and far less than in the manufacturing sector, and that the same applies, to an even greater degree, in the information sector.

As always with 'new ideas', a vast amount of talk precedes action, and it would not be unfair to say that this is the case with regard to quality issues in the service sector in general, including the information services area. The two extremes of the debate reflect delight and downright cynicism, with the middle ground including those who either regard quality management as necessary for survival in an increasingly competitive climate, or (perhaps reluctantly) as something which cannot be ignored. Perhaps the two ends of the spectrum can be illustrated by a management consultant and a librarian, traditionally seen as trusting and conservative stereotypes. The first wrote:

> Management consultants seek a 'holy grail' product. To fit the bill it should be recurring, authoritative, profitable, widely in demand and lead to further work .... Quality certification shows signs of satisfying the properties of the holy grail product, and with its current growth rate exceeding 35% annually, it is capable of turning over £3 billion a year in the UK.[2]

Clearly threatened by such rhetoric, a leader in the UK journal *Library Association Record*, opined:

> Total Quality Madness, or TQM, is the latest private sector mania to hit public libraries. Armies of management consultants are marching into town halls, pontificating on services, producing reports and submitting bills.[3]

The fact that both of these statements were recorded in 1992 underlines just how early in the debate we find ourselves, as well as the need to continue that debate in a more informed and balanced manner. At the moment of writing, not very much of this debate has been formally recorded and the literature is somewhat sparse, at least in the information sector (with which the rest of this chapter will be mainly concerned). There are several reasons for this, which include the following:

1. There is not yet much to talk about, beyond intentions and general descriptions of how to get started in quality management, certification etc
2. Early practical examples are somewhat tentative in their conclusions, and certainly incomplete in cost–benefit analyses; these are unlikely to become clear until the new procedures have been running for at least three years
3. Most of the serious applications appear to have been effected in the private sector. A few commercial information services have been proud to announce the implementation of TQM or certification; but managers of in-house services

rarely have the time or inclination to write up their experiences.

It is largely because of the feeling that more is happening than is being recorded that a number of study projects and research programmes have been initiated. These will be outlined later in the chapter.

The information environment

It is not surprising that ISO 9000 (and its equivalents) has been criticized for its bias toward the manufacturing sector, because this is where the concept was born. A large part of the philosophy is still rooted in the statistical approach to quality control and other relatively hard techniques, such as value analysis. It is, however, becoming perfectly clear that the basic principles are just as properly applied in the service sector. For example, only a few words and emphases need to be modified in Deming's famous 14 Points (also referred to as Obligations). It would, for example, be foolhardy to deny that 'The consumer is the most important part of the production line', and those in the information sector – above all – should welcome 'There is no substitute for knowledge'. But it is the implications behind these 'Obligations', and the hard work needed to turn them into practice in specific environments, which will demand attention.

ISO 9000 provides an excellent starting point and framework, but it must be adapted for each sub-sector. One organization that has successfully struggled through this process is the UK-based Marketing Quality Assurance (MQA). MQA spent five years developing measurable requirements specifically for the marketing function, and it is interesting to note that of the 58 requirements in the MQA specification, 23 are in ISO 9000, while the other 35 are specific to marketing.[4] This will give some idea of the task confronting the information sector if they choose (as they should) to go down this road, particularly as it may well be that the information services area has unique characteristics to be considered.

Gilchrist[5] has argued that one vital characteristic of the sector is the 'information chain', wherein the 'commodity' is subjected to a number of transactions in its passage from the originator to the user, and that each supplier/user interface in the chain is of equal potential importance. At the least there should be no corruption of data at the interface; at best there can be significant added value. Figure 14.1 shows the simplest configuration of the information chain, while Figure 14.2 displays one complication wherein the primary publisher bypasses the database producer by supplying machine-readable text direct to the host, or CD-ROM to intermediaries (or, increasingly, to users). It is important to recognize in this picture that each of the components in the chain is both a supplier and a user (even, it can be argued, the authors and the users). Furthermore, each user in the chain may be a user of a single 'up-stream access point', with little or no interest in how his or her enquiry has been met by the collation of, and enhancement to, a range of inputs from other suppliers. Another obvious aspect of this chain is that it is not only inter-organizational, but is almost certain to be international; yet, there is no key player in the chain, no obvious

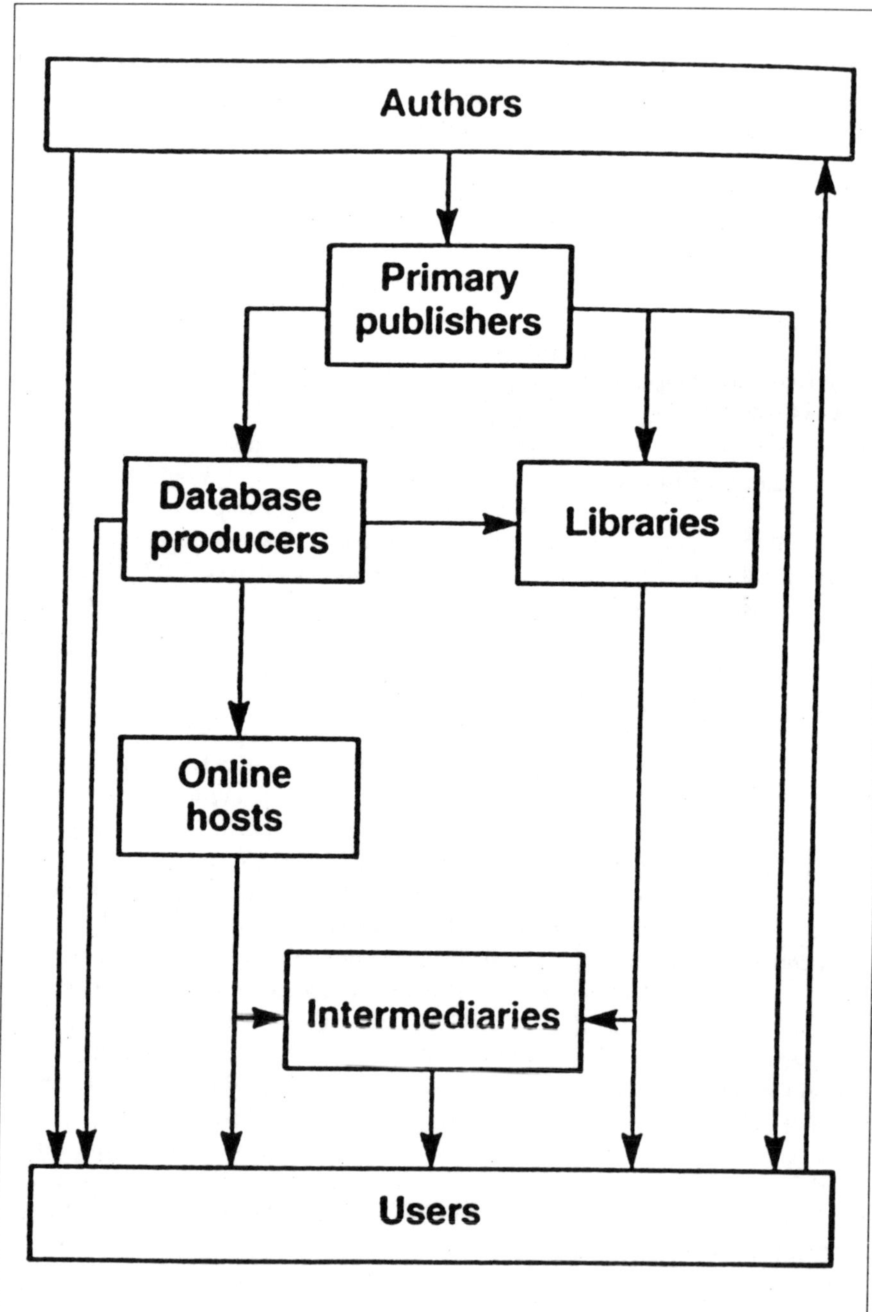

Figure 14.1 *Information chain – simplest picture* (from Aitchison, T. M. (1984), 'Online and the database producer,' *Journal of Information Science* **9**(2), pp. 75–80.

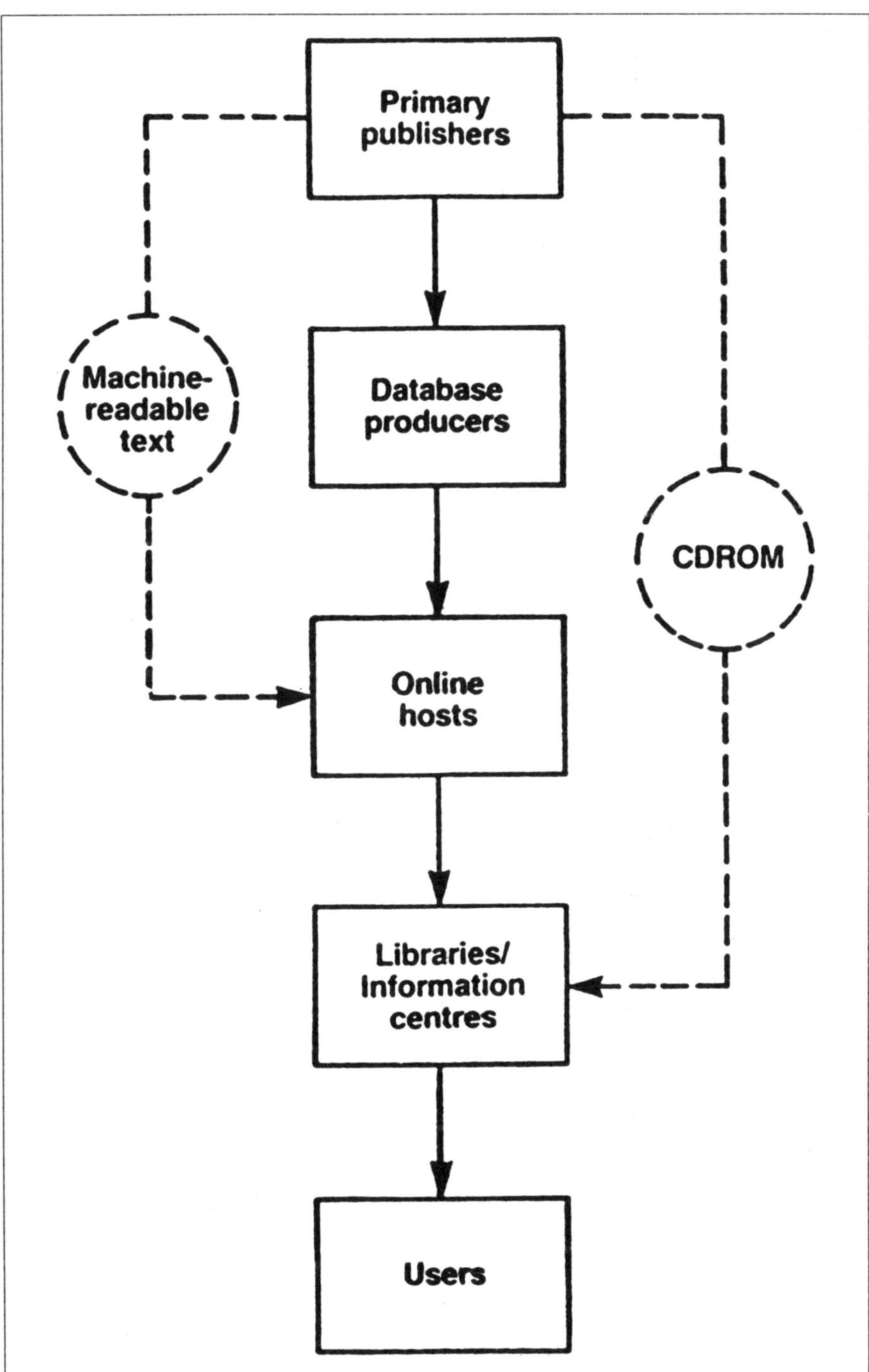

Figure 14.2 *Information chain – added complexity* (from ibid).

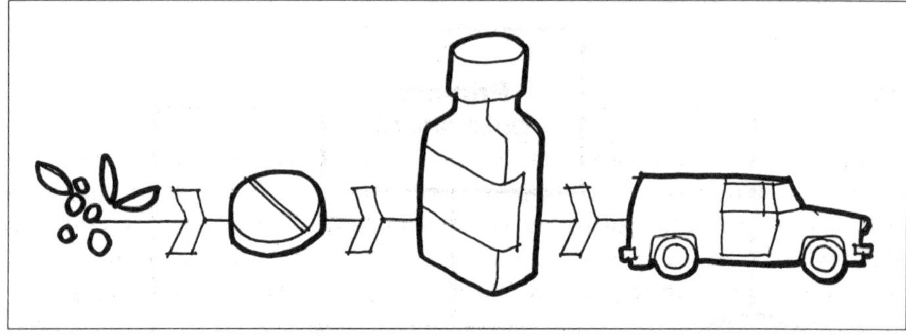

Figure 14.3 *Standards in the supply chain – pharmaceutical industry*

setter and guardian of standards. In another paper, Gilchrist[6] demonstrated this with two diagrams contrasting the information chain with the manufacture and distribution of pharmaceuticals. From Figure 14.3, it can be appreciated that the pharmaceuticals manufacturer (represented by the tablet) can impose strict technical standards on the suppliers of raw materials, packaging and distribution in order to ensure that the product is, and remains, of high quality. On the other hand, a look at Figure 14.4 shows that the standards in the information chain pertain either to formatting or to transmission, but not to the handling of the content. The consequence of these arguments would appear to be that it is the information industry itself which should seek to identify and codify the requirements for the

Figure 14.4 *Standards in the supply chain – electronic information seller*

effective application of ISO 9000 and the consequent measurable sets of performance criteria.

A snapshot situation report

For reasons stated above, it is too early to be able to present an objective overview of what is happening in the information sector with regard to quality issues; but some trends are discernible.

First of all, it would appear that there are two separate movements: the first led by intermediaries concerned with database quality, and the second comprising a range of organizations concerned with various approaches to quality management. The Finns claim to be amongst the earliest communities concerned with database quality[7], which possibly stems from the fact that they are an information-conscious people who understand the extent to which they rely on foreign databases. For some years, the Finnish Society for Information Services has maintained a Committee on Database Quality. Another early initiative was taken by a joint action sponsored by the UK Library Association and the UK Online Users Group (UKOLUG), who held an open meeting on the topic which gave birth to a Task Force on Database Quality. Subsequently, the UKOLUG Annual Lectures at the London International Online Meetings in 1991 and 1992 were devoted to this theme; the UKOLUG Annual Conference of 1992[8], devoted six papers to a session on quality assurance. It was at this conference that UKOLUG and the Southern California Online Users Group announced their intention of working together, and with the European Online Users Group (EUROLUG). It is clear that SCOUG have made the most significant advances in this area with regard to identification of performance criteria;[9,10] while this work has not yet been translated into a programme of monitoring, it has attracted the interest of the database producers, and meetings have been held between them and SCOUG. The last part of this chapter includes mention of plans to build on this work, initially within a European research programme.

The second movement, the application of quality management within organizations, is both larger and wider, in that there is now some evidence of its application by commercial information providers, public and academic libraries and information services (LIS), government and special LIS, as well as infrastructural support from professional institutions. Early signals of activity in these areas are to be seen in the health sector,[11] wherein LIS was sucked into the wider issue of patient care, and in an awareness-raising conference[12] organized jointly by the UK Institute of Information Scientists and Task Force Pro Libra Ltd. (a UK-based company offering services to the information sector, and currently undergoing certification to BS 5750).

One of the few surveys to be conducted in this area was funded by the UK British Library Research and Development Department and published late in 1992.[13] The survey covered public and academic libraries and showed (Figure 14.5) that involvement in quality management was in its very early stages and encompassed a wide range of approaches. The author of the survey also commented that these

	Public	Academic	Total
Quality assurance	32.3	32.5	32.5
Quality improvement	40.0	37.5	39.0
TQM	18.5	20.0	19.0
Customer care	87.7	52.5	74.3
CQI	35.4	27.5	32.4
BS 5750	16.9	10.0	14.3
None of the above	7.7	32.5	17.1

Figure 14.5 *Involvement in quality management*

initiatives had been developed in isolation, without input from other LIS, and that they were weak in the critical area of performance measurement. It is significant that almost a third of academic libraries were not involved in any quality initiative, and that the most popular approaches were the relatively easier options of customer care (74.3 per cent) and quality improvement (39.0 per cent), while the more exacting TQM and the relatively costly certification option scored 19.0 per cent and 14.3 per cent respectively. Furthermore, with a response rate of only 52 per cent, the actual degree of involvement is almost certainly considerably lower.

The government sector in the UK has for some time maintained a strong and coordinated interest in performance indicators. Early in 1993, a person who had been heavily involved in this activity, and in promoting quality concepts in the Ministry of Defence Library Services, was appointed Quality Manager at the MoD Headquarters Library service. John Brockman had already carried out a study tour, including a visit to the US Department of Defense and other government bodies in the USA, and is now actively applying suitably anglicized DoD techniques within the MoD. Consequently, Brockman is a regular speaker and author on quality issues.[14,15,16,17]

Special libraries have been less forthcoming, and little is known in the UK about their quality efforts except for two cases, both in the construction industry, of certification to BS 5750. The Nordic countries appear to be rather more advanced; two companies which have started out on serious quality management programmes have agreed to become the subjects of in-depth case studies. One is the Norwegian firm Norsk Hydro AS, and the other is the Danish Jutland Telephone Company.

News from other European countries suggests that the UK picture reflects the situation elsewhere. There is serious and informed interest in the Nordic countries, particularly Denmark, Norway and Finland. Following a central German government campaign to promote interest in quality assurance (starting in 1992 and budgeting £140 million over a four-year period), the information sector has responded, and a conference on quality management was held in May 1993 under the direction of the Deutsche Gesellschaft für Dokumentation (DGD). In the Netherlands, again spurred by government concern, the public libraries are beginning to address the issue. France, through its professional body, the Association Française des Documentalistes et des Bibliothecaires Specialises

(ADBS), have long taken an interest in the application of management techniques to LIS, and have contributed their experience of the application of value analysis.[18]

Action programmes

Various initiatives and conferences have already been mentioned, notably the LA/UKOLUG foundation work, the conferences and seminars in Rotterdam, Helsingborg and Guildford, and most recently the launch seminar of a new Special Interest Group devoted to quality issues set up by the Federation Internationale de L'Information et Documentation (FID). These have all shown that, by and large, progress in addressing quality issues in the information sector has reached similarly tentative stages in all the countries participating in the above events. Furthermore, these institutional initiatives have pointed to the desirability of mounting international action programmes to promote awareness, to share experience and to collaborate in research.

The first such research programme to attract funding was launched at the beginning of 1993 with a grant from NORDINFO. Initially, this programme was intended to involve all the Scandinavian countries, and it is hoped that this plan may yet be realized. At the moment of writing it is a two-country project involving Denmark and Norway. Under a small steering group, the project is being conducted from the Royal School of Librarianship in Copenhagen, in conjunction with the Danish Technological Institute.[19] The core of the project consists of two in-depth case studies of TQM in action, one subject being the LIS function of the Jutland Telephone Company in Denmark, the other a more generalized information service of Norsk Hydro AS, which also operates an internal consultancy service including the implementation of TQM in its portfolio. The project duration is currently 20 months, though it must be hoped that this can be extended for as long as may be necessary in order to get past the TQM implementation phase and into problems of evaluation. In the meantime, the project is examining various approaches and techniques deployed in the services sector, with a particular interest in the problems of performance measurement.

Previous work in Denmark[20] suggests that it should be possible to construct a Customer Satisfaction Index appropriate to the LIS function. A pilot study across a company offering a range of cleaning services concluded with a list of only ten quality characteristics divided into five main groups. Initially, the list contained more than 75 items, and it will be interesting to see whether the list of characteristics which will be identified and considered for information services is capable of a comparable reduction. It may end with a larger list, or perhaps even a more hierarchical and structured list; but the next stage will be to determine the optional ways of collecting, analysing, weighting and interpreting the results. Above all, it is appreciated that customer satisfaction must be measured on a regular basis. Also under consideration is an alternative approach which focuses on 'gaps' in the service provision model, a sort of 'Customer Dissatisfaction Index'. This approach is exemplified in Figure 14.6, taken from one of the few textbooks currently available

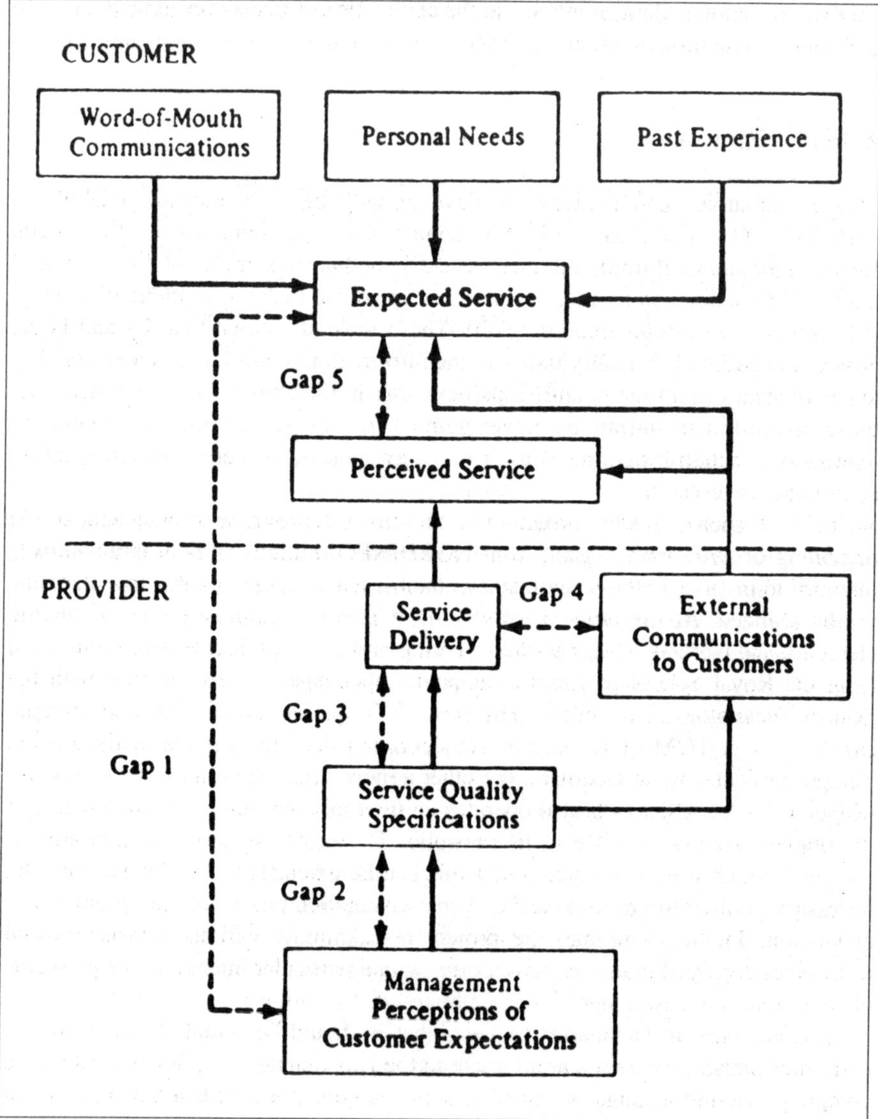

Figure 14.6 *Conceptual model of service quality* (from Zeithaml, V. A., ref 21)

on quality issues in the service sector.[21]

In parallel with the successful attempts of the Nordic Group to attract funding, a consortium of organizations within the European Communities put forward a proposal for an action programme to the Directorate General of the European Commission concerned with the information market. The consortium comprises EUSIDIC (a European association which brings together users and suppliers in the information industry), EUROLUG (the European Online Users Group) and GAVEL (a European consortium of information consultants). At the moment of writing DG XIII was still considering the proposal, but some foundation work has started and formal agreement has been made with the Nordic group to share information and experience. (It is planned that this will result in one or two guidebooks scheduled for publication in December 1993.)

This programme is somewhat more ambitious in that it will attempt to make a bridge between the information providers and intermediaries as well as with users. The roots of this project are to be found (as mentioned earlier) in the interest stirred up by the LA/UKOLUG actions, and in the TQM Seminar organized by EUSIDIC in Rotterdam. The first thrust in this programme is being initiated by EUROLUG, which is investigating the possibility of monitoring database quality, based on the SCOUG criteria, and operating through EUSIDIC in the same way that EUSIDIC and EUROLUG so successfully monitored the effectiveness of correction to databases offered by the European PTTs. The second thrust will follow up the EUSIDIC spotlight on TQM. The intention here is, initially, to mirror the EUROLUG approach so that perceptions of quality (and the identification of performance criteria) may be simultaneously considered by practitioners as they look upstream to their suppliers and downstream to their users.

In the longer term, the programme aims to work with the Nordic Group towards the construction of a Customer Satisfaction Index (or some similar vehicle), together with the concomitant procedures for collection and analysis of data. Here it is hoped that the programme can build on previous work supported by DG XIII in its Materials Database Demonstrator Programme. The same message comes through in this work with regard to quality measurement: that the three main aspects of technical data systems which contribute to satisfying the expectations of a potential customer are:

1. the description of the system
2. the contents of the system
3. the service provided to deliver the contents of the system.

Though the measurement component of quality management is vital, it must be incorporated into a framework provided by the quality manual; this should be another product of the action programme. As mentioned previously with regard to the MQA, such a manual should be based on ISO 9000, but must be adapted and augmented as necessary. The EUSIDIC programme will also conduct case studies of TQM implementation, but not in such depth as the Nordic project, the immediate aim being to compile a practical and useful guide to experience in the field.

In October 1992, before its bi-annual Congress, FID Council agreed to the formation of a Special Interest Group devoted to Quality Issues. This was formally launched at a seminar in London in March 1993, an event sponsored by the British Library Research and Development Department. The seminar was open only to invited delegates (though the Group itself will be open to all FID members and accredited non-members), and it was encouraging to note that the 24 delegates represented no less than 14 countries. Each country presented an informal account of its national situation (some of which is featured earlier in this chapter) and it seemed clear that all were at similar stages of development. The meeting agreed that the Group should work through a network of national focal points, currently being established. Also, because it is more likely to be effective operating as a clearing-house and champion of causes, the meeting agreed to support, and where possible to follow, the action programmes being initiated by the Nordic Group and EUSIDIC.

It should be emphasized, however, that the Group will not operate in a passive mode. It has set as its first target the production of tangible results to be presented to a FID/QI seminar preceding FID's Congress in Tokyo in the autumn of 1994.

Conclusions

Inevitably, this chapter must be incomplete and piecemeal, concerned as it is with nascent movements in the application of quality management. Consequently, the reader must feel some frustration at being told that the exciting part of the story is just about to happen. How it will develop is still open to question, but there can be no doubt that quality issues are here to stay, and that the application of quality principles within the information industry will have a significant effect. Some claim that those organizations that do not initiate quality management will not survive; others claim that, as information technology and the new economies bite deeper into our working environment, quality management is one of the great catalysts for organizational and cultural change. To those who regard it as a 'new management fad', the answer is simple: it is not new, it is merely the culmination of a series of developments that has included Management by Objectives, Organizational Development, Quality Circles and a range of other approaches. In many respects it can be argued that the time is exactly ripe for quality management, customer-oriented services and empowerment of staff. Disregarding, or perhaps looking underneath, the political hype, it is no coincidence that governments are investing large sums of money in promoting quality management, and that award schemes are spreading. Following on from the original Deming prize and the Baldrige National Quality Award, there came the US Presidential Award for Quality (confined to the public sector) and more recently the Northern Ireland Quality Award, the UK Prime Minister's Award for Total Quality and the European Quality Award (administered by the European Foundation for Quality Management). While these clearly have a promotional value, they also provide a widespread discipline, based as they are on ISO 9000. It is interesting to note that in 1992, 300,000 organizations applied for the extensive Baldrige documentation, while only 100 submitted themselves for judgement. In other words, a very large number of organizations appear to be taking quality management seriously, even though they may have no intention of seeking awards or certification.

Finally, an aspect of these awards, which should be of great interest to the information sector, is beginning to emerge. All the award systems allocate points for different aspects of quality management. The Baldrige scheme is typical; Figure

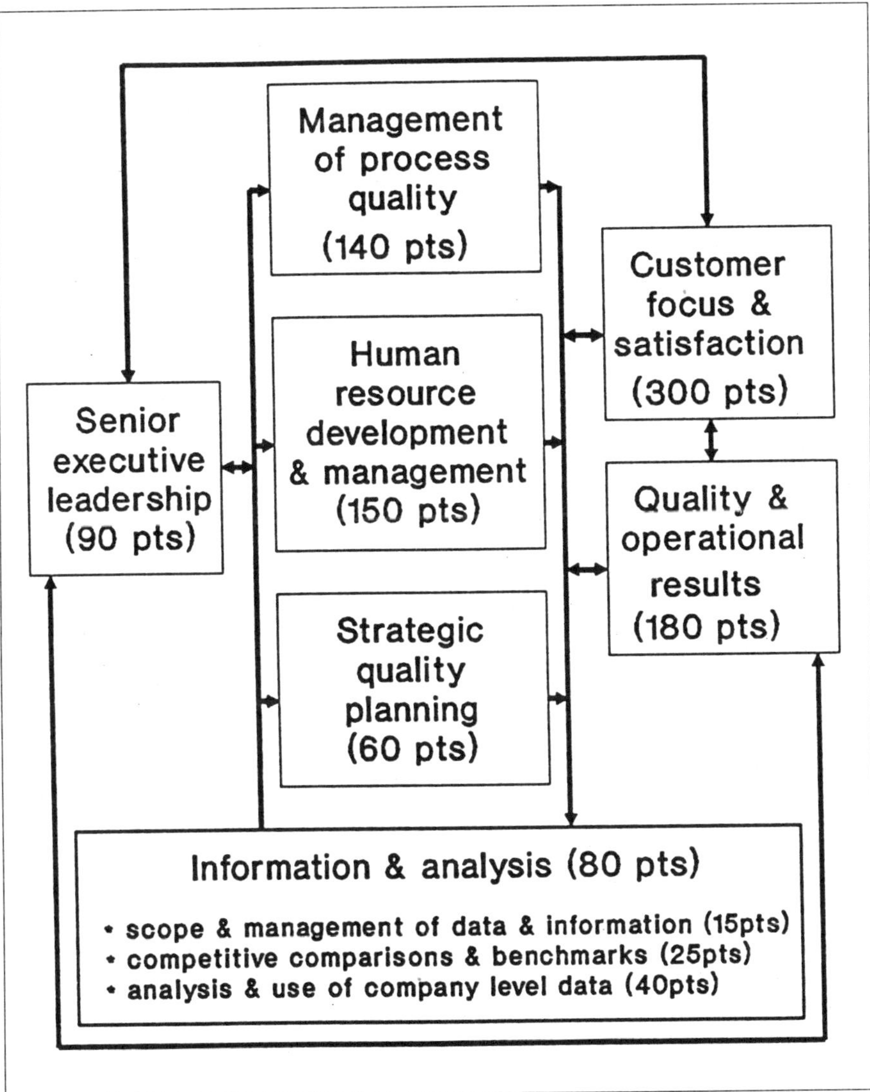

Figure 14.7 *Baldrige Award criteria framework – dynamic relationships*

14.7 shows the points allotted to each activity. Some observers, for example the US Society for Information Management, have concluded that the Information and Analysis component, although scoring only 80 points out of the total of 1000, is a critical factor in the success of the organization. Conversely, Cruise O'Brien and Voss,[22] in an assessment of 42 British organizations using the Baldrige criteria, concluded 'Management and Information Systems have become highly sophisticated and an integral part of management in most firms. However, the managers reported that few of these systems were yet geared to quality measures'. Thus, the information sector faces the challenge not only of putting its own house in order but of raising the whole level of information management within the organisations they serve.

Notes

1. British Standards Institution (1987), Quality systems. Specification for design/development, production, installation and servicing BS 5750 : Part I : 1987.
2. Mainelli, M. (1992), 'Certification Boom Spells Good Business', *Management Consultancy*, March, pp. 57–61.
3. The Commoner (1992), 'Total Quality Madness', *Library Association Record*, November, p. 714.
4. Griffith, Ian (1992), 'Completing the Quality Equation', *Management Consultancy*, April, pp. 63–5.
5. Gilchrist, Alan (1992), 'Quality issues in the information sector – old ideas, new pressures', in K. Adler, *et al.*, (eds) *Proceedings from the 8th Nordic Conference on Information and Documentation, 19-21 May 1992*. Helsingborg. TLS. Stockholm 1992.
6. Gilchrist, Alan. Paper presented to EUSIDIC 1992 Spring Meeting: 'TQM in the information environment', Rotterdam, (unpublished).
7. Juntunen, Ritva *et al.* (1991), *Quality Requirements for Databases – Project for Evaluating Finnish Databases*. London. Online Information.
8. Armstrong, C.J. and Hartley, R.J. (1992), *Database 2000. UKOLUG State-of-the-Art Conference, 1992*, Oxford. Learned Information.
9. Basch, Reva (1990), ' Measuring the Quality of the Data: Report on the Fourth Annual SCOUG retreat', *Database Searcher*, pp.18–20.
10. Granick, Lois (1991), 'Assuring the Quality of Information Dissemination: Responsibilities of Database Producers', *Information Services and Use* **11**, pp. 117–36.
11. Haines Taylor, Margaret and Wilson, Tom (eds) (1990), *Quality assurance in libraries: the health care sector,* Ottawa. Canadian Library Association.
12. Brockman, John R. (1991), 'Quality Assurance and the Management of Information Services. Report of a one-day seminar organised jointly by the Institute of Information Scientists and Task Force Pro Libra Ltd.', *Journal of Information Science*, **17**, pp. 127–35.
13. Porter, Lydia (1992), *Quality initiatives in British Library and Information Services*, London, BLR & DD.
14. Brockman, John, R. (1992), 'First Steps in Implementing Quality Management in Library and Information Services', *State Librarian* **40**.
15. Brockman, John R. (1992), 'Just Another Management Fad? The Implications of TQM for Library and Information Services', *Aslib Proceedings*, **44**, pp. 283–7.

16. Brockman, John R. (1992), 'Total Quality Management: the USA and UK compared', *Public Money and Management* **12**, 4, pp. 6–9.
17. Brockman, John R. (1992), 'TQM and Government Departmental and Agency Library and Information Services', *Proceedings of the Annual HERTIS/TFPL Conference*.
18. Michel, Jean (1990), 'VAID – Value Analysis Applied to Information and Documentation Services and Products, *IATUL Quarterly* **4** (2), pp. 82–9.
19. Johannsen, C.G. (1992), 'Danish Experiences of TQM in the Library World', *New Library World* **93**, pp. 4–9.
20. Kristensen, Kai, Kanji Gopal, K, and Dahlgard, Jens J. (1992), 'On Measurement of Customer Satisfaction', *Total Quality Management* **3**, pp. 123–8.
21. Zeithaml, V. A., Parasuraman, A. and Leonard, Berry (1990), *Delivering Quality Service: Balancing Customer Perceptions and Expectations*. New York: Collier MacMillan.
22. Cruise O'Brien, R. and Voss, C. A. (1992). 'In search of quality. An assessment of 42 British organisations using the criteria of the Baldrige Quality Award'. *London Business School Operations Management Paper 92/02*, London: London Business School.

Index